BIRDS
of an Iowa Dooryard

A BUR OAK BOOK

BIRDS

of an Iowa Dooryard

By Althea R. Sherman

Edited by Fred J. Pierce

Foreword to the 1952 Edition by Arthur J. Palas

Foreword to the 1996 Edition by Marcia Myers Bonta

University of Iowa Press ▣ Iowa City

University of Iowa Press, Iowa City 52242

International Standard Book Number 0-87745-568-6
Library of Congress Catalog Card Number 96-60645

Birds of an Iowa Dooryard is published with the gracious
permission of the State Historical Society of Iowa, Des
Moines.

"Althea Rosina Sherman: Ornithologist of an Iowa
Dooryard," from *Women in the Field: America's Pioneering
Women Naturalists* by Marcia Myers Bonta, is reprinted
courtesy of Texas A&M University Press.

Dedicated by Fred J. Pierce and Arthur J. Palas
to the cause of scientific bird study for which
Althea R. Sherman worked so assiduously

CONTENTS

The Johnson County Songbird Project : ix
Barbara Boyle

Althea Rosina Sherman:
Ornithologist of an Iowa Dooryard : 1
Marcia Myers Bonta

Editor's Note : 11
Fred J. Pierce

Foreword to the 1952 Edition : 13
Arthur J. Palas

I. Watching the Birds of Our Dooryard : 23

II. Feeding Winter Birds : 32

III. The Home Life of the Chimney Swift : 40

IV. Birds Near at Hand : 62

V. The Phoebe : 89

VI. The Nest Life of the Western House Wren : 100

VII. The Cuckoos : 115

VIII. Habits of the Short-billed Marsh Wren : 121

IX. Notes on the Rails : 133

X. Eleven Days in the Life of a Catbird : 139

XI. The Strange Flycatcher : 149

XII. The Nest Life of the Sparrow Hawk : 152

XIII. Nest Life of the Screech Owl : 167

XIV. Down with the House Wren Boxes : 184

XV. The Old Ornithology and the New : 196

XVI. Experiments in Feeding Hummingbirds
     during Seven Summers : 207

XVII. Are Birds Decreasing in Numbers? : 223

XVIII. At the Sign of the Northern Flicker : 237

A Bibliography of the Published Writings
     of Althea R. Sherman : 266

THE JOHNSON COUNTY SONGBIRD PROJECT

From her early childhood Althea Sherman learned all that she could of the natural world. She lamented that her parents' generation had not even more carefully observed and documented the native plants, birds, and wildlife. This would have at least provided a record of what had been lost in the encroachment of white settlement. Sherman was dismayed by people in general and ornithologists in particular who took for granted or ignored the habitat requirements of birds. She recognized more than ninety years ago that loss of habitat was the fundamental cause worldwide of the decline in numbers and species of birds. Sherman would no doubt be heartsick today to see yards shaved just one or two inches high, roadsides mowed edge to fenceline, streams straight and naked, and prairie and forest nearly everywhere supplanted by beans, corn, and cattle. She could not have imagined miles and miles of malls, superhighways, grandiose homes, and housing developments.

In 1915 Sherman drew wide attention with her design and creation of her twenty-eight-foot-tall, nine-foot-square chimney swift tower, which enclosed a two-foot-square wooden chimney, a winding staircase from bottom to top, and four floors or levels. The tower brought visitors from around the world and remains a testament to the imagination and determination of this pioneering Iowa woman and to the local carpenters who carried out her plans. Four oak posts in the center were set in cement and prevented the tower from toppling in the strong Iowa prairie winds and storms. These posts rose to fourteen feet and supported the fourteen-foot wooden chimney rising above. Stairs were built around the posts through the first and second levels and encircled the chimney on the upper two levels. Doors allowed entrance into the chimney, and numerous peepholes and windows which jutted into the chimney in a V allowed observation without frightening the swifts. Enclosed bookcases lined the walls on all four floors.

The tower's small, irregularly placed windows may seem a bit odd when viewed from the outside, but inside it becomes apparent that these were strategically located to allow light onto the stairs and into the chimney itself. Small boards and pegs nailed to the oak posts and to the edges of the chimney were placed for hanging the kerosene lanterns Sherman used in her night studies of the swifts. A platform that Sherman called her opera seat was built below a second floor window, and from here she viewed the various nesting activities in the treetops outside the tower. A window seat at the top level is situated between a door into the chimney and a window of the outside wall. Here Sherman watched, weighed, measured, and drew the swifts at all stages of nest life. A large shelf at the top of the window seat may have served as a work area. No one before Sherman had ever witnessed the entire nesting cycle of the chimney swift, and her swift journals, covering eighteen years and four hundred pages of research, may offer the most extensive study of this species in existence. Several historical accounts claim this structure is the only one of its kind.

Recently, Althea Sherman's chimney swift tower was near to falling or being razed but was instead donated to the Johnson County Songbird Project for the purpose of restoration. The organization's ultimate goals include the acquisition of a historically appropriate site with land conducive for a bird sanctuary and living laboratory, restoration of the tower (itself a museum), and establishment of a Sherman interpretive center. The tower will be used again as a nesting site for chimney swifts, for continuing Sherman's work, and as a historical and educational tool for schoolchildren, scholars, and the public. A fund-raising campaign is ongoing for site acquisition, tower restoration, and research and development of the Sherman center. Educational programs are available on request. Donations and inquiries are welcomed by the Althea R. Sherman Project, 1320 Grabin Road NW, Oxford, Iowa 52322, phone 319-628-4824.

While the site search continues, other facets of the Sherman legacy have now been preserved. Sherman's chimney swift journals, along with her many other bird and historical journals, have been microfilmed by the State Historical Society of Iowa, which also holds 250 of Sherman's paintings and drawings. In addition, several private Sherman collections have been gathered and microfilmed by the Johnson County Songbird Project. Althea Sherman is increasingly being recognized in historical exhibits and in the literature of ornithology, history, and nature, as evidenced here in the republication of her *Birds of an Iowa Dooryard* by the University of Iowa Press.

Barbara Boyle

ALTHEA ROSINA SHERMAN:
ORNITHOLOGIST OF AN IOWA DOORYARD

The ornithologist from National, Iowa, was notorious for her biting wit, her implacable battle against house wrens, and her chimney
swift tower. Althea Rosina Sherman, born in 1853 in the first frame
house on the Iowa prairie north of Dubuque, had four sisters and one
brother. Her parents were pioneers who had trekked west from New
York State to Prairie du Chien, Wisconsin, in 1843 and had then
moved on across the Mississippi River to Iowa two years later.

Her father, Mark, was a cobbler and an investor in farm mortgages,
and her mother, Melissa, was a pioneer mother with strong Victorian
beliefs. They must have been unusual people for their time and place,
since they sent all their surviving children to college. Their son,
Mark, became a lawyer, two daughters were medical doctors, and
Althea was an artist-teacher for the first twenty years of her adult life.

She received bachelor's and master's degrees from Oberlin College
and remained a loyal alumna all her life. From there she went to teach
in a country school for a few years, making a deep impression on at
least one former student, who remembered her forty years later.
"There was never another teacher like her. She took us into the
woods . . . showed us how flowers grow; how seeds ripen; how leaves
are constructed and how they breathe; how to know trees by the
bark."

However, Sherman's burning desire, at least as a young woman,
was to be an artist, so she gave up her general teaching and went back
to school, first at the Art Institute in Chicago and then to the Art
Student's League in New York City. From 1882 to 1895 she taught
art at a number of places, including Carleton College in Minnesota
and in the city schools of Tacoma, Washington, as a supervisor of
drawing.

But in 1895 she was called back home to tend her ailing parents.
Her father died the following year, her mother in 1902. Dr. Emily
Amelia, her older unmarried sister, returned to the homestead in
1902 to practice rural medicine, horse-and-buggy style. For better or
worse, the two sisters lived together there for the rest of their lives.
To hear Althea tell it, it was mostly for worse; Amelia, as she pre-

1

ferred to be called, was as tightfisted as her father had been. He had left them both a substantial income, but while Amelia pinched every penny, Althea was known for her generosity to educational, religious, and charitable institutions.

Althea had continued to take art lessons off and on while she had tended her parents, and once she was freed of that responsibility, she began painting more and more. But the landscapes and still lifes were gradually supplanted by charming portraits of the birds she had started to observe. Whenever she had a chance, she would watch the bird life in the acre around her home grounds and in an adjoining pasture and swamp. Much of her time was taken up with mundane tasks, such as cleaning a smoking stove, baking, picking berries, tending a huge garden, and generally keeping up a large home without running water or an efficient heating system. Amelia, however, "that lazy, shirking, domineering miser," as Althea called her in a letter to ornithologist Margaret Morse Nice, frequently "dons her most charming mood and tongue-lashings in order to *do* nothing" herself.

Apparently Althea never outwardly showed her resentment as housewife to Amelia's more masculine role of chief breadwinner. All Althea's feelings about those she believed had wronged her were revealed in letters and journals. To the world she appeared friendly, optimistic, and enthusiastic, a contrast to the gloomy and doom-saying Amelia. Neighbors and friends respected Amelia for being a wonderful, caring doctor, which she was, and Althea for her artistic talents, bird studies, and housekeeping and cooking abilities. There is no doubt that Amelia often helped Althea, at least with her bird studies, and could identify the various species with an unerring ear as well as eye. Althea, whose hearing diminished rapidly as she grew older, often relied on her sister's sharper ears to pick up the first calls of returning birds each spring. They lived in a white New England–style home with green shutters. Behind some of those shutters lived bats, which Sherman studied for fourteen summers. Vernon Bailey and his wife, Florence, visited Sherman one summer; he came to study her little brown bats, while Florence came to see Sherman's flicker houses attached to the large old barn. After encouragement from Vernon, Sherman wrote about the bats, in her sole article on mammals for the *Journal of Mammalogy*.

Of all the thirty-eight years she spent in bird study and of all the species she observed at great length—screech owls, eastern phoebes, red-winged blackbirds, gray catbirds, brown thrashers, American robins, alder flycatchers, sora rails, house wrens, chimney swifts, ruby-throated hummingbirds, American kestrels—the flickers were her favorites. She called them the "species that afforded me more hours of pleasure than any other bird," in a 1933 letter to Dr. Shaver. To Margaret Morse Nice she said, "If I should have only one family of birds saved from total destruction I should chose [*sic*] the Woodpecker, since they have given me more pleasure than any other."

In fact, her first long published study on one bird species was devoted to the flicker. "At the Sign of the Northern Flicker" appeared in the *Wilson Bulletin* in 1910. Although flickers had been living in a hole in the Sherman barn since 1897, Sherman began her detailed studies in 1908, when she took wooden soap boxes and attached them inside the barn wall behind three flicker holes. On the eight-by-twelve-inch floor of each box she spread excelsior. In the tops of the boxes she drilled an observation hole to let her look down into the eighteen-inch-deep "nest" she had made. Near the bottom of the nest she drilled a large second hole, through which she could reach in to remove nestlings for weighing, painting, and photographing when she needed. A trap door hid that hole from the flickers.

Her many hours of observation and meticulous notes were later appreciated by Arthur Cleveland Bent when he wrote his *Life Histories of North American Birds* series. Using her "very thorough studies," he realized that her statement on the incubation time for flicker eggs, eleven to twelve days, corrected earlier work by other ornithologists stating fourteen to sixteen days. Edward Forbush, whose *Birds of Massachusetts* was considered a classic work in ornithology, was not respected by Sherman. His "ignorant trash" regarding flickers, she told one friend, was probably caused by his "Massachusetts complex," which "always prevented him from reading anything printed west of the Alleghany [*sic*] mountains. Like many of his neighbors . . . probably he thought . . . none but Indians live there." Bent, however, did read widely and accepted her incubation figures as well as much of her other original material regarding flickers. He used her "very good description of the naked and blind nestlings" verbatim and quoted a number of her careful observations of the young.

Her paintings of young flickers were also attractive and accurate, for she continued her artwork while she observed. A catbird in its nest, four brown phoebes roosting, a chimney swift on its nest, three young brown thrashers—year by year her portfolio and her reputation grew. In 1922 she was asked to exhibit her bird paintings at the

American Ornithologists' Union's annual meeting in Chicago. How pleased she must have been when America's foremost bird painter, Louis Agassiz Fuertes, told her that her brown thrasher had more life and personality than any bird he had ever painted.

Certainly she had a way of portraying some of her favorite songbirds with great charm and affection. But she was, unfortunately, part of the old, judgmental school of natural history, assessing good and evil in human terms, a not uncommon malady among some ornithologists even today. The "good" birds were prey, the "bad" ones predators or pest species. Her list of those she actively opposed included house sparrows, bronzed grackles, European starlings, house wrens, screech owls, ring-necked pheasants, and American kestrels— all birds that she had carefully observed and found wanting.

Again Bent respected "the careful observations of Miss Althea R. Sherman," quoting her figures on screech owl egg-laying and incubation and her description of nestling plumage and habits. Sherman, though, was more concerned about what screech owls ate. To her distress she discovered that song sparrows and juncos were favorite foods, as well as goldfinches, and vesper, savannah, white-throated, tree, chipping, field, and swamp sparrows. Twenty percent of their sustenance was gained from songbirds, and so Sherman made her decision. "Their ravages were so great that it was decided if we desired a little bird paradise where all good birds were welcome through the summer time there screech owls could not be encouraged to remain." Her solution was to give away the owlets as pets, but after that experience she became judge and jury where screech owls were concerned, killing three of them when she discovered that they had killed a family of southern orioles.

Sherman's "Acre of Birds," as she called the area around her home where she did her observing, was definitely managed. House sparrows were killed, dressed, and fed to her cats, house wrens were shot by neighbor boys she enlisted and supplied with an air gun, rabbits and woodchucks were trapped and removed, and she urged her neighbors to shoot ring-necked pheasants "that are filling our acres in the township. It is an outrage, a crime to breed this pest on valuable Iowa land, then suffer the rabble to run over us and shoot this game. I have a big fight on hand, but I mean to fight." Even naturalist-writer Aldo Leopold fell under suspicion, "that minion of the diabolical work of the ammunition makers," who "had been in this region" in 1932 "under the guise of restoring prairie chicken and bobwhite" and

was instead "working for the spread of the ring-necked pheasant."
Though unreasonable, judgmental, prejudiced, narrow-minded, and sometimes even vindictive, Sherman did remarkable work, driven to learn all she could about birds. There is no doubt that she loved the outdoors, even though her terms were strict. "The woods," she wrote, "are always alluring and I often spend a day of unalloyed pleasure there." Sherman also loved her Iowa homestead. She believed Iowa a "splendid state to be born in and to study its birds, especially if one sticks to country living." She insisted that her yard was not a garden but an orchard, mostly of plum trees, because birds liked to nest in them. There were apple trees, shade trees, mulberry, gooseberry, raspberry, and elderberry bushes. One visitor called it "a tangle of bushes and native and cultivated trees." Sherman admitted that it was run-down, but it was a place the birds liked. She attributed the number of species she had identified over the years (162) to its location near the watershed between the Mississippi and Turkey Rivers. As the farmers plowed up the land, even the marshy areas, bird diversity decreased; Sherman, by keeping her land as wild as possible and by gradually buying up nearby abandoned lots, created an oasis for birds.

One source of joy was a marshy area three hundred feet from the house, where she built a wooden blind on posts to observe the marsh birds, particularly rails. The blind had a door on its east end and a window on each of its other sides. The forty-six-inch-square blind lasted twenty years, and over that time she watched 110 species of birds from it. Sherman estimated she had spent two to three hundred hours studying rails—far more time than other people, she asserted. Sora, king, and Virginia rails were all observed, but soras were the common species. In 1909 they nested in her marsh after a courtship that reminded her of boys playing leapfrog.

That same blind attracted the screech owl family the following year, and in 1912 American kestrels or sparrow hawks, as they were then called, moved into the box. With agony of mind Sherman faced her dilemma. Yet her scientific curiosity, as always, won out over her fears for her "harmless, little feathered friends," and she settled down to make still another outstanding study of a nesting species. She darkened the windows of the blind and observed them through a peephole sixteen inches from where the female kestrel brooded. Day by day she weighed the eggs and then the birds. Long hours were spent "standing noiselessly upon a box with head scraping the roof of the blind." Not an easy task even at first, later "it became almost insupportable with the heat of an afternoon sun beating upon the blind, and with the stench from a nest whose walls were thickly encrusted with excrements."

Facing the question again of what they ate and fed their young, she found one scientific paper that claimed 18 percent of their food consisted of songbirds. Reasoning that the same percentage had applied to screech owls and that despite it, some small birds had survived, she decided to give the kestrels a trial. She also helped them along by feeding the young thirty-three dead house sparrows. Mostly they ate fledglings just out of the nest, she discovered, along with ground squirrels and meadow mice. And "sparrow hawk" seemed an apt name as far as their favorite birds were concerned. But despite her dislike of the fact that they consumed sparrows, she let them stay around the rest of the season. *The Auk* published her "The Nest Life of the Sparrow Hawk," and once again Bent quoted her account at length in his own work.

Sherman's life was not all drudgery in the kitchen and bird observation outside. She was a member of fifteen scientific societies, including the American Association for the Advancement of Science, the Wilson Ornithological Club, the National Audubon Society, the Biological Society of Washington, and the American Ornithologists' Union, although she had only bitter words about the A.O.U. She wrote to Nice, "I have said and believe it, that no woman will ever be made a Fellow of A.O.U. . . . No, man nature must change before a woman is a Fellow." She also subscribed to twenty-six magazines, many related to her interest in nature, but others, including the *Mississippi Valley Historical Review*, *Wisconsin Archaeologist*, and the *Journal of History and Politics*, reflected a wider world view. In her notebooks she mentions attending an Equal Suffrage meeting at the schoolhouse in May 1916. She was the first woman, along with a neighbor who accompanied her, to be entertained at the Explorers Club in New York City in 1919.

Sherman also gave talks about her bird work; locally, she spoke on "Our Birds and Ourselves" at a Farmersburg school program and read her "Birds Close at Hand" in Elkader High School, and nationally she was invited to speak on "Birds of an Iowa Dooryard" in front of the esteemed Linnaean Society of New York. Sherman was no stay-at-home. Whenever she could get the money she attended meetings as far away as Saint Louis and Boston. She often went to Chicago, particularly to read and study in the excellent John Crerar Library, which specialized in natural history. When she visited New York City she went to the American Museum of Natural History and observed birds in city parks and on the then-bucolic Staten Island.

Probably the most exciting time in her life occurred from November 7, 1913, until August 26, 1914, when she took her long-anticipated trip around the world. It was unfortunately curtailed by the advent of World War I, but during those ten months she visited twenty countries in Europe, North Africa, and parts of southern Asia. When she returned she wrote four articles about her bird observations there for the *Wilson Bulletin*. The first, "Birds by the Wayside in Europe, Asia, and Africa," mostly recounted her time in India, which she crossed twice by railroad and mail train. Sometimes she used rickshaws as conveyances, although when she reached the village of Mount Abu, she found a better mode of travel. "It suited my purpose better to go afoot and alone in the neighborhood of the village and to confine the rides to two half days. I found the rickshaw as heavy as a buggy, and when empty it was hard to pull up hill, therefore I walked on the upgrades and let the rickshaw boys draw me when the road was level or down hill." She regularly arose each morning at dawn and observed birds for two hours before breakfast.

In Egypt she spent five weeks traveling by train, boat, carriage, hand cart, and donkey, "none of which yielded the satisfaction in bird viewing that was experienced on the few occasions when I could go on foot and alone," she wrote in "Birds by the Wayside in Egypt and Nubia." She finished her accounts in Palestine, where she went from Jaffa to Constantinople, and Greece, which she had been wanting to visit for over forty years. Her articles discussed in detail many of the birds she saw and proved that she was familiar with many foreign species through prior reading on the subject. By then World War I had begun, and her ship was forced to dodge German submarines as it carried her prematurely back to the United States.

Once she reached her Iowa acres, she launched her most impressive and innovative bird study. Hiring a local contractor, she laid out her plans for building a chimney swift tower. Three carpenters constructed the original structure in 1915. Made of white clapboards to match the house, it was nine feet square and twenty-eight feet tall. An artificial chimney of rough pine was built inside, two feet square and extending fourteen feet down into the tower. A door opened into the chimney, and a built-in ladder reached to the top so that the chimney could be opened in the spring before the chimney swifts arrived and closed in fall after they left. Auger holes on two sides served as peepholes, while the other two sides had windows with frames that met in an obtuse angle. This left a space jutting into the chimney where Sherman could put her head and have a clear view through glass both to the bottom and the top of the chimney without startling the birds. At night a paper screen was placed over the window with a lamp behind it, so Sherman could still watch the birds' activity.

It took three years before chimney swifts discovered the tower, but in the summer of 1918 the first chimney swift nest was built. Luckily the swifts located the nest in a favorable viewing spot just under the right-hand corner of the window, fifteen inches from Sherman's observing eyes. In her usual thorough way she recorded every facet of the nesting, hatching, and raising of chimney swifts. She was particularly interested in proving that the young chimney swifts were not fed at night, and after many evenings of watching and seeing no feeding activity, she was certain that the noises in the chimney at night were caused by the birds shifting their positions. She also found that both parents incubated the eggs, and one year she observed a third, unmated bird help out with the domestic chores for the entire season. To her delight, the young swifts were never quarrelsome; in fact, "no evil has been detected in its relations with its own or with other species." Therefore, Sherman declared, the chimney swift should be the "bird that properly might be chosen as the emblem of peace."

Year after year her observations continued. In 1928, when she was seventy-four years old, she made four hundred visits to the chimney to observe the longest occupancy the birds had ever made—130 days. She estimated she had climbed twelve thousand steps throughout the season to reach her observation window. In addition, she had taken 133 visitors to see the swifts and written thirty-two pages of notes.

In 1928 ornithologists T. C. Stephens and William Youngworth made a visit to the Sherman homestead, where they camped outside overnight in their umbrella tent beside the chimney swift tower. Sherman had insisted they take an upstairs room, but Stephens, an old friend, knew that she was merely being polite. "The sisters," he informed Youngworth, "did not like to entertain menfolk under their roof for the night." That moral issue settled to the Sherman sisters' satisfaction, they accompanied the men to an ice cream social at the fairgrounds. Later the men visited the chimney swift tower and were given a tour of all the other bird nests and nesting boxes in the yard.

Then Sherman showed them her paintings and sketches and told them just how she had discovered her subjects. Despite her pride in her paintings, it was her bird notebooks she was most anxious about. She wanted very much to complete them for publishing.

By then she was suffering from arthritis, although her domestic work load never lightened. When she finally completed her chimney swift studies in 1936, she had filled four hundred notebook pages, which was only a small part of her total output. It proved to be too complex for a woman in her eighties, who still had to draw fresh water from a windlass well every day, to organize coherently. So the chimney swift notes were not published during her lifetime, and Bent did his chimney swift article without the benefit of her research.

He did, however, make passing reference to her indictment of house wrens, the battle that split bird lovers into factions. In 1925 three articles by Sherman on the subject appeared. *Bird-Lore* entitled its piece "The Problem of the House Wren," and the *Wilson Bulletin* published "Down with the House Wren Boxes," followed by "Additional Evidence against the House Wren."

It was not the house wren she opposed but the artificially high numbers that were thriving because every backyard bird lover had been erecting house wren boxes. House wrens, she wrote, were far more destructive to songbirds than house sparrows. The males spent much of their time entering the nests of other birds, piercing their eggs, and then throwing them out of the nest. Such depredations had caused a great decline of songbirds in many places. Furthermore, she cited renowned ornithologist Robert Ridgway and other prominent experts who had observed and commented on the house wren's destructive practices. She exhorted people not to kill house wrens but to tear down all the nesting boxes and let the population dwindle to a reasonable number. But she began poisoning them to redress the balance.

Sherman's battle against the well-loved "Jenny Wren," who sings so beautifully, was uphill at best. Even Alfred Otto Gross, who contributed the chapter on house wrens to the Bent series, called her stand against the wren a venomous one and declared that "Miss Sherman's paper stimulated the writing of many of the articles for and against the wren that followed." Naturally, Sherman took every attack as a personal affront. "Of course Bighead Baldwin was there running over the sewer spout about his lousy wrens," she wrote to Nice. "Did he attack me in his usual shyster lawyer role in his defense of the wren?" As part of her scorn toward those she called "bird lovers" as opposed to ornithologists, she wrote a bitter, sarcastic paper, "The Old Ornithology and the New," comparing the scientific work of ornithologists to the "bird talks" of uninformed bird lovers. Undoubtedly her indictment of their ignorance was not exaggerated, because the "nature fakers" were still writing the same incredible "twaddle" that T. R. Roosevelt had objected to several decades earlier, including, in Sherman's opinion, Gene Stratton Porter, who wrote "sentimental trash."

But the "scientific approach" Sherman advocated appalled the scientists as well as the sentimentalists. Only the good birds were to be "loved and protected." Those not fitting her idea of good—the predators and pests—were to be eliminated. Certainly Sherman never saw that her own feelings toward birds were equally sentimental. She was a member of the "old ornithology," along with William Brewster, whose scientific work she admired. Unfortunately, after her house wren articles, she wrote only short bird notes for the rest of her publishing career, and in 1933 even those notes stopped.

Old age and old ideas conspired in the end to stem the outflow of excellent bird studies from her pen. Although she outlived her sister Amelia by five years, dying alone in the old house in 1943, she never accomplished her fondest dream—to write a book about all she had learned and seen over her remarkable lifetime. But she did the next best thing. In her will she left $7,500 to publish "a book as a monument to the memory of Testatrix and as a means of making available to the public some of the literary efforts and scientific accomplishments of Testatrix. . . ."

In 1952 *Birds of an Iowa Dooryard* by Althea R. Sherman was published. Her friend Fred J. Pierce had labored long and hard through her sixty handwritten notebooks to produce the work, and Margaret Morse Nice helped publicize it.

Although her old-fashioned Victorian morality toward birds has long been replaced, there is no doubt she was sincerely motivated by her belief that in birds "we see reflections of human conduct. It is this mirroring of our own natures in a dim way that awakens our interest in them." For all her scientific studies, it was her emotions that ruled her conduct. The wonder of it all is that even so, what she observed and recorded of bird life has never been contradicted by contemporary ornithologists.

Marcia Myers Bonta

EDITOR'S NOTE

Althea Rosina Sherman was an exacting observer whose painstaking accuracy is reflected in all her writings. She was meticulous in her record-keeping. Her greatest ornithological interest was the study of nesting birds, and it was here that she did her most important work. Her patience seemed limitless. This is attested by the thousands of hours spent in watching at close range the nesting of birds which she found on her home acres at National, Iowa.

It was Miss Sherman's desire to publish a book on her nesting studies. The plan to write such a book evidently came late in life—too late for her to complete the actual work or to outline what she wished to include in it. Hers was a busy life, with numerous distractions from her bird work. The years rolled by all too rapidly and did not leave enough time for the book which she often mentioned. Thus this task was left to another to finish.

The editor's problem, in preparing this book, was to select suitable material from a vast amount of information. Miss Sherman left about sixty notebooks, closely written in longhand, as well as a number of chapters for the intended book. These latter papers were in various stages of completion. Some were apparently finished; of others there were first, second

11

and third drafts, while with still others whole sections had been cut out and could not be found. Since the notebooks were so voluminous and made up almost entirely of day-to-day recordings, only a small amount of material from this source could be utilized.

My objective in the selection of material was to use as many of the nesting studies as possible, as this was the field in which Miss Sherman excelled. Besides the original chapters which I was able to make up, we were kindly given permission to reprint a number of articles from the *Auk* and *Wilson Bulletin*. These are quoted *verbatim*. This supplementary material helps to round out the book and to convey to the reader the broad scope of Miss Sherman's work. Also included are several chapters which show some of the other angles of her bird work, as well as the wit and satire which she occasionally employed.

Fred J. Pierce

Winthrop, Iowa.

FOREWORD TO THE 1952 EDITION

From the earliest period of white settlement an area in Clayton County, Iowa, became known as the Garnavillo Prairie. It extends roughly a length of about twelve miles from south of the town of Garnavillo northward to the villages of Froelich and Giard, average width about five miles. The deep loam is underlaid with clay subsoil, so crops withstand extended periods of drought. Being gently rolling in contour wet weather is not especially harmful. It is one of the rich agricultural areas in the agricultural state of Iowa; rich not only because of the productivity of the soil but also on account of the financial resources of its citizens. The greater portion of the early settlers on the area were immigrants from Germany and Ireland, but among the earliest arrivals were a good many of pioneering inclinations from the Eastern States and New England. Among these were Mark B. Sherman and his wife Melissa Clark Sherman. Mark B. Sherman's kin extend back to Roger Sherman, a signer of the Declaration of Independence; to Roger Conant, founder of Salem, Massachusetts; and to James Conant, a former president of Harvard University. Mrs. Sherman was a daughter of Myron H. Clark, nineteenth governor of New York State (1855-1857).

Mr. and Mrs. Sherman had lived for a few years at Prairie du Chien, Wis. They came to Iowa in 1845. Here they built one of the first homes on the Garnavillo Prairie. The structure still stands and is now serving as a machine shed. Near them was forming the village of National to which they moved after twenty years of farming and built the Sherman Home-

13

stead. For a living Mr. Sherman cobbled boots for his farming neighbors. To the same neighbors he loaned money and increased his possessions from the interest accruals. As an investor in farm mortgages Mr. Sherman was very successful. He made loans with discretion. When borrowers became enmeshed in financial difficulties he gave wise counsel. He usually collected the prevailing high rate of interest. Seldom did he have to resort to severe measures to liquidate a loan. He was well regarded by those who dealt with him.

Mr. and Mrs. Sherman reared to manhood and womanhood five daughters and one son. One of the daughters died as a young woman. The others received a college education. The son received a legal education. Two of the daughters became doctors of medicine at a time when that attainment was rare for women. Mr. Sherman died in 1896 and left a substantial estate to his family. A daughter, Miss Althea R. Sherman, author of this work, was born on October 10, 1853. After receiving a bachelor's degree from Oberlin College she taught for several years in the public schools. After post graduate work at Oberlin she received her Master's degree and spent several years in the study of art. For a time she was instructor in drawing at Carleton College and then supervisor of drawing in the public schools of Tacoma, Washington. In 1895 she returned to her ancestral home to help care for her aging parents.

Any reference to the life history of Miss Althea R. Sherman is quite deficient without including a word about Dr. E. Amelia Sherman. The two sisters never married and from the time of the passing of their mother in 1902 until Dr. Sherman's passing in 1940 they occupied the Sherman Homestead together. Very few changes were made in that home during the seventy years preceding the death of Miss Althea R. Sherman on April 16, 1943. At Miss Sherman's passing there was still in use the open well from which water was drawn by windlass. Born in 1881, on the same Garnavillo Prairie, this writer has never seen another open well with windlass, rope and bucket. The parlor was kept dark by tightly closed shutters. The beautiful paper on the walls was in excellent condition after seventy years. A stern frugality was a part of the life of Dr. Sherman as it had been of her parents. In her will Dr. Sherman provided: "My property represents the savings of a lifetime and my shares of the estates of my parents, savings of three lifetimes of industry, economy and self denial, and I wish it used wisely, not wastefully—extravagantly, nor to encourage idleness or luxurious living." That Miss Althea R. Sherman felt and at times chafed under the severe economy is apparent from some of the daily notes which she recorded.

Dr. Sherman made contributions to her profession. She kept membership in state and federal medical societies until her death. She appeared on their programs and contributed articles to their publications. Many of us well remember Dr. Sherman travelling the countryside with white horse and top buggy as a country doctor.

Though both sisters were positive characters and had widely different interests, they were able to adjust such differences as might be expected to arise. It can be said with certainty that after their parents were gone, the only person that influenced either of them was the other of them.

Miss Sherman never acquired her father's and her sister's taste for financial matters. Though conservative by nature, she travelled in foreign lands, and made substantial donations to educational, religious and charitable institutions. She paid dues to numerous scientific groups and when away from home did not deny herself the things generally considered as necessities. She seemingly made some loans without sufficient investigation where the family name of the borrower bore a good reputation. She made some excessive loans for the security offered. She unnecessarily surrendered substantial values where borrowers wanted to liquidate. Some of these things may have transpired because she disdained her sister's excessive frugality.

When visiting with the sisters, one was soon impressed with the different directions in which the conversation was directed by them. Dr. Sherman was likely to comment on the wayward behaviour of young people, about the excessive use of tobacco and intoxicating liquor, and the speed of automobile traffic. The conversation with Miss Althea tended to a more optimistic outlook. The beauties of the season, if it fit the facts, or some interesting current event was more likely to receive attention, and if the conversation was with a fellow bird student, it would be about the arrival or departure of certain species, or the thrill she had experienced in some unusual bird observation. From this it might be implied that Dr. Sherman was uncompromising and Miss Althea the more tolerant. That was not the case. Dr. Sherman was not accustomed to express or exhibit any ill will, not even toward those who had evidently disappointed her. Miss Althea did not overlook any wrongs and some of the wrongs were evidently not real.

When rural mail delivery was established by the Post Office Department the post office in National was abandoned and the community was served through McGregor. Not so much the Post Office Department, but the people of McGregor and the town itself, became the objects of Miss Althea's scorn. From then on she was unduly critical of everything said or done by the citizens of McGregor. When a letter was addressed to her, the writer was informed that thereafter all mail to her was to be directed to "National via McGregor." If the writer did not heed the first admonition he was likely to regret the oversight.

Miss Sherman attained some recognition as an artist. Her paintings included some of birds as they are usually seen, partly obscured by lights and shades. Their reproduction on colored prints is not likely to prove satisfactory. Her art efforts were not in the direction of modern art. Much of modern art is not to paint what is seen, rather to have the work of art carry a thought or theme, something to carry the mind of the observer beyond the pigment and its arrangement upon the canvas. It is doubtful that she would ever have depicted cheerfully what she had not seen. Her mind was of scientific bent. In her paintings and drawings as well as in her writings she tried to present to us, as nearly as she could, what she actually observed. Her theme was the truth and truth was thrill enough.

As soon as Miss Sherman returned to the parental roof she devoted much of her time to drawing and painting. Birds were a part of her subjects and then was formed the determination to make an intimate study of the birds about her home. Some of her former pupils in the public schools have told of her interest at the time in nature lore, how she took them into fields to have them see at first hand how all life exists, grows and propagates itself. Painting of the birds, then, was not the beginning of bird study for her, but it was an agency to lead to a life's work.

Miss Sherman's work is convincing proof that no one need lament not having opportunity to travel in foreign lands for nature study. Miss Sherman made a

unique and valuable contribution to the knowledge of
birds, and she studied them where we all may do so, at
our very doors, and she recorded facts not theretofore
known.

Not only did Miss Sherman make valuable reports
of her studies, but she possessed a rare ability to express herself. Her writings are decidedly readable.
She never wanted for an interesting word to record
her findings. This should not be called a gift, for she
had prepared herself. Those who were familiar with
the way she worked knew that she never gave up her
studies. She had at her elbows, and she used what
she had, a number of books on how to use words and
phrases and how to appeal to readers. She made a
study as to how to report scientific facts and she adhered to the rules. If we want to think that she had
a gift of expression it probably was her pungent wit,
but if she had such a gift, she also improved it by constant study. By wit, irony and ridicule she could disarm
an opponent. She used that ability, not personally, but
always with cutting force.

When a scientific group of which she was a member
at an annual meeting adopted a statement of purposes,
and resolved, among other things, to protect all of
native life, Miss Sherman wrote an open letter which
was published in the organization's publication. She
demanded that at the next annual meeting of the association the word "all" would have to be removed from
the resolution. She would not agree to tolerate rattle-
snakes upon her grounds, nor would she agree to
propagate obnoxious weeds.

A young lady, whose father was a member of the
state legislature, and being interested in birds, asked
a young lawyer to draft a bill for enactment into law.
It was to the effect that a specific day of the year be
set aside as a bird day to be observed by the public
schools, during which day some time should be

devoted to the study of birds. The bill was drafted just as the young lady had specified. To the consternation of the young lawyer the bill was passed without the change of a word. It is still a part of the law of the State of Iowa. No doubt most school authorities of the state are not aware of the existence of the law. Neither the proponent of the law, nor the drafter of it, had the knowledge, insight and experience possessed by Miss Sherman as to how to study birds. In her powerful style Miss Sherman wrote a criticism of the law. She argued: Why a bird day? Why birds only? Why not a day for each form in the animal, vegetable and mineral kingdoms? Would there be enough days in the school year for that? Why should not a special day be set aside for the study of worms, since worms have been so intimately connected with man since the beginning of recorded history? Nature study, not birds alone, needed to be studied and that the year round. The law was useless and impractical, she argued. Her predictions came true. The lawyer (not young now) still wonders if Miss Sherman ever knew who drafted the bill; he did not have the temerity to admit it to her. She never indicated in her criticism that she knew how the law came into existence. She may have known. She won her point without letting it become personal.

The people who came to visit the Sherman home, (and there were many during the months of May and June, just when nesting activity was at its peak) never knew how much Miss Sherman begrudged the time taken from actual observation, during the days when she was busy from dawn to dusk, during the sixteen hours of daylight. In her charming way, she received all visitors, but in her bird notes she at times made the observation that the tramps were on the highways again. When one realizes all the work she did during such periods of the year it is not surprising that she made such notations in the records for herself, but it is astounding that she could remain such a charming hostess under such trying circumstances.

None of Miss Sherman's writings aroused more interest and discussion than her paper: "Down With the House Wren Boxes." Most bird students agreed that she had presented the facts correctly. Not all agreed with her as to the drastic remedies she advocated and resorted to. The article not only had the attention of bird students. Extracts of it appeared in farm journals and in the public press. Miss Sherman received many letters about the article. Some of these writers had not made a special study of bird behaviour. Some questioned Miss Sherman's knowledge of the subject! Such unwarranted criticism she could not ignore. She followed the matter with several succeeding articles and vehemently defended the position she had taken. For several years there had been on the Sherman grounds a Purple Martin house of a popular make. Unfortunately the builder of these houses also questioned whether Miss Sherman had drawn her conclusions after sufficient observation. Miss Sherman wrote to this man that he was probably blinded by mercenary motives which kept him from seeing the depredations by the House Wren. The beautiful bird house was cut down and thereafter received asylum in the barn hayloft. On the House Wren issue Miss Sherman would be heard after her death. In her will she provided that those receiving the Sherman Homestead should not allow House Wrens to nest thereon. During the last years of Miss Sherman's life, when she was no longer able to interfere, House Wrens were defiantly building their nests and cheerfully singing on the premises. Even if the beneficiaries under her will would seek to abate the declared nuisance as directed, the mischievous and resourceful House Wren would no doubt find some way to circumvent the injunction against his presence.

The summing up of the House Wren issue had better be left with Arthur Cleveland Bent, Bulletin 195, page 115, *Life Histories of North American Nuthatches, Wrens, Thrashers and Their Allies:*

"The relations of the House Wren to other birds make him a much more interesting even though it be a less desirable personality. His aggressions toward other birds have not been recently acquired but constitute an old and well-established trait. His behaviour is evidence of his superior intelligence in the battle of the survival of the fittest. He is activated to secure and dominate a definite area during the reproductive season for the sake of his own preservation. For this reason this small enterprising midget making his way in the world often against superior odds deserves our respect rather than our condemnation. If man upsets the balance of nature by his interference, for example by erecting too many nesting boxes, then man alone is to blame for the conditions which prevail in certain localities."

If it may be said that Miss Sherman could not tolerate adverse criticism, that is but human. Many great men and women have not been able to disregard unfavorable criticism, just or unwarranted.

During the active years of Miss Sherman's bird studies she appeared on programs of the American Ornithologists' Union and the Wilson Ornith. Club. Those who heard and met her at such meetings never forgot her. Her inimitable mannerisms, her charming personality, her forceful and pungent wit, her knowledge of the subject treated and her ability to present it interestingly, made her appearance on a program an attraction. She was known and beloved by the leading contemporary ornithologists of the United States and Canada.

Postville, Iowa.   Arthur J. Palas

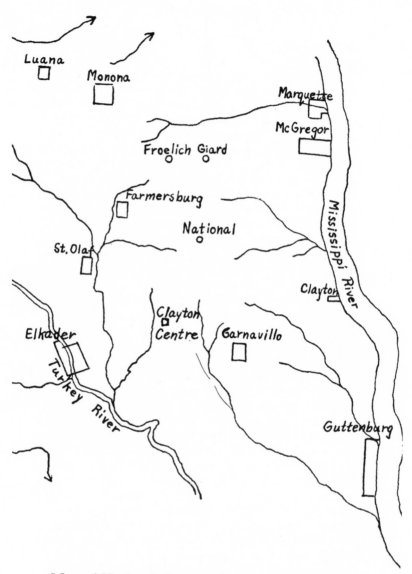

Map of National, Iowa, and surrounding territory.

CHAPTER I

WATCHING THE BIRDS
OF OUR DOORYARD

The dooryard which I am describing is situated in northeastern Iowa, 6 miles west of the Mississippi River and 3 miles south of the 43d parallel of latitude. It contains an area of about one acre. According to good American usage, we have various kinds of yards or fenced enclosures, such as dooryards, barnyards, stockyards, chickenyards and numerous others, and according to the same usage, in speaking continually of our dooryard or houseyard, we abbreviate it to yard. This I did in one of my published papers, and when 'The Ibis' reviewed it, the reviewer put yard in quotation marks and proceeded thereafter to call it a "garden." Now our dooryard or our *yard* is not a garden, which signifies a cultivated place for flowers or vegetables, or both. But a very small part of it is devoted to vegetables. Buildings occupy a part of it, and still another part is given over to the orchard, a large part of the trees of which (at present) are plum trees, bearing harvests mainly of birds' nests. There is toleration for plum trees for several reasons: They take care of themselves and are thorny and brushy about their trunks, thereby offering desirable sites for bird nests. Besides the plum trees, there are a few apple trees, shade trees, and the mulberry, gooseberry, raspberry, elderberry, and a half-dozen other kinds of bushes that have grown from seeds dropped by the birds. So without aid from mankind, the birds are responsible for much that is attractive to themselves.

This land sixty years ago was open prairie devoid of tree or shrub. It lay at the southern extremity of a small village which grew no more in that direction; consequently there has always been farmed land to the south and west of our place. For two reasons I cannot give the early history of bird life in this dooryard, which began in 1866. In the first place, I knew very little about birds, and in the second place, I was sent from home to school in a distant state at the age of fifteen years, and my time for upward of twenty-five years thereafter was spent in study or teaching away from the parental roof. My return to it dates from 1895. At that time the shade trees, ornamental shrubs and orchard trees of the neighborhood were well grown. As my observation of birds grew keener, it was very evident, when returning from trips to the woods or similar outings, that we had more birds than nearby places, and this remark was frequently made: "If one wishes to see the birds, one should stay at home." The reason for this was long sought. After twenty years of study of the problem, this solution of it is offered: The village site is near the watershed between the Mississippi and the Turkey Rivers. That makes it near the headwaters of streams, which a little lower down cut deep channels but near their sources spread out into marshy meadows. There, in migration time, may be seen some of the shore birds: the Wilson's Snipe, Solitary Sandpiper, Yellow-legs, the King and Virginia Rails, while among the breeding species are the Sora, Red-winged Blackbird and Short-billed Marsh Wren. It may surprise some people to hear the Short-billed Marsh Wren spoken of as a back-dooryard breeding species, yet such it has been with us.

Recently there occurred the death of a pioneer who came to our Clayton County, Iowa, in 1838, when eighteen years of age. Had this pioneer been a careful observer of birds, what a history of wonderful changes could have been given us! Our county a century ago was one of magnificent distances. Bounded on the east by the Mississippi River, on the south by Dubuque County, it stretched on the west to undefined limits in the Rocky Mountains, and on the north it reached to Canada, embracing within its area all of the present state of Minnesota. St. Paul was one of its few voting precincts. The Territory of Iowa had been open to white settlement for only a short time. Wildlife flourished in its original abundance. Those were the days of countless water-fowl and of the Prairie Chicken, the Passenger Pigeon and the Wild Turkey. So exceedingly numerous were the Wild Turkeys on the banks of one of our rivers, it was named Turkey River—a name which it still bears.

We who are children of the pioneers of Iowa, ought to be able to give a better account of the changes that have occurred in our bird population. For myself I can say this: The Barn and Cliff Swallows were *the birds* of my childhood on a farm where I lived until nearly twelve years old. These two species, but more especially the Cliff Swallows, were very numerous, yet now they are rare, thanks to that hated alien, *Passer domesticus*. I do not know that either the Catbird or Brown Thrasher had reached us then, for the mewing call of the former and the thrashings given by the latter would have left indelible impressions on the memory of a child. On unfenced portions of prairie, where herds of cattle grazed, and many beautiful wild flowers bloomed (now gone forever), were to be found the eggs or young of ground-nesting species. Rail fences together with a lack of trees and telephone poles accounted for the absence of Northern Flicker and Red-headed Woodpecker now so abundant. In fact, almost all the birds of village, farm and orchard that have succeeded the original avian occupants, have followed the trail of the white man. The species that they have supplanted, have disappeared entirely or have become very scarce—not because of intentional harm done them by mankind, for very little shooting or trapping of birds has been done in the last half century. The effects of land cultivation may be plainly seen upon a number of species of the bird population.

Most of our farmers practice the three-year rotation of crops system, which appears to be uncongenial to the birds. This seems to account in large measure for the fact that about our village certain birds have been more abundant than elsewhere in our region. The small pastures of the villagers, the cemetery, the churchyards, and the twenty acres constituting the County Fairgrounds have remained in grass year after year, and apparently in consequence of this Meadowlarks, Bobolinks and Song Sparrows have been more numerous than in the surrounding country. In studying the effects of rotation in crops upon what I am permitted to see of bird life, it has been learned that large autumn records are certain for those years in which my farmer neighbors have planted corn in the fields adjoining our lands.

For upward of fifteen years the village was decadent, and now is nearly obsolete. For several years, when many of the houses were uninhabited, the study of bird life was at its best. The bad boys and the cats having left, the birds in an unmolested state tenanted the deserted homes of man.

In recent years we have added several abandoned village lots to the original acreage of our homestead, and in the expression "our place" all this land is included, yet there has been little seen on the entire place, that has not had a duplicate in the dooryard also. Either on our place or in the air overhead there have been identified 162 species of birds. The largest number of species seen for any one year is 109, and the annual average for twelve years is 103 species. The Rock Wren is one of the very few species seen on the place, but not in the dooryard. Its coming was hailéd with joy, for it not only added a new species to the list, but it moved the limit of the range of the Rock Wren 200 miles eastward.

The comparison of records is a game I am forced to play alone, because of lack of other observers in the region. A comparison of the daily average for each month has much interest as well as some value. People with little knowledge of birds are heard sometimes to say that we do not have as many birds as we did a few years ago. Daily records of the species seen and the averaging of them month by month, established the truth of this impression. Ten years ago, when bird life was more abundant, the daily average for June, July and August was twenty-five species, but in more recent years this daily average has dropped.

The number of species that have been found nesting on our place is thirty-three. The Prairie Horned Lark and Vesper Sparrow have nested just over the fence on neighboring acres, and it is hoped that their nests may yet be found on our land, where, no doubt, they have been placed unobserved. The names of the breeding species are given below.

Sora
Killdeer
Bob-white
Mourning Dove
Screech Owl
Sparrow Hawk
Yellow-billed Cuckoo
Black-billed Cuckoo

Red-headed Woodpecker
Northern Flicker
Chimney Swift
Kingbird (Eastern)
Phoebe
Bobolink
Cowbird
Red-winged Blackbird

Eastern Meadowlark   Migrant Shrike
Western Meadowlark   Northern Yellow-throat
Baltimore Oriole   Catbird
Bronzed Grackle   Brown Thrasher
Goldfinch   Western House Wren
Chipping Sparrow   Short-billed Marsh Wren
Song Sparrow   Robin
Dickcissel   Bluebird
Barn Swallow

All the birds named except four, viz.: Sora, Killdeer,
Western Meadowlark, and Short-billed Marsh Wren,
have nested within the dooryard. Besides these, within
a radius of a quarter-mile, ten or eleven other species
have nested, some of which in the future may come
to us. It may be noted that a majority of these species
are such as have followed man to his home on the
treeless prairie and availed themselves of the buildings,
trees and shrubs that he has placed there.

Within the past fourteen years the advent of a
hitherto absent species, the Cardinal, has been watched
with intense interest by all bird lovers. The brilliant
colors of the Cardinal attract the attention of almost
everyone. This, taken together with its winter habit
of coming to dooryard or chickenyard, has helped in
the collecting of data concerning its northward movement and its slow spreading across the northern portion
of Iowa. In some places it has become a common breeding species, "as common as the Robin" in the estimation
of some people. It is now a resident about my home,
and we hope soon to add it to the list of breeding
birds of the dooryard.

Enough circumstantial evidence has been collected
to convince us that certain winter visitors such as
Cardinals, Hairy and Downy Woodpeckers, Chickadees and White-breasted Nuthatches have returned

winter after winter to our wind-swept dooryard for
the sake of the food offered them. No doubt trapping
and banding would change the circumstantial evidence
to proof positive.

The coming of spring brings with it the opportunities
to study the courtship and mating of various species
of birds about the dooryard. Once I thought I witnessed a mating proposal on the part of a Brown
Thrasher as he walked with his enamorata in front of
a window. He picked up a brown leaf and a moment
later the Lady Thrasher picked up another brown
leaf. Translated into human behavior and language,
it would be equivalent to the young man saying as he
picks up a brick: "See this pretty brick! Let's build
a home!" And she responds as she lifts another brick:
"Yes, let's do it!"

After courtship comes the selection of nest-site. The
rather conspicuous behavior of Mourning Doves and
Brown Thrashers at such times is very similar, due
very likely to the similarity of their nesting needs. The
exchange of place on the nest is very quickly done by
both species. The bird returning to the nest must have
an easy access to it, and the sitting bird likewise needs
opportunity for easy exit; therefore both doves and
thrashers have been seen enacting what appears to be
a rehearsal of these movements in the proposed nest
site. The thrashers jealously guard the chosen nest
site and have been known to "scold" a person approaching it before a single stick has been laid. The Phoebe
often chants for days the merits of a location that
seems suitable to him, but which his mate obstinately
refuses to accept.

Following long and careful study of both Flickers
and House Wrens, a certain theory appears very
reasonable: The males have come first in spring and
have selected boxes placed for them. Since to human

eyes the males look alike, and to human ears their songs sound alike, a strong suspicion is engendered that these males with the ready furnished homes hold undue importance in the eyes of the females. It has been hinted that something similar to this has happened in the human family. And has not Emerson written: "Nature is full of a sublime family likeness throughout her works . . . Nature is an endless combination and repetition of a very few laws."

One year I observed a pair of Barn Swallows making use of an old nest built by the Phoebe, thus saving themselves the labor of building a nest of their own. Several times Catbirds have built in a dwarf plum tree which grew in front of one of our windows. The Catbird nests, placed 2 feet from the window-pane, have been watched through old-fashioned, outside house blinds, and in addition to this a drawing of the mother bird on the nest was made from the same vantage point. The study of these nests was filled with absorbing interest; so great was my interest in them that almost my entire time for days was spent in sight of them. Very near the site of these Catbird nests were placed the nests of Brown Thrashers and Song Sparrows. A violent storm destroyed the nest of the former before the eggs were hatched, while the fate of the Song Sparrow was a mystery. There are so many mysteries that bird study chances upon, one is fortunate when he finds an unlocking key. A number of years ago, I had opportunity to follow part of the nest history of the Mourning Dove, when one of its nests was built in a tree less than 10 feet from a window of my bird tower. I had been an onlooker when an egg was hatched. When that nestling was about four days old, I rose early and at about five o'clock in the morning arrived at the watchout with an armful of sewing, expecting to spend the entire day there. The watching of a Mourning Dove's nest is a dreary task, unless one can do something besides watch. If one knits, that is an excellent occupation, for the eyes must be lifted to the nest at least once a minute, since the exchange of the place on the nest is done so quickly and quietly it easily escapes detection. At about half past seven o'clock that morning, while I had shears in hand, I saw the feathers elevated on the back of the dove, then saw a red squirrel climbing the tree trunk. An instant later I was out. I screamed and threw the shears, but of course did not hit the squirrel. Afterthought showed me that I could easily have caught him by the tail, while he was swallowing the first nestling. The second one he took in his mouth and mounted to a higher branch. Luckily I had some neighbor boys, who shot him there.

Many observations of nesting birds have been made within the limits of our small grounds and dooryard. These are described at considerable length in the other chapters of this collection of nesting studies of Iowa birds.

CHAPTER II

FEEDING WINTER BIRDS

In summer it has been remarked by strangers that, to them, our place does not look like a favorable resort for birds, their idea for such a resort being a thickly wooded spot, such as does not maintain one-fourth the number of breeding birds as does our dooryard. However, the presence in winter of any bird, except occasional transients, might well be a matter worthy of comment, especially when the exposed, wind-swept location of our home is considered. Still more surprising is the fact that, with a few exceptions, the birds that spend the entire winter months with us are woodland dwellers, and have exchanged the sheltered spots of their summer habitats for the bleak, open prairie in winter. Among the few exceptions to be mentioned are the Redpoll, Goldfinch, Tree Sparrow and rarely a Slate-colored Junco. One winter a Northern Shrike made his headquarters in our orchard. Three species of owls occasionally make visits. Both the Cedar Waxwing and its northern cousin, the Bohemian Waxwing, have tarried for a few days or weeks. In the days when the Bob-white was numerous a wandering covey would stay near for some time.

Of the eighteen species of birds that have found food which induced them to linger for periods measured either by a few days or all winter, only seven of them have made the longer stay. These have been the Hairy and the Downy Woodpeckers, Blue Jay, Tree Sparrow, Cardinal, White-breasted Nuthatch and Chickadee.

For a dozen or more years many experiments were

made to learn the winter bird boarders' choice in foods. All like nuts and suet, but there is a mixture that almost always is preferred to suet. In preparing the mixture we take a cupful of corn meal, a cupful of lard cracklings or chopped suet, a half cupful of chopped walnut meats, three or four table-spoonfuls of corn syrup, and enough water to wet the mass. This is cooked for a few minutes and may then be filled into the holes of a feeding-stick or spread upon cards of corrugated pasteboard with thread or twine bound about to hold the food in place. These were called "food cards" long before the World War occasioned the use of another style of food cards. The food cards are fastened to shingles or to the inside curve of pieces of galvanized iron, and hung in various places. If fastened to a picket fence, they are hung vertically; if fastened to branches of trees or snowball bushes, they hang face downward at an angle considerably away from the perpendicular. That pest, the English Sparrow, fears the motion of the shingle, but such desirable boarders as the woodpeckers, nuthatches and chickadees cling to the shingles without apparent inconvenience when once the food has been found.

Were I required to choose from all the birds the single family that has afforded me the greatest amount of pleasure, my choice would fall upon the woodpeckers. Certainly as songsters these birds do not rank high, though the merry calls of the Flicker and Red-headed Woodpecker are jolly and cheerful sounds. As a rule, the Flicker is with us for six months and the Red-head is with us four months of the year; four others of the Picidae remain the year around in northeastern Iowa. Three of these have come to our home in winter. The Red-bellied Woodpecker, whose habitat is in deep, wooded ravines, very rarely is seen upon the prairie. To have one come in mid-winter, find food, even to visit the feeding-stick and linger about for three weeks, was as pleasant as it was unexpected.

The Hairy Woodpecker occurs much less frequently than the Downy. That individuals of both species have been boarders here in winter and have nested the following summer in the woods two or three miles away, seems proved by them in several seasons. Some of our winter food usually remains in the spring after our boarders have left; whether suet or a mixture of several materials, shreds of food will stay in the feeders for weeks. When at intervals weeks afterward in May or June, a Hairy or a Downy Woodpecker unexpectedly appears and flies directly to a food card on a suspended sheet of metal or to a feeding-stick and helps himself to the food thereon, he plainly proclaims himself a boarder of the preceding winter. This has happened enough times to make convincing the theory that these woodpeckers nest in the woods two, perhaps three, miles away, yet near enough to permit occasional returns for meals. The reason I feel confident that they go so far is because such birds do nest there, and between their feeding place and the woods there are but three farm houses; these have about them a very limited number of trees. In passing these farmsteads in spring I have usually stopped long enough to learn what birds were there, and have seen neither of these species about. It is quite credible that a winter boarder Downy of mine once raised a brood in an orchard, distant two miles by air line measurement. The nest was in the trunk of a dead apple tree about three feet from the ground. The orchard borders a strip of dense woods from which a supply of food could be obtained. Such timber environs are selected for nest sites by both the Hairy and Downy Woodpeckers, even by the very same birds that choose to be prairie dwellers for the remainder of the year.

Contrasted with the arrival of spring in our southern states, the coming of our northern spring often suggests the marriage proposal, which, though long and confidently expected, upon arriving is declared "sudden." Whether this coming be earlier or later than normal, about March 21 our woodpecker boarders begin to betray signs of the strong physiological urge, the impellent for posterity, that has brought the earliest migrants northward. It is then that Downy begins to go gadding. He may not have missed a meal the whole winter long, but near the time of the vernal equinox he is off to the woods for the day. For two or three weeks he returns for supper about five o'clock, and stays for an early breakfast the next morning; no doubt, he sleeps in his old winter quarters. Unfortunately, I have never been able to follow him to the woods, where his wooings have progressed favorably. The mate chosen, or, more correctly, the one that chose him, may have the fickle nature of the female Flicker and requires watching in fair weather, when a rival might be abroad. Stormy, disagreeable weather seemingly releases Downy from work and watchfulness. At all events, on such days his return to the feeding-stick is expected, and he does not disappoint us. There have been Aprils in which on several successive days these returns for meals have been made, and in two seasons visits in May have occurred. In one cold, backward May the visits did not cease until the 26th. After this the curtain falls on Downy's activities and is not raised until the last days of June, when he returns to his boarding place with an offspring. On one day it may be a son he brings, and on the next a daughter, or it may be a son and a daughter together that he leads directly to the ancient piece of suet from which he tears pieces with vigor and stuffs them rapidly into the waiting mouths. It is the paternal role of Downy that strikes people as exceedingly droll; his small size and juvenile traits have failed to give the impression of a grown-up, and it is not strange to hear people refer to him as "the little imp."

I have never known the street and number of Hairy's winter sleeping room, which at times appeared to be near. With Downy it has been different, many of his rooming places having been known, some of them in dead limbs of plum trees, quite as many in fence-posts. In the middle of October, 1919, he was seen at work excavating a hole. The same cavity provided an acceptable nesting place for Bluebirds in the two successive springs following. On September 3, 1921, he was busily digging out lodgings, which were soon finished. Eight days afterward a gentle knock brought him to his doorway, but twelve more days passed before he was seen at the feeding place. His faith that a food supply would be maintained brought him from the woods to hollow out a chamber for a winter residence. Such faith ought never to be misplaced, but on two successive winters our home was closed and a break came in woodpecker history as far as my records were concerned.

Often the woodpeckers forage for themselves quite successfully until near the middle of December. In the autumn of 1911 a Hairy Woodpecker fed for some time on the soft kernels of a late planting of sweet corn. In the middle of October suet was put up in several places near the garden, but not until Christmas day was a Downy seen as the first visitor to it. The following January opened with below-zero temperature which continued for sixteen days without a break, the mercury hovering between 4 and 32 degrees below zero. Five other below-zero days came later in the month. Judging from their behavior, both the Hairy and the Downy present feared an exhaustion of the food supply, from which the former drove his smaller cousin. Each, watchful of his rival, had his favorite location on the south side of the neighboring apple trees where he clung when the mercury was capering about the mark of 18 degrees below zero. Jealousy concerning the food supply seemed to be the only explanation of this conduct. The customary spot for placing food for birds is east of the house in two large clumps of snowball bushes. Here two pieces of suet had hung for weeks. Downy found this food first. Ten days later Hairy also discovered it to the great distress of Downy. His concern, expressed by much fluttering and spluttering through the bushes, was of the most vigorous character. In the sharing of food generosity is not a strong woodpecker trait.

Except when his larder runs low, Downy does not go to the ground in search of food. Yet two or three rather unique acts on his part have been witnessed. Once when on his feeding-stick, he pulled a piece of suet from a hole and it fell to the ground. He immediately flew down after it, carried it up to the hole and neatly tucked it back in place, then proceeded with his meal. Halved squash seeds are usually scattered on the ground, and a few times he has been seen to take one of these, wedge it under some suet remaining in a hole where he could manage to extract the half kernel.

Thus far the pronouns referring to Downy have been of the masculine gender, singular number, from which it should not be inferred that for twenty-five or more years the bird has been one and the same. In the line of boarders breaks must have often occurred, breaks not easily recognized. Quite often there have been two male boarders of this species, one of which quailed and fled before the overlord. The next winter the timid one may have become the master with an understudy of his own. Once there was unquestionable certainty about the line of succession: For four or five years a certain Downy had returned each autumn. In 1923, on June 30, after an absence of forty-six days, he appeared on the feeding-stick, accompanied by a daughter; the following day both were back and his young son was with them. Sonny's crown had an unusually large spotting of red, which served easily for distinguishing him from his father; this crown marking persisted for several weeks after his father's final disappearance. Here was a case of family inheritance among birds: Not only did Sonny succeed to the feeding-stick of his sire, but also at roosting time was he seen to occupy the cavity that Daddy was seen digging in the previous autumn. Of his sister's fate there was less certainty. The next winter a female was seen occasionally, and in the fall following a female claimed the feeding-stick immediately upon the disappearance of a male believed to be Sonny. She was the only Downy visitor for the remainder of that winter.

Seldom has a female Downy been a boarder when a male was here. The treatment accorded her has never been so rough as that bestowed upon the second male, but it has been far from cordial, and sufficiently hostile to make her visit a short one. One female had a longer written history: once she was seen to chase a male Downy. She stayed until the regular leaving time in spring. The following December she was the first of her species to appear, and was very soon eating from the food supply. It was in the days when the food was fastened to shingles and metal shields where it was not quickly found by strangers. In her first winter this Downy had interesting experiences with English Sparrows. Few things irk me more than to see these detested aliens get a morsel of the prepared food; it was to keep them from it that the food-card shields were hung at a sharp angle downward. While Downy clung to the strings of a food card enjoying her meal, a gang of these outlaws gathered about her, uttering all the swear words at their command. She would dash at them, scattering the crowd, but they soon returned to again enact the scene. At last a smart one learned to hang on, soon all of them could do it. It was an unmistakable demonstration of the way in which wild birds learn to get food through observation and imitation. For two or three winters these sparrows caused much trouble, after which the wise ones died or forgot their lesson, since in more recent years the food has been safe from them. This was a matter for rejoicing for it took four hours to prepare a supply of the mixture that lasted only fourteen days.

CHAPTER III

THE HOME LIFE OF THE CHIMNEY SWIFT

By standing on a box placed on a chair and aided by a hand-mirror thrust through a stove-pipe hole into a chimney, one may learn a little about the home life of the Chimney Swift *(Chaetura pelagica)*. Or one may have a still better chance such as was enjoyed many years ago by Mary F. Day, in New Jersey *(Bird-Lore,* Vol. 1, 1899, pp. 78-81). It was her good fortune to watch a nest built a trifle above the stove-pipe hole, which was about 2 feet above the floor. She made such good use of her opportunities that the data she collected were most accurate. However, many things were left unseen by her which better facilities for viewing might have revealed. Some of these things I am now able to describe.

Many years ago I planned a building which was not built until 1915. For lack of a better name, it is called the Chimney Swifts' tower. Its dimensions are 9 feet square and 28 feet to the top of the chimney. The artificial chimney is 2 feet square, and runs down the center of the tower to a depth of 14 feet; the chimney was built of pine flooring with the rough sides of the boards turned within. A door opens into the chimney and a stationary ladder may be climbed for closing and opening the top of the chimney in fall and spring, respectively. Auger-holes serve as peep-holes on two sides, while on the other two sides are windows. The frames of these windows are not vertical but are in two planes which meet in an obtuse angle. Into this space which juts into the chimney one's head can be

introduced, and through the glass a view to the bottom
or to the top of the chimney may be obtained without
unduly frightening the birds. A paper screen often is
placed over one window and back of it a lighted lamp
or lantern gives sufficient illumination for one easily
to watch the swifts' home life at night. The illumination is even a little better than it is by day. Although
my chimney was planned without a very full knowledge
of Chimney Swift life, after many years of use and
observation made within it, I have failed to see how
any improvements could have been made in the plan-
ning of it.

The Flicker seems to think itself a privileged bird
on our place—that it has the right to occupy any and
all buildings except our house. When two-thirds of
the siding had been placed on the tower, a male Flicker
was seen inspecting the building. When the tower was
completed this or another Flicker frequented the chimney, and perhaps roosted there; at any rate he did
much hammering in it by day. For three summers he
is believed to have kept the Chimney Swifts out. In
1918 the Flicker did not return and the swifts built
their nests there in June—three years after the tower
was built. Very likely they resorted to the wooden
chimney after having had another nest destroyed.

It was the busy summer of war time, when everyone
was expected to work to the utmost limit. Work so
occupied my time that for a few weeks I neglected to
visit the chimney. That was the time the nest was built.
The first summer the nest walls were so low that a
newly hatched swift rolled out and was drowned in
the rain-pan, which rests at the bottom of the chimney
and is designed to keep the rain water from running
down into the bottom half of the tower. The second
year an egg rolled out. The nest was used for the next
five summers, and each year its walls were raised a

little, until the increment amounted to about a half inch. One year only a few sticks were added, and these were broken off before the nesting was over. This building up of the nest wall is done after egg-laying has begun. Before that a few sticks are stuck against the wall below the old nest.

By the best of luck the nest was built in the spot most favorable of all for the viewing of it. That place was in the middle of the north wall and under the right-hand corner of the window. Thus it is brought within a distance of 15 inches from the eye of the observer looking through the east window. It can also be seen through the auger-holes made for that purpose, and of course the chimney can be entered through the door at any time, although that is undesirable after the young begin to fly.

The Chimney Swift's nest measures only 4 inches from right to left, and 3 inches from its front edge to the wall back of it. It looks very frail and bends some-what under one's touch, and is more flexible in damp weather. The first year of its occupancy I had spasms of fear whenever it rained, but after I saw the nest sustain the weight of six well grown young ones and both parents, I had greater confidence in its strength!

To catch the rain that falls through the hole in the top of the chimney a zinc pan was made in the size of the chimney floor. This rain-pan has served another purpose. By cleaning it every day in spring and fall, it can be ascertained if the swifts have passed the night in the chimney, since there are sure to be a few excrements left in it if they have roosted there.

One year the swifts arrived on April 29, but that is a week earlier than the average date of spring arrival. There were two of them that year—a mated pair beyond question. They circled above the chimney for about an hour, but it was still closed. It was opened during the forenoon and about sunset I saw one of the birds drop into the chimney. Excrements left on the rain-pan showed that both swifts had roosted there. Their custom is to hang to the wall, side by side below the nest, until incubation begins, and at this location one continues to roost except at such times as it shares the nest with its mate. Not infrequently both swifts have been seen on the nest, and it may be a common habit. A person can hardly approach the nest without making a little noise, which may cause one bird to drop to its place on the wall.

Except when frightened neither the old birds nor the young frequent any other place in the chimney other than the small space to the left and below the nest, which comprises no more than a third of a circle with a radius of 12 to 14 inches from center of the nest. This is their "home, sweet home" all summer long, and to this spot two birds return in the spring.

As has already been stated, the first nest was a month late and, presumably, was built after a first nest had been destroyed. In the second and third years egg-laying began on June 1; in the fourth year on May 30; in 1922 on May 20, which was only 22 days after the swifts arrived. In 1922 the swifts arrived a week early, on April 29, and the beginning of their nesting was ten days ahead of any previous year. Eggs have been deposited on *every other day* except in 1922 when there was a curious exception to the rule. It was on the morning of May 26, when I expected to find the fourth egg in the nest, that only three eggs were found, the same number that had been seen there on the two preceding days. On the floor of the chimney were the remains of a soft-shelled egg. The fifth egg was in the nest on the morning of May 29, *three* days instead of *two* days from the preceding laying, and the sixth egg was in its place on May 31, egg depositing having extended through twelve days. A curious coincident happened on May 28, the day the fifth egg was due but failed to be laid. That day in the barn nest no egg of the Phoebe appeared. In this place I have watched nearly forty Phoebe nests, and this was the first time a Phoebe had ever been known to skip a day in egg-laying. A search for remains of a soft-shelled egg was made, but nothing was found. A line of speculative thought was started: Phoebe is seldom seen on the ground and the Chimney Swift almost never. Both species then must get their supply of lime for egg shells from their insect food. Just here there is need of the entomologist and the chemist, the former to tell us what insects constitute the food of these flycatchers, and the chemist to give his analysis of the insects and of the egg shells. Bearing directly upon the case of the soft shells is the fact that we were having four quite rainy days in succession at that time, when for the flycatchers there was a scarcity of insects in the air. To this rather than because it was Sunday—the day of rest—the omission in egg-laying must be attributed.

The first year of Chimney Swift nesting in my tower, four eggs were laid; the second and third years there were five; and the fourth and fifth years there were six eggs laid.

During the period of ten or twelve days occupied by the egg-laying, a swift is seldom found in the day time in the chimney, and very rarely is one seen on the nest for a few minutes. Real incubation appears to begin a little while before the last egg is laid, since usually the hatching of one is a little later than that of the others. Both swifts share in the incubation and the brooding of the young. Occasionally the eggs are left uncovered for a short time. When the nest was new and the sticks on both sides curved upward to the same height, there were but three positions possible for the sitting bird's head. It could be held upright or bent to the right or to the left. The returning bird grasped the front edge of the nest and instantly dropped to the eggs with its breast against the chimney's wall. This was true of the first season. After the sticks near the top of the left side of the nest were broken off the swifts could sit crosswise of the nest, which they seemed to prefer to do. Certainly they looked comfortable that way, while they did not look comfortable the other way.

The nest duration from the laying of the first egg to nest-leaving has been 42, 45, 47, 45, and 50 days for a five-year period, giving an average of 46 days. Of this period incubation has taken 18 days for the first and second years and 19 days for the other three years; 19 days was the time in the nest watched by Miss Day.

As the eggs hatch the shells are not carried out, but are tossed to the floor of the chimney. These shells suggest that the head of the embryo swift must lie in the egg in somewhat different position from that of all other species known to me, since other birds' shells are divided in the middle, while the division in the swift's egg is scarcely more than a third of the way down, the large end portion suggesting a lid for the remainder of the shell.

Structural similarities in the Chimney Swift and Flicker led ornithologists to place the two species near each other in classification. Although there are striking differences to be noted while studying the home life of both species, still there are equally striking similarities. In both species the young when hatched are perfectly naked, there being no vestige of natal down. In both species there is a continuous infant crying or moaning by the young when they are unbrooded. Both are fed by regurgitation; both make a great clamor when the parents come to feed them; both sleep hanging to the wall, although the swift has never been seen to sleep with head turned backward and bill hidden in the feathers of the back. Both species are free from lice or vermin of any kind. Unlike the Flicker's, the swift's feeding is done with gentle movements and is finished quickly, though at times two or three nestlings may receive a part of the meal brought in. Unlike young Flickers, the swifts are never quarrelsome. During the many summers of intimate living with the Chimney Swift, I have never found it a subject for criticism in any respect—no evil has been detected in its relations with its own or with other species. In short, it appears to be a paragon of perfection—the bird that properly might be chosen as the emblem of peace.

During my early study of the Chimney Swift I made the very broad assertion that the bird does not feed its young at night. My subsequent years of study of this species have in no way caused me to alter my opinion. During numerous summers, with lighted lamp before their window, I have frequently sat up in night-watching of the swifts. I have chosen the nights most favorable for their going out—when there was bright moonlight, many insects abroad, and the young were large and needing their greatest supply of food. Not once has a swift left the chimney. I know that others have told us that have seen swifts go out at night. I do not dispute such statements, but what I do contend is that the parents do not feed the young at night. From twenty minutes to a half hour after sunset is the latest in the evening that I have seen the parents bringing food. It is dusk then within my chimney, the hole of which is twice as large as that of an ordinary chimney.

In the first place, the young are sufficiently fed dur-

ing the day time. My notes show that there is plenty
of time for more feedings by day if it were necessary.
Moreover, the hard-worked swifts have another way
of meeting exacting requirements. None of us has forgotten that the summer of 1921 was extremely hot
and dry. That was the season our swifts raised six
young ones, the feeding of which may have overtaxed
their parents' energies. One day while I was watching
them, an old bird came in, fed, and remained to rest.
Very soon another bird did the same, and a few minutes
later a *third* swift came in, fed, and rested also. I
looked and counted again. There was no mistake—
three adult swifts were hanging on the wall, while the
nest held six blind nestlings. This was the first time I
had seen this phase of Chimney Swift life, which Miss
Day also witnessed in her New Jersey nest. The third
swift continued in the role of nurse-maid. The lamp
before the window showed that she stayed with the
family at night. When the young had left the nest all
nine swifts could be counted on the wall. The third
bird continued to act as nurse-maid for at least several
days. So beautifully ordered was the family life that
no one could tell which was the willing servitor, but I
guessed that the two hanging under the young were
the parents, and the nurse was the one at the side of
the young. One cannot help speculating as to the
manner of the introduction of the nurse-maid into the
family. Was she invited or did she come as a volunteer
missionary? I have always thought that it was a
female swift—quite likely an old maid. That there
are old maids among the birds is as probable as that
there are old bachelors, widows, widowers and grass
widows and widowers, of all of which we have had
ocular proof.

Many people have the Chimney Swift nesting inside
their chimneys. If you ask them their opinion regard-

ing the night feeding of the young, they are pretty confident that it is done, for very often from their bedrooms they have heard a noisy chatter exactly like that heard in the day time when food is brought. By my night watchings I have learned that a very slight movement made by one swift starts all the young ones to chattering. Not until some one has witnessed an actual feeding at night by good artificial light, shall I believe that such a thing takes place.

The most striking thing in the appearance of a newly-hatched Chimney Swift is its very large eyes, showing through the thin skin. The eyes begin opening at the age of fourteen or fifteen days, and the young begin the nest-leaving three or four days later. In the hot summer of 1921, with six youngsters in the nest, three of them began climbing out on their fourteenth day, when no crack of eye-opening was visible. On their first nest-leaving the young rest a short time on head or shoulder of a parent, then return to the nest. The permanent nest-leaving takes place two to four days later, when the young are nineteen or twenty days old. Although hanging close beside the nest, they do not return to it except in cases of fright or great excitement, and the stay is very brief.

The nest is in the exact center of the wall, yet the young leave it from the left side and both parents and young hang beyond the left side of the nest or below it. A photograph taken by H. K. Job shows young swifts hanging to the left side of the nest. In my study of both the Little Brown Bat and the Large Brown Bat, I find them in nine cases out of ten choosing the upper left-corner of windows for roosting places. These facts are mentioned because the bats and swifts appear to have 'left-hand' inclinations.

The space to the left of the nest being the "home base," we naturally expect that more meals will be delivered from the left side of the nest. This has proved true, for the records show that the feedings have been somewhat more than two and one-half on the left side to one on the right. After the young are out of the nest, occasionally a parent feeds from above, or again from below the fledgling. When the old birds arrive they drop a distance of about 30 inches below the nest, then climb the wall to it or to the bunch of fledglings, which remain in their place on the wall, awaiting the meal to be brought to them, instead of flying to the old bird.

Many observers have noted the frequent feedings of Chimney Swifts toward evening, when there is a meal for each nestling brought in every six minutes, and again every nine minutes; but during the day there is often great irregularity. For each nestling the time between meals is sometimes twenty minutes, again it is forty minutes, and still again it is two hours. The average time seems to be about an hour. The longest watch maintained in one day was eight hours, when twenty-one meals were served to three fledglings, averaging a meal for each bird every one and one-seventh hours. Often the stay of a parent after the feeding is very brief — a minute, sometimes less than that; again the stay may be for a half hour, and occasionally for an hour.

During these daytime rests as well as at night, the parents usually take their places below the young ones, pushing their heads upward until lost to sight. In this position their heads and shoulders must give considerable support to the young ones above them. Often one or two of the fledglings take this position in reference to their mates.

We have noted that swifts can collect a meal in six minutes. What then are they doing during an absence of an hour, even two hours or more? What are they doing in the spring when absent the entire day? And in summer after the brood is on the wing? The whole family returns to the chimney to roost for a fortnight or thereabouts after they have vacated it in the day time. Then for another week or ten days only two return for the night. These I take to be the parents. They are there for the night only. Not a swift is seen during the day, and they perhaps go to another chimney or hollow tree to rest. I suspect that they hurry off to town. I see many flying over our river towns, when none are about my chimney.

I have been much interested in the stimulus that awakens the feeding reaction in very young birds. In the case of the Chimney Swift I have found that this stimulus is a noise, as it is with young Phoebes. I suspected that the vibrations of the air caused by the parents' descent into the chimney might be another factor. Since my chimney is large enough for me to enter, I have stepped within and fanned the air violently, but not until a slight noise was made were the swift nestlings aroused.

While my Chimney Swifts have left as early as August 15, observers in nearby towns within the county have seen them during most of September and even as late as October 1. During the years the chimney tower has been their home for 102 to 131 days. In a typical year they were there twenty-one days before egg-laying began, and sixty-four days elapsed from the laying of the first egg until the young could feed themselves; the parent swifts occupied the chimney for fifty-three days when not actively engaged in caring for nest and young. The expression, "home life," seems literally true for the Chimney Swift.

Excerpts from Chimney Swift Notebooks

July 31, 1918. My first visit to the nest was made at 5:40 a.m. I found both swifts sitting side by side on the nest. The tails and wings of both were at the same angle. On the 27th I thought both must do some of the incubation, that is, cover some of the eggs, but before that one sat in nest while the other one clung to edge. No wonder that left side of the upward arching piece of the nest has broken off with two birds crowding into it at the same time. It was the last part of the structure built so may not have hardened so well as the other side. Next visit was 1¼ hours later; one parent at nest and it was feeding. A Red-headed Woodpecker came to top of chimney and drummed long and loudly, but swift appeared not to notice it.

August 7, 1918. Temp. at 5 a.m. was 71°. Soon after that I had reached observation station beside chimney. Just at sunrise, about 5:15 o'clock, a parent came to feed, hung from west edge of nest to do it. This side has fewer sticks projecting outward from it. After feeding, the bird brooded. The young now pile so high in nest that the brooding bird looks very uncomfortable, and is in nearly an upright position, its tail coming down around lower edge of nest. Yesterday and today it is so warm, brooding is not continued after early hour. Pin-feathers stick out all over the birds, quills of wings projecting about three-eighths of an inch beyond flesh. Very often the nestlings throw their heads about and go through the preening motions, though there is nothing to preen. For an hour, 6:15 to 7:15 p.m., except for several minutes when I was busy with supper-getting, I had chimney under observation, and parents entered eight times. For three of the visits I was watching in tower. First time parent lit on front edge of nest. One young one reached over rim and was fed, and old bird left immediately. Sec-

ond time parent lit on west edge well up and two
reached toward it. Bird stayed three or four minutes.
Third time parent lit west side of nest, below it evidently, for two hung their heads down over edge of
nest. Between times the young swifts kept up a slow
chatter, making it shriller and more rapid when a
parent came. When I made considerable noise with
door, their cry was fuller, louder and like the fear cry
of Flicker. After these three feedings it became pretty
dark inside of chimney. I came to house and saw five
entries into the chimney. In most of them the bird
stayed scarcely a minute. The last one went in after
the other one and neither came out again, though it
was still light enough outside to see birds or other
objects.

August 14, 1918. After 10 o'clock (a.m.) Amelia
came up but did not see a feeding. She stepped inside
the chimney, touched one and caused a great commotion in the nest. One fell out. This shows that since
young have their eyes open fear drives them from
nest when they are touched. Before eyes were open
they stuck tight to nest and stiffened themselves. When
not touched no movement of my hand back and forth
over their heads close to their eyes brought any response, neither did vibrations of currents of air caused
by moving a newspaper noiselessly. The shrill, scolding
note that I have compared to both that of the Flicker
and the wrens, is an indication of fear the same as
with the other species. Now the young swifts are still
except when a parent comes. The least motion of the
old bird calls forth a chorus of chatters or peeps, and
a slow but pretty constant flow of solo remarks is kept
up as long as the parent stays.

August 20, 1918. It is now 9:45 p.m. I have been
in tower since 7:15. Both parents had *retired* when
I came up with big metal lamps so there might be plenty
of light in the chimney. Moon is nearly full and shines

clear, so the night is about as bright as is possible here
at this season. (Moon is full August 22.) The inside
of the chimney is brightly lighted so the parents could
see to feed in case they ever do such a thing at night.
This is perfectly absurd—as if they could work all day
and all night, too. Whenever the parents move there
is a great twitter, same as is made when they are fed.
Such was the case when parent on right (under the
nest) moved over to the left of bunch at 8:30 p.m.
Again at 9 p.m. there was much noise when a parent
moved, and some outcries at other times since. For
the most part, the young are quiet and the old birds
are less disturbed than one would think, considering
all the noise we have been making. Amelia came up
about 9:30 o'clock. The swifts were in close arrangement. One parent had a youngster on its head, but
Amelia could not make it out. I raised the screen over
the window and one dropped 15 to 20 inches below its
former place. Amelia had scarcely reached the bottom
of the stairs when the bird crept back to its place. All
began to preen. I saw all five heads at once, on the
move. This morning I began watch at 9:45 o'clock and
continued it until 11:15, when I saw the first feeding.
Bird came to E side, fed and left at once. In the afternoon the parents never stayed more than a minute;
generally it was no more than one-half or one-fourth
minute. I came at 3:12 p.m. and left at 5:12 p.m.
Feedings were at 3:12, 3:41, 3:47, 4:04, 4:10, 4:32,
and 5:04. After 4:04 feeding I heard a thump. I
rushed to the south peep-hole in time to see a young
swift creep up to its place with the others. I was scrub-
bing floor and cleaning the tower at the time. I intended
to stay by chimney until midnight. But what's the use?
It certainly is plain that swifts do not feed at night.
It is now 10:32 p.m. The swifts and I both need rest
for tomorrow's work.

August 21, 1918. Feedings today were at 9:26,

9:26½, 9:39, 10:15, two before 10:57, 11:25, 11:34, 12:17, 12:22, 12:45, 2:21, (absent from 2:22 to 3:30), 3:57, 4:09, 4:42, 4:54, 5:16, 5:47, 5:52, 6:14, 6:17. As soon as parent left at 11:39 the young began to fly. I found one under nest, on east wall of chimney and one on window frame. One flew to west side nearly up to corner brackets. I saw that one descend. It would vibrate its wings, drop 2 or 3 inches then repeat the operation. As the swift hangs to the wall its toes are level with its throat, sometimes appearing above the shoulders or top of wing. I find that when I stand with my face against the chimney and put my hands and forearms up against the chimney, my hands come above my shoulders just about the same as swifts' feet do. Almost proportionate part of the swift's frame hangs below its feet, as in our case would hang below our hands could we cling to a wall by our finger-nails. This manner of its clinging makes it easy for the parents to push under the young ones, as is their habit. Three times a Red-head came to the top of chimney, drummed and screamed. The first time the young swifts were frightened into uttering the scolding cry of fear similar to that of Flickers.

August 27, 1918. Was up at break of day, which was 37 minutes before sunrise and by our time it was five o'clock (temp. 54). Saw a swift enter chimney 17 minutes before sunrise. Did not go to tower until about 9 a.m. Light still was poor. I could see two swifts together, and a third one may have been there. I heard noise of swifts as if they were fed and again a noise just before I started to leave. I stopped to look through south peep-hole and found the swifts' home vacant. After searching the chimney thoroughly I felt certain that only one young swift was there. It was on south side not much more than 2 feet from top. I decided to remain and watch through east window. The youngsters in a short time flew home. Before and after they came, the young one called softly. It showed much uneasiness by moving sidewise back and forth in the square foot of space which seems to be the home of the family; after a while it stopped its moving and peeping. I had a dull time waiting, but at last a parent came in with two young ones and there was an uproar. There was louder and stronger begging than I had heard heretofore. One got into nest and made a great clamor. I notice it is when they get excited that they get into the nest. They have done it when I have disturbed them, and now when bidding for the meal brought in. The parent and the three young settled for a rest. I could wait no longer. As I passed around the chimney I frightened out the three that had just come in, leaving but one behind. In afternoon I looked in and found two or three at home.

June 11, 1920. Toward evening yesterday I saw a swift flying against dead branches of plum trees as if trying to get twigs. It made as many as three trials, but did not go into chimney. This afternoon I examined the nest carefully and found that several newly added sticks had been placed on front edge of nest. Am certain no repairs on nest were made before the laying began, and these fresh sticks were not added until lately; possibly some of it done as early as June 7.

July 7, 1923. I stepped inside the chimney and stirred up the nestlings by putting my fingers on them. As for several previous days three of them had heads over the edge of the nest. An adult swift was in the chimney. It flew up and kept flapping its wings. When it found I was not frightened but kept poking the young ones, it came down and lit on the front of my dress, about as high as my knees, and hung there until I moved to leave.

May 13, 1924. The nest that has stood the wear and tear of the rearing of six broods in that many summers, I found this spring had become insecure. The east side of it (about one-third of it) had become loosened from the board to which it was attached. To secure the prospective nesting of this year, I put very oily putty back of the detached part, then with a screw-eye to the right, another over the nest, and a small staple to the left of the nest, I sewed the nest in place with No. 8 black thread. I don't think it will fall. [On May 28 she noticed a few sticks added to a foundation nest started in 1920. Building began on this and a new nest was completed during the period of egg-laying.]

June 22, 1924. Incubation is well under way. This evening I went twice to see the nest. First time sitting bird only was in. On second visit nest bird and a *very long* one under the nest were seen. Soon a swift came, went to left side of nest and appeared to feed the bird on nest. In five to ten minutes it scrambled down to a place below the nest and measured considerably less than the "long bird."

July 1, 1924. Three swifts in tower tonight: two on nest and one hanging below nest.

July 2, 1924. Three again tonight. They flopped about and only one was on nest when I got to peep-hole.

July 3, 1924. Three and *all three were on nest* at 10:30 p.m. when Miss Jordan had first view of them by lantern light. Two flew down, leaving one to cover the eggs. This is the first time three have been found on nest during incubation.

July 4, 1924. Three in chimney at 9 p.m. Believe I saw two on nest, and am sure one left nest and another took its place.

July 17, 1924. Three adults were brooding the young, and they certainly made a funny show of it.

Nest is full of young so these old ones have hard
work holding on. [The third adult was observed until
August 4, and it appeared to have as much interest
in the brood of young as the parents.]

July 25, 1925. At 7 a.m. I found only one swift in
the chimney, none in the air. It is a cold, cloudy, lower-
ing morning, such as would urge birds to stay in, therefore it seems strange that it was chosen for wing trials.
At 8 a.m. three young were in chimney. This early date
for flying outside leads to the looking up of data.
Flying outside: 1918, age 30 days; 1919, age 23 days
(*frightened* out); 1920, age 30 days; 1921, 28 days;
1922, 30 days; 1923, 32 days; 1924, 29 days; 1925,
25 to 31 days. So it proves that the earliest age (except
in 1919 when they were frightened out) for *flying
outside* has been twenty-five days. At 12:30 p.m. six
swifts were in chimney, probably both parents and
the four young. I could see no difference in size. Went
again at 9:20 p.m. and found the usual formation of
the four young hanging above the parents.

June 2, 1927. Raining; temperature stands at 51°.
About 8 a.m. I found both Chimney Swifts hanging
below nest, close together. About 4:30 p.m. I went
to tower to look for birds to the westward. Three
Chimney Swifts were flying, often passing between
dead branches of the plum tree. I heard a swift enter
chimney but for nearly five minutes did not go to look
at it through peep-hole. Bird was sitting on east edge
of nest, holding in its bill a stick about 1½ to 2 inches
long. I thought (but was not sure) I saw stick shifted
in its place in mouth. After three or four minutes the
swift deposited the stick on west edge of nest up near
the wall, then for fully five minutes the bird worked
its bill back and forth over west edge of nest with
motion similar to that of a person working putty or a
cake frosting into a crack with his finger and doing a

thorough job of it. Toward the close of the work I
thought (again I am not quite certain since the light
was poor) I saw the stick being moved a little toward
the front of the nest where most of the fluid had been
poured. As the swift worked, the edge of the nest
grew to look wet and shiny. As soon as the bird left
I opened the door, touched the edge of the nest, and
it *was wet and shiny.* I think that from twelve to
twenty drops of the fluid glue had been poured on it.
It dries very fast. The swift was in the chimney fully
fifteen minutes.

Summary for 1928

Chimney Swifts were here on 130 days.
My visits made to their chimney were 400.
Number of steps up taken, approximately 12,000;
   height of risers in the steps, mostly 7 inches. If all
   were in one continuous ascent they would reach
   1 1/7 miles up into air.
Number of visitors taken to see Chimney Swifts, 133.
Pages of notes written, 32. Number of words written
   (estimated), 8640.

Data on the Chimney Swift

Use of Nests

1st nest used 1918, 1919, 1920, 1921, 1922, 1923.
2nd nest used 1924; fragment of it removed May
   26, 1933.
3rd nest used 1925; broken off (by hail?) May 13,
   1926.
4th nest used 1926. Built on site of third nest.
5th nest used 1927.
6th nest used 1928 and 1929.

7th nest used 1930; fell in 1931.
8th nest used 1931.
9th nest used 1932.
1st nest used again 1933.

Incubation Period from Laying of Last Egg

	Last Egg days	Next To Last Egg days	Clutch eggs
1918	18	19	4
1919	19		5
1920		19	5
1921	18	19	6
1922		21	6
1923	17½	19	6
1924	18	19½	5
1925	19		5
1926	18		5
1927	19	6th egg, 20 days; 7th egg, 19 days	8
1928	18	5th egg, 19 1/3 days	6
1929	18	19½	5
1930	18		6
1931	18	20	5
1932	18	19	5
1933	18	19	5
1934			5
1935			4
1936	18	20	5

Chimney Swift's Stay at National, Iowa

	Date First Seen	Date Last Seen	Days Spent Here
1915	May 5	Aug. 1	88
1916	May 12	Sept. 6	117
1917	May 12	Sept. 2	113
1918	May 16	Sept. 8	115
1919	May 8	Aug. 23	107
1920	May 5	Sept. 23	141
		(Chimney Aug. 15)	102
1921	May 7	Aug. 27	112
1922	Apr. 29	Sept. 7	131
1923	Apr. 28	Aug. 20	114
1924	Apr. 29	Sept. 4	128
1925	May 11	Aug. 19	100
1926	May 1	Aug. 24	116
1927	Apr. 30	Aug. 25	117
1928	May 2	Sept. 9	130
1929	May 7	Sept. 5	121
1930	Apr. 29	Sept. 2	126
1931	May 2	Aug. 22	112
1932	May 2	Aug. 18	108
1933	May 12		
1934	May 4		
1935	May 11		
1936	May 8		

Visitors Taken To See The Chimney Swifts in Tower

	Number of People	Different Parties
1918	100	26
1919	68	17
1920	121	35
1921	127	35
1922	160	46

1923	110	30
1924	99	34
1925	81	22
1926	100	31
1927	131	33
1928	133	44
1929	88	33
1930	79	27
1931	133	46
1932	187	47

No record after 1932

Editor's Note

Miss Sherman's "Chimney Swift Tower" was designed for the sole purpose of making a systematic study of the nesting habits of this species. This very unusual structure was probably the only one of its kind in existence. Her studies were methodically conducted over a long period of years, from 1918 to 1936, and were finally concluded only when her advanced years and failing health prevented continuation. Her day-to-day observations of the Chimney Swift filled two notebooks—a total of 400 pages and approximately 91,000 words written in longhand. It is an extremely interesting document and is doubtless the most complete and detailed study ever made of the nesting habits of this bird.

The purpose of the present volume is to present as many of the nesting studies of various birds made by Miss Sherman as is possible in one book. We could do little more than touch the surface of the Chimney Swift studies. The Chimney Swift journal, which is now the property of the Iowa State Department of History and Archives, Des Moines, is a unique and valuable record which is worthy of publication in its entirety. It is to be hoped that some day this may be accomplished. In order for bird students fully to evaluate and interpret the data on this bird, the observations for each year, set down in detailed form and unbroken continuity, should be available in a printed volume. —F. J. P.

CHAPTER IV

BIRDS NEAR AT HAND

When the nights are bitterly cold, the mercury ranging from 20 to 30 degrees below zero, when we should very soon perish out of doors if not well wrapped, we are wont to think of our little bird boarders and to wonder at their ability to survive the extreme winter cold. We may know that the Chickadee is well sheltered in the feather-lined nest of a House Wren, for 'round about three o'clock we watched him retire, as usual, into the bird-box; and we may be equally confident that Nuthatches and Downy Woodpeckers are comfortably housed in holes in the trees; but the Cardinal, the bird of the southland that recently moved to our northern homes, roosts during the frozen night in the bare branches of a snowball bush in our front yard.

Still more remarkable than the endurance of our winter birds is that of sixteen species for which the winter climate of Iowa is far too mild; for to the north of us there live sixteen species that have never been known to come as far south as Iowa, even in winter. There are forty-three species of birds that find the region about the mouth of the Mackenzie River much too warm for them and go to the icy lands north of that latitude to nest and raise their young. Nineteen of these species pass through Iowa in spring as they journey north, and one of these nineteen, the Golden Plover, is one of the greatest travelers in the world, making a round trip annually of 20,000 miles as it flies from its winter home in Argentina to its circumpolar northern breeding range. It is known to cover 2,500 miles in a single flight.

For most of us the habits of the birds about our homes are very interesting, for in them we see reflections of human conduct. It is this mirroring of our own natures in a dim way that awakens our interest in them. We find that bird life is a compend, an epitome of human life. This fact is voiced by the poet, as well as by the philosopher and the naturalist. Tennyson said:

In spring a fuller crimson comes upon the Robin's breast,
In spring the wanton Lapwing gets himself another crest.
In spring a livelier iris changes on the burnish'd dove,
In spring a young man's fancy lightly turns to thoughts of love.

Think of that! "In spring a young man's fancy lightly turns to thoughts of love." Maybe it is true in England, where Tennyson lived, that spring is the season for the turning of the young man's fancy, but any American mother with a grown-up son can tell you that the seasons have no influence on her son's fancy; that 30 degrees below zero is temperature just as favorable as balmy weather of June for the sprouting of the love fancy. She detects the first signs of it above ground, when he spends a quarter-hour in parting his hair, a half-hour in tying his necktie to suit his newly acquired, fastidious tastes. Then none of his clothes are good enough. He needs a new suit. How precisely like a bird he is in this! The bird, too, appears in a brighter coat during the courting season.

Sometimes, in certain species, the male wears a worn suit exactly like the female in winter, but on the approach of spring a very great change in appearance takes place. Among these birds are the Bobolink,

Indigo Bunting, Goldfinch and Scarlet Tanager. In the north the Goldfinch is the only one of these that we are permitted to watch while he changes his colors. Mark well that I said "while he changes his colors," and did not say while he changes his suit or coat, for there is not change or molt of feathers. This fact has been established by captive birds. The Scarlet Tanager without dropping a feather has changed from the winter olive-green to the red of summer, and before the time for returning south in autumn has molted and donned again his modest olive-green attire. This truth makes highly amusing the attempt of a writer in a popular magazine, to give a touch of nature to his story by speaking of "the red feather dropped by a Scarlet Tanager as it winged its way southward."

In February, 1918, there came to our place a flock of about twenty Goldfinches. They stayed until May. For several weeks the males and females looked alike, thereafter the males could be distinguished because of their brightening color. By April 4th the golden hue of some of them had become prominent, and it increased in brightness until the clear, yellow color of summer was reached. How this comes about without molting, or without the feathers changing colors as do the leaves in autumn, has been demonstrated by Dr. Joseph Grinnell with a series of skins of the House Finch. These show that the change is produced by a gradual wearing away of the gray tips of the feathers until the bright rose red lying beneath is exposed.

In case there is a difference in the plumage of the two sexes it is the male, as a rule, that wears the more brilliant dress. However, most rules have exceptions, and the Wilson's Phalarope is one of these. For it is the female of this species that has the gayer plumage, and does the courting. Her less conspicuous mate builds the nest and sits on the eggs while she flaunts her fine feathers far from home. When the eggs are hatched she helps in the care of the young, thereby showing that matters are not so bad as they might be.

Reflect a moment, if you will, upon the vastness of printed matter — fiction, mostly — that deals mainly with courtship and marriage in human society. The students of animal behavior have been busy in recent years with studies of the phenomena relating to the mating of the lower animals. From 'The Courtship Display of the Palmated Newt' (which is one of the water salamanders) we may learn that the male of the species is far more handsomely colored than the female, and his antics to attract her attention are as conspicuous as those of the most demonstrative birds.

The flashing of fire-flies on a summer evening is an exhibition familiar to all. Yet few people realize that they are witnessing a genuine "sparking" scene. It is a curious fact that the use of the word "sparking," meaning courting, did not originate from an understanding of the import of this insect's habit, for the expression is an old one, whereas the significance of the glow or flash of the fire-fly has been a discovery added to knowledge within very recent years. Only a few years ago so eminent a naturalist as Professor Mast, of John Hopkins University, experimented throughout the summer with various tests upon the courtship display of the fire-fly. The world as a whole is heedless of many great nuptial affairs that are of common occurrence. Among these may be mentioned the marriage-flight of ants: these are truly marvelous occasions when for one brief day millions of winged ants leave their humble underground homes to fly in the blue ether of the heavens, where their marriages are consummated. Returning to earth, they break off their wings, for one flight, one trial of aviation, is all they ever make.

If, when he would a-wooing go, your son is like a
bird in preening himself and donning fine raiment, he
is like a bird in another respect: he thinks he must treat
his lady-love to ice cream, or if that is not convenient,
then to nuts and candy. If he has her here this evening,
you may be sure he has one or both of these sweetmeats
in his pockets. Several years ago we had Blue Jay
boarders that we named Sir William and Simple Susan.
The food given to them was for the most part black
walnuts. Throughout the winter Sir William paid small
attention to Simple Sue further than to drive her from
the food. But in early March a change came over him.
He carefully picked the nut meats from their shells,
and began to stuff the lady jay, while she, poor, silly
creature, accepted the nuts with a great fluttering of
wings and a helpless air, as if she had not been able
to forage for herself all winter! The solemn-looking
Screech Owl—the emblem of wisdom—also has his
romantic hour. That hour is when the dusk of evening
is thickening into the blackness of night. Then he comes
to the neighborhood of the nest and the instant his low,
quavering notes are heard, his mate scrambles from
the nest-box and joins him for an outing and a hearty
supper.

Both dancing and dueling are prompted largely by
amatory impulses. Only a few bird species are noted
for their courtship dances, but duel combat is frequent
among many, though few birds fight to the death.
Almost anyone may witness a cock Robin fight, that is
renewed at intervals for several days. The Bobolinks
clinch and fight with vigor and persistence, but as a
source of amusement for onlookers the Northern
Flickers in their courtship contests lead all the rest of
our common birds. After years of living on the most
intimate terms with this species, and after long search-
ings for reasons for certain amatory behavior, there

still remain puzzles not fully solved. Of one thing I am confident: that among all our common birds the Flicker's heart is the one most impressionable to the charms of the opposite sex. So deep is this susceptibility that there is almost no association together of the sexes in the late summer and fall after the young can take care of themselves. A flirtation is certain to follow an accidental meeting of male and female. At that season the coming of a female to our place is announced by Flicker calls, which are followed by the customary courting antics of drumming, bobbing, and bowing. The reason for the males abounding on our place is easily explained. Nine years ago the bird-boxes in the barn were increased to seven. As roosting places these boxes are occupied by the males. Should a female attempt to roost in a box, she is promptly driven forth by the very male that shouted, and drummed, and hammered all day long in spring to coax her to that box to nest.

Until Flickers nested in our barn the details of their domestic life had been hidden from all human eyes. Through peep-holes in the nest-boxes placed for Flickers in the barn many visitors have seen chapters of that life. As for myself, the sum of the time spent watching them would total weeks, if not months. For a dozen years the nest life must have been nearly normal, then followed a period of abnormal (perhaps ultra-normal is a better designation) that has illustrated the effect of changed environment in the life of birds.

A brief sketch of a normal nesting of a pair of Flickers reads like this: a pair of Flickers have chosen each other for better or for worse. The male begins to drill the nest-hole in a tree or stump. Its location should be some distance from other Flickers' nests for the female of this species seems to be a weak-minded, incon-

stant, frivolous creature, that is called from duty by
the notes of any stray male. It seems a very great pity
that William Shakespeare did not live in America and
know the characteristics of this bird before he wrote
his aphorism on inconstancy, which, beyond doubt, then
would have read: "Frailty thy name is female Flicker."

In the first days of nest-making the male spends
much time chasing off after his light-minded spouse
and rewooing her in the face of interloping rivals.
Sometimes Mrs. Flicker is induced to take a look at
the hole that is in progress; and she may tarry to hew
and throw out a few chips, then she is off again. If
the truth must be told, the female is a downright
slacker. Not only does most of the digging out of the
hole fall to the male, but he is the better parent in
the care of the eggs and the young. At night he is
the one that incubates, and later broods the young;
and he does more than half of the feeding of the
nestlings.

One spring, owing to carelessness on my part, a
catastrophe happened. The peep-hole in the top of
the Flickers' box was left open, and our young cat
amused himself by thrusting his paw into the hole.
He could not reach nor injure the sitting bird except
through fright—the latter he did most thoroughly.
The terrified male beat about the box, leaving numerous bloodstains. During the forenoon his mate came
to entrance hole repeatedly and called in sweetest *wick-
i-wick* notes for him to leave and let her take her place
on the eggs. Finally he went out but did not return.
Doubtless his widowed mate announced that she could
not and would not go on alone with the nesting. At
all events she soon was proclaiming her bereavement
from the housetops. In that she did not differ from
many other widows. Her grief was short-lived. From
another barn-box she soon began to call, to hammer,

to drum. In a day or two she had drummed up two males. (One may have been her old mate, recovered from his injuries, but on that point I could not be certain.) Failing to get either male to nest with her in one of the barn-boxes, she compromised. A bird-box mounted on a post was selected instead, and a brood was successfully raised in it. If this were a fable instead of a perfectly true story, I should conclude in this way: This fable teaches that the art of courtship can be mastered by a female as readily as by a male, if she is disposed to try.

Let us return for a moment to the normal nesting of the Flicker in the hole dug to the depth of 16 or more inches in the tree, where its translucent, white eggs are laid on the nest bottom without any of the soft nest linings such as most birds use. If it had not been for the nests, watched in the barn-boxes, we would have very poor ideas of what goes on in the closed up nest in the tree. We should be making dozens of blunders and mistakes from guesswork. But the peep-holes in the box-nests admit of clear viewing of the nest activities at a distance of 16 or 20 inches from the eye. The light in any box is sufficient for the reading of ordinary newspaper print. A hand-hole in the side of the box allows the removal of eggs or young for marking, weighing or general study. In addition to the Flickers, these boxes have afforded nesting places for Screech Owls, Sparrow Hawks and House Wrens, all hole-nesting species whose nest secrets were for the first time viewed on our place and the discoveries in their nest-history added to ornithological science. For results the study of birds near at hand seems to be the only method worth while.

Rarely can the charge of polygamy, or more accurately bigamy, be brought against our birds. Nevertheless there is one of our common birds that is a true polygamist of the Latter-day Saint stripe—of the genuine, dyed-in-the-wool, a-yard-wide sort. This bird is the Red-winged Blackbird. The behavior of one of these was so marked as to make it certain that the same bird was with us for several summers. He was named Brigham, though he was by no means young. His vindictive, insolent manners were acquired one summer in his early life, when one of the nests was visited daily by me. At times other visitors were led over the quaking bogs and through the water of a ravine to see the eggs or young. Though neither eggs nor nestlings were ever touched, he seemed to regard me as his arch-enemy and always battered me to the best of his ability. It was noticed that his hostility was reserved for me alone, and that he did not touch my sister the few times she was present, though he struck me again and again—many times. His bellicose attitude toward me continued for more than a week after the young had left the nest. One day before visiting his ravine my sister and I exchanged clothing. Over this Brigham seemed nonplussed and sat rather sheepishly on a fencepost, but finally hit my sister a few rather feeble blows, the only ones he ever gave her, while he refused to touch me. From this it was clear that he recognized the disturber of his peace by the clothes she wore.

Something very like this happened, when a pair of Sparrow Hawks nested in my bird-blind. They came to know me as the person who carried the key to their castle, and the female would begin to scream the moment I came in sight. In fact the neighbors said they could tell whenever I was out of doors by the screaming of the hawk. Brigham's antipathy against me survived the nesting season mentioned. Two winters subsequent to it were spent in New York City and my return home in spring was very much later than Brig-

ham's arrival. Both springs the instant I appeared in
the back yard he came up from the ravine shouting
defiance, and, perching in a treetop, he flaunted his
red badge of hostility as was his custom throughout the
summer as long as he lived. No other Redwing either
before or after Brigham has been guilty of such offensive behavior.

In strong contrast with the behavior of Redwing
and Sparrow Hawk is that of birds that recognize
the people who feed them. Many instances have been
known of Chickadees, Nuthatches and a few other
species, that have come to the hand that feeds them.
My own experiences with Ruby-throated Hummingbirds have been interesting. There were evidences for
several summers that the same hummingbirds returned
each year. It is now certain that their drinking of
syrup from bottles was a habit started by the accidental
finding of the syrup, or from seeing others drinking.
The accidental finding of the syrup has not proved
easy in recent years. Eleven summers of experiment
in feeding Rubythroats not only has made it clear that
the same birds returned to our dooryard year after
year, but also that one of them after an absence of
almost eleven months recognized the one who fed her.

The spring of 1907 was extremely backward. Probably it was the late growth of vegetation in the ravine
that caused a female Redwing on May 22 to build a
nest near the top of a plum tree standing about 60
feet from our house. The following day was rainy
and the Redwing worked busily from dawn till dark
on her nest. Her maxim seemingly was, "Make the
nest while the grass is wet" in contradistinction to our
"Make hay while the sun shines."

That spring was the third one we were certain of
Brigham being with us; and it was none other than
Brigham, himself, that with his most gallant manners

was showing a second female through the treetops a few days later. A nest-site for No. 2 was selected in a tree 25 feet from that of No. 1. Only a week after the locating of No. 1 Brigham with his customary ostentation was showing female No. 3 all the suitable nest-sites that were unoccupied. The treetop she chose was 27 feet from No. 1's nest and 66 feet from the house. It was two weeks after this that No. 4 was settled in the tree in which No. 1 had built, whereupon the supply of females seemed to have been exhausted.

There was no Ann Eliza the 19th to apostate and tell us the secrets of Brigham's harem, yet this was not greatly regretted, since anyone from the house windows could watch the proceedings of this unique seraglio. The opportunity was most unusual, for Redwings very, very rarely build in the tops of trees so tall or so far from low land. The male Redwing often helps to feed the young and we hoped to see if Brigham showed partiality—if he helped one wife more than another. But hopes are sometimes dashed to the ground. This time they were dashed to the ground along with the eggs of nests No. 1 and No. 3. Soon after the eggs were laid in these nests violent windstorms lashed the pliant branches of the trees and tossed out the eggs. Female No. 2 had placed her nest in a stiffer twig that bent less before the storm, and No. 4's nest was not completed. Nest-life for No. 2 was over before the eggs of No. 4 were hatched.

From the house windows near by many observations were made upon the behavior of Brigham in relation to his concubines and their husbands he had displaced, and to his share in feeding the nestlings of wife No. 2. Very little, if any, antipathy was shown by one female toward another. All lifted up their voices in greeting of Brigham when he came to their neighborhood and sang his customary *"Bobaree"* call. Their note sounded somewhat like *"twit-twit-twitter-chee-chee-chee,"* and was uttered not only when they saluted Brigham but also by each female upon reaching or leaving her nest, and she was sometimes answered at such times by the other females sitting in their nests, also when she flew above their nests. There was nothing hidden in this seraglio, nothing secret. Each and every movement was proclaimed from the treetops.

Brigham certainly was a masterful old blackbird, and before the eggs were hatched spent most of his time and strength in driving off other birds. There were two or three male Redwings that were probably the lawful mates of the females he had stolen from them. He spent hours each day on the wing driving the males away. When a rival rested at some distance from the nests he also rested, perhaps stationed on top of a fencepost from which he shouted defiance, and unfurled his red flags of war, which fairly blazed with color as they showed to greatest advantage. After the windstorm destroyed the eggs in nests No. 1 and No. 3 the rivalry between males ceased, and it seemed more than likely that the owners of the ruined nests went away with the Redwings that Brigham had been chasing so constantly.

After the eggs were hatched in nest No. 2 Brigham shared in the work of feeding the young and cleaning the nest, but he did no brooding. For a male creature he did fairly well, though the record kept shows that he did somewhat less than half of the feeding; nevertheless he did almost all the blustering and shrill screaming when a person approached the nest.

Soon a spring came when Brigham returned no more. Though he behaved like an enemy, we had looked upon him as a friend, and missed him. When other springs return with their birds, we are happier if they are unmarked, if from their numbers no old acquaintances are missing.

Success has attended the use of a tent, or cloth blind, to conceal the observer, while studying the nest life of birds near by. This is a method that appeals to few people except those bent on scientific research. For most bird students the concealment afforded by their home walls has greater desirability; therefore, if near to a window there are vines and bushes suitable for nest-sites, the birds will be pretty sure to use them, and the watching of them will be easy. In addition to such places there is the house porch, where the Phoebe, Barn Swallow, and rarely the Cliff Swallow may build at times.

One year the porch nest of the Phoebe was occupied by a pair of Barn Swallows, after a slight remodeling. For seventeen nights before the swallows began repairs on this nest they roosted outside on a molding of the cornice of the porch. They were obliged to sit length-wise, since the top of the molding is only 1½ inches wide. Their dark plumage rendered them conspicuous against the white painted surface. After work on the nest began they roosted beside it on top of the porch post.

The corner of the porch formed two sides of the nest. A wall of mud and straw described an arc of a circle from one side of the corner around to the other side, but no mud pellets were laid against the wood of the corner. The work of lining the nest with feathers began on the second day. There has been much sentimental talk about the Robin (as well as some other species) molding its cup-shaped nest by pressing against the mud with its breast. There may be more gushing sentimentality in such language than in saying that she kicks the material into shape with her heels just as a hen does, when making her nest in a straw-pile. If anyone needs convincing that it is kicking with the heels instead of molding with the breast that the bird does, he should have watched that Barn Swallow. Most of the time her breast was pressed against the wooden sides of the corner while she vigorously kicked the nesting material into place.

On the morning of May 28—only four days after repairs were begun on the nest—the first egg was laid, and four others were added on days that followed. As soon as incubation began there was promise of many, pretty little domestic scenes. With twittering calls the male would fly to the nest and appear to insist that his seemingly reluctant mate take her outing, while he sat upon the eggs. The nest-site has always been safe from cats, but the poor swallow did not know it, and would swoop at our cat which was loafing on the porch floor. Before condemning the cat to solitary imprisonment a watch was kept to see if he struck at the bird. It is believed that a neighbor cat, which was in the yard, caught the Barn Swallow, for he disappeared.

Could the little widow without aid from a helpmate carry the nesting to a successful termination? The necessary period would be at least thirty days, as indicated by previous observations. For the first three days of widowhood she was left in peace, but on the next two days two male swallows were flying about the nest, and on the succeeding day—the sixth day since she lost her mate—I found one egg pierced and removed from the nest. Four days later—on June 13— the first young swallow was hatched; two more appeared the next day, and by the evening of the 15th all were hatched. The little widow evidently was proving equal to the task of caring for the entire family.

By June 18 there could be no doubt that three male Barn Swallows were wooing and trying to win the little widow. They flew back and forth under the porch.

One carried a bit of dead grass in his bill and progressed so far in his attentions as to alight beside the nest and on other perching places near by. The next morning the program was repeated with additional features. Twice a male carrying a straw lit on the nest and left the straw there, whereupon the little widow drove him away. Truly, affairs had reached an exciting pitch! About half-past ten o'clock my sister called my attention to the fact that a male swallow appeared to be killing the young. Rushing out, I found the smallest nestling lying on the porch floor, apparently dead, its head raw and bloody; three other wounded little creatures were in the nest, but thought to be dead. This supposition delayed action for a little time. Meanwhile the murderer was watched at his atrocities. The dead, smallest bird had twice been restored to the nest after having been thrown out, when the villain returned. He pecked at it thirty times by count, and swallowed the pieces of flesh pecked off, after which he dragged it out and threw it to the floor for the third time, then flew away twittering sweetly. This small one was thrown out five times, and the next in size four times, the thud when striking the floor heard 40 feet away in the house. After a time it was learned that two nestlings were alive, owing their lives very likely to the shielding furnished by the dead bodies I had replaced in the nest. The baby-killer was driven off many times in the next four hours, but during an interruption of the watch he returned and emptied the nest of all the young. Despite their fall and other injuries, the two larger nestlings were still alive.

By this time plans for constant guarding of the nest had been formulated. The task of guarding was continued for eight days. These were June days—the longest of the year. The watching of the nest commenced ten minutes before sunrise and ended at 8:15

in the evening, a duration of about sixteen hours. The short nights gave scarcely enough time for sleep, yet it seemed sufficient for the Barn Swallows, which were on hand sometimes when the sun rose.

Two, and often three, males were present, but only one was believed to have been of the baby-killing type. He soon learned to be wary and to shun the din of the pounding of tin pans and dodge the sticks of stove-wood flying through the air. A reign of terror was inaugurated. On the first afternoon of defensive oper-ations, even though I sat no more than 12 feet from the nest, the murdering little demon came many times and was driven away. As already stated, the nest could be seen from four rooms, but not from all parts of each room, nor during a trip to the cellar; there-fore at times brief lapses in the watching occurred, of which he took advantage. On the second day of keeping guard he reached the nest no more than a dozen times, yet twice he began his bayoneting, and once, having a nestling by the neck, he attempted to drag it out. The following day he succeeded in alight-ing on the nest edge four or five times only, and but once was caught assaulting the young birds. On the fourth day this murdering male came as often as once an hour, but found no chance to alight on the nest. On the fifth day he gained access to the nest for about one minute, yet that was long enough for him to leave bleeding wounds on one nestling. There was no attack on the sixth day and on the seventh day only one, when he again attempted murder during a five-minute sus-pension of watchfulness. This was his last opportunity and seemingly there was no abatement in his blood-thirsty intentions.

The nest had been treated with sulphur and pow-dered borax and no vermin was seen about it, but the mother bird often burrowed into the nest as if catching something. To allow her this attention as well as a chance to brood, made necessary the watching for eight days. At the end of eight days the mother had ceased to brood and the nest could be screened in. A frame had been made that covered the nest corner. On this was tacked wire screening in which was a hole large enough to admit the mother's head. It was thought that if she would do the feeding, some one could remove the frame daily and clean the nest, but, quite beyond expectations, the little mother attended to that matter also. Once a male swallow lit on the wire screening, but made no attack on the young birds. When the frame had proved a success a great sense of relief was experienced, for I had felt at times as if *three swallows* might make an entire summer for me.

Aside from the deadly attacks on the nestlings of the little widow, not much thus far has been told concerning her three suitors. They came early and stayed late, as suitors often do. Sometimes one, sometimes two, and sometimes all three were present. They favored a place on the telephone wires, which was a resort also of the little widow, while resting from nest duties. They would sidle along a wire toward her, pouring forth their most seductive lays or twitters, to all of which she usually appeared oblivious; if she did respond it was with wide open mouth and a hostile attitude, which seemed her sternest form of disapproval. It was thus she protested, when the satanic swallow was killing the nestlings. At ten minutes before sunrise on June 23, she was found sitting on a telephone wire with a male. My notes that day say: "He made courting demonstrations, whether she turned a deaf ear to these blandishments I can not say, but am sure she is not quite free from blame. Had she fed her young more frequently, and remained on the edge of the nest as she did later in the forenoon, it would have *looked* better. But for nearly four hours she was altogether too much in the society of the three males."

After the frame was in place she could not sit on the nest edge as was her custom, but was obliged to rest on top of the next porch-post. To this place a suitor would come and twitter at her, while she turned a deaf ear and a blind eye to him, or more literally she turned her back on him. Later, the enamored male, unseen by me, brought mud balls and bits of straw to this spot, the foundation of a nest, as it appeared certain.

At daybreak one morning the frame, which for a week had protected the fledgling swallows, was removed. Their enemy made no attempt to hurt them, and they had one joyous day, perched on the rim of the nest. The following morning they took flight, the day being the American "Glorious Fourth of July." A minute after the second bird had flown, the mother came to the nest and acted unusual when she found nothing there. Twice within the next forty minutes she brought food to the empty nest. This reaction to the nest had little suggestion of "coaxing" the young birds out.

If the little widow raised another brood that year, it was not done on our place. On July 29 and August 24 a female came to the old nest, and on the afternoon of the latter date seven Barn Swallows came within the porch, perching on a post-top and over a door. It may have been a farewell call. Nothing similar to it has happened before or since.

The catastrophe that sometimes befalls bird nesting can not always be traced to cats, though the first misfortune of the Barn Swallows undoubtedly had that origin. Because their nest was near at hand where most of their activities could be seen, there was no unsolved mystery. Every spring there are so many despoiled nests, so much fighting among the birds, that one is made utterly heartsick, especially when the whole world of mankind is also waging war (World War I). One year three successive nests of the Brown Thrasher were destroyed. The eggs were pierced by a bird's bill and left in the nest, thereby indicating that it was not the work of an egg-eating species.

At our home we realize the folly of having a place too attractive for the birds. The guerrilla warfare, the bushwhacking that follow too crowded conditions cause us great disquietude. After years of studying the subject my convictions are that much of this bushwhacking warfare is waged by one member of a species against another member of the same species— Barn Swallow against Barn Swallow, Brown Thrasher against Brown Thrasher, Flicker against Flicker. Of bushwhacking birds the Brown Thrashers are among the greatest sinners. All may go as merrily as marriage bells, when only one pair of Thrashers is nesting. A second, even a third or fourth may come in quietly and settle to nesting; but trembling seizes us, when the greatly admired song of the Brown Thrasher joins the bird chorus. If it continues for a few days we know what to expect—the finding of all the eggs in a Thrasher's nest punctured by a large bill. Very likely every Thrasher's nest in the yard will meet a like fate. No one can tell what exchange of mates takes place nor which one of the males is driven off before domestic tranquility is restored in the Thrasher family.

To be sure, there is the House Wren, a very demon of destruction, that spoils the eggs of many species, such as the Black-billed Cuckoo, Phoebe, Chipping Sparrow, Catbird and Robin, together with those other criminals, the Bronzed Grackle and Blue Jay. Overcrowding an area with birds is a common cause of trouble. One box for House Wrens is sufficient; more breed disaster, and the name of these disasters is our "dear" little wrens.

Some species, as for example the Purple Martin, are social in disposition and live happily in apartment houses. But "sexual jealousy" is strong in most species and several pairs in a neighborhood need to nest some distance apart—a distance of feet, yards, or rods, according to the bird. Even then there appear at times hooligan males (perhaps females) that, failing to secure mates or a desired nest site, run amuck and break up the nests of their brother kind.

One spring a Robin built conspicuously in a willow tree. Presumably it was an owl that found her there and left her feathers scattered about the nest. My grief was keen for thus a male Robin was set free and I feared for the constancy of another female that had just finished her nest on a window shelf placed in the bird tower, where I could watch through a peep-hole the nest operation only 12 inches from the eye. My fears were justified. The female deserted her nest as was anticipated. A bit of good fortune befell this nest the following spring. It was put out on the window ledge, and possession was taken by a white-tailed Robin. She relined the nest and had laid two eggs before they were thrown out by some bird fiend. This Robin with a white tail then went to another nest built by another Robin, whose eggs also had been destroyed. There White-tail raised a brood. Her third nest, which she built herself, also had a successful issue.

One year I decided to increase the number of Flicker boxes in the barn to seven. One object was to afford more roosting places, but the main purpose was to learn if more than one pair at a time would nest in the building. During the experiment some surprising things were learned about the Flicker—which under normal conditions had proved himself a perfectly good bird. Within the next three years the species had increased in numbers to an unusual extent, and nesting areas were crowded. In the spring of 1913 there was a long fought battle for possession of the barn by Flickers. That it was to gain the barn and not mates seems established by the fact that the contest was waged by two apparently mated pairs. First the males fought, while the females looked on, then, one male having been driven off, the females fought in like manner. The battle raged early and late for a week, until one pair was left in full possession.

A month from the day the fight opened the first egg was laid in a box named "M." All went well until the morning for the fifth egg to be laid. When I visited the nest at an early hour a Flicker was calling and drumming in box "S" on the south side of the barn, suggesting that at last we were to have two nesting pairs. For nearly two hours I watched beside the nest. The sound made by the newcomer seemed to be the cause of great perturbation in the female occupant of box "M," and the fifth egg had not been laid at 7:30 o'clock. I was detained in the house for fifteen minutes and found the nest empty when I returned. No trace of eggs remained in it. Two days later, about 200 feet from the barn, most of the egg shells were found. They bore my number marks, which made positive proof. There was one unnumbered shell; this showed that the fifth egg was laid before the nest was raided. Except for the Flickers in box "S," there were no other birds about that could or would have done the deed.

Apparently these nest robbers were driven away within a few days, and again five eggs were laid in box "M." All but one of them were carried off, but this time the looting was done at intervals. Then the

box was used for a third nesting by the same pair, and
four was the number of eggs. All hatched. The young
were of good weight, healthy, and active at first; but
they grew slowly, then shriveled and .died — clearly
from starvation. Four weeks earlier, in a nest in a
tree-trunk a quarter of a mile distant, a half dozen
well grown nestlings had died, very likely from the
same cause. Subsequent years gave opportunity for
study of similar cases.

Each spring brought the fierce struggle for possession of the barn. The question of nest site being settled,
the noise of Flicker courtship died away. Quiet reigned
for a few days, egg laying began, then the nest would
be despoiled, often when two eggs had been laid.
Thereupon bedlam broke loose once more and spread
throughout the neighborhood. Sometimes the upheaval
followed the destruction of a nest tree by a windstorm.
A summary of the tragedies in the barn nests shows
that in 1915 the nest in box "M" was raided, when
there were only two eggs. Nesting was transferred
to box "S," which also was broken up after the depositing of the second egg. The Flickers then returned to
box "M" where seven eggs were laid. Three were
infertile, three hatched. The young birds did well for
two weeks, when they were allowed to die soon after
a noisy pair of Flickers took up their home in box "E."
There four eggs were laid, two hatched, and the nestlings soon died from starvation, while exciting Flicker
courtship was going on outside. The summary for 1916
is very similar. The first nest was in box "S," which
was ravaged of its two eggs. Box "E" was then occupied and was despoiled after the clutch of five eggs
was completed, thereupon the birds returned to box
"S" to nest. Out of six eggs laid there, only one
hatched. The nest was guarded with vigilance, and devoted care was given it yet the lone nestling died when

about two weeks old, seemingly from lack of food for it weighed only 1000 grains when its weight should have been 1500 grains. This time the cause of death was not so clear—the case was different from all others —for the mother Flicker was often at home in the nest. I knew of but four successful nestings that summer among the dozen or more pairs of Flickers in the neighborhood.

The reason was sought for the shrinking away and subsequent death (apparently from starvation) of young Flickers in the nest. The behavior of the parents as well as that of other Flickers in the vicinity was carefully watched, and the psychology of this strange conduct was probed. The interpretation is summed up in this explanation: the Flicker, like many other species, becomes silent and secretive as soon as nesting begins. All goes well when the nest is beyond earshot of other nests; otherwise should disaster befall a nest within hearing distance the uproar started by the afflicted pair proves too disquieting for the self-control of mother Flicker. She seems unable to withstand the merry music of the opposite sex. Perhaps she simply rushes off to see where the fire is, or what harm it has done. At all events she neglects her family. Her faithful mate stays by the nest until the last nestling is dead. He feeds them little, if any, and spends most of the time at the nest-hole, probably looking for his recreant spouse. In order to react to the duties of the nest the Flicker seems to need the responsive cooperation of the mate. One bird will not carry on the work alone. These are a few of the facts gathered during four years of superabundance of Flickers, when they raised very few young, and their method of race suicide was made clear. Some very surprising traits were revealed. After that their numbers returned to normal and for the two succeeding seasons their behavior has been normal also.

Mention was just made of the starvation of young Flickers, when no food was brought. Starvation also occurs in broods that receive the normal care and devotion of both parents. This happens in cases where there is a difference of a day or two in ages of the first-hatched ones and the youngest. The young are fed by regurgitation and this feeding at first is by numerous gentle insertions of the parents' bill into the nestling's mouth. The bill is grasped at right angles and is soon held firmly while the parent pumps vigorously. These first-born ones grow amazingly fast, their mouths grow wider, their necks longer, they jostle the youngest baby to one side and its strength fails. If it does seize the parents' bill it has become too weak to suck with a strong pull and is dropped for one that draws with greater strength.

In 1921 an old bachelor among the Flickers came to our place and dug a hole in a maple tree. He called long and loudly for a mate. Now and then a female came near and his antics were of the most lively sort, but they failed to win him a mate. He returned the following spring and for many days fought another Flicker for possession of the barn. He was the defeated one. He then began digging a hole in a plum tree, next tried a willow tree, after which he chose the box in my bird blind. To this he brought a mate early in June—a June bride. Five eggs were laid. A week later they were a most beautiful sight. The usual translucent, gem-like appearance of the fresh egg was enhanced. Those who are familiar with Flicker eggs during incubation know that they should have been dark with embryonic life. The hope of posterity kept this pair of Flickers to the duty of incubation for thirty days—two and one-half times the period necessary to hatch out fertile eggs.

In discussing the psychology of the Northern Flicker

it is hoped that no one will infer that I dislike the bird. On the contrary I am extremely fond of it. As a subject for notes it has given me material for filling hundreds of pages in my notebooks—two or three times as much as any other species. For years we have lived very near to each other. I have stood or sat beside its nest-box, while every phase of Flicker nest life passed within view, during which time I there combed my hair, ate my meals, and once dressed for a visit to the county seat. But in spite of this intimate living some things have escaped me, some puzzles still are unsolved!

Perhaps young fledgling occupants of nests in trees or bushes realize as we do that if they fight they will fall out. Since no such danger threatens young Flickers they fight vigorously at meal time. In marked contrast with their behavior is that of young Sparrow Hawks. When their mother brings in a ground squirrel or a bird all stand in perfect decorum against the walls of the nest while she tears the prey and gives each its share.

Experiments in feeding young birds brought up the question of how great a role has environment played in shaping the nature of the stimulus needed for securing a feeding response from very young and blind nestlings, whose food reaction is instinctive, and not the result of learning. I find that the Phoebe, whose pristine home was in the shadow of a great immovable rock responds to a very slight noise, while the newly-hatched Catbird gives the feeding response of throwing up the head and opening the mouth, when it feels the vibration of the nest-bush, caused by the parents' approach. Experiments in the case of very young Flickers have shown that the darkening of the nest by placing a hand noiselessly over the hole was all that was needed to arouse from sleep the ever-hungry

"The wild rose—the state flower of Iowa. The Goldfinch—the state bird of Iowa." 1936.

"Northward Bound, a Chestnut-sided Warbler."

"Alder Flycatcher and Young." 1931.

"Scene with Stream."

"His Mother Knows That He Is Out."

"After Dinner Rest Awhile."

Catbird on nest. 1906.

"Birds from Nature: Young Male Rose-breasted Grosbeaks." 1902.

"Those the Cats Love Die Young."

Blue Jays.

"Young Downy Woodpecker."

Young Catbirds.

Thrush on milkweed.

"Moonlit River."

Adult Chimney Swift on nest.

Flicker "Hurling a Derisive Yelp." 1910.

brood. It was after no amount of shaking of the artificial nest, no clicking on my part, nor any other device
served to call forth the feeding response in very
young House Wrens, that the effect of the father's
singing was noted. To this paternal song alone they
responded after their return to the true nest. To my
mind it is clear that young Prairie Chickens hatched
under a barnyard hen die from lack of the natural food
stimulus, which may be a characteristic call or cluck
which is unknown to us.

The mating antics practiced by a few species of birds
have been interesting to me. These gyrations are indulged in by the males alone, in the presence of the
females of their kind. The term dancing has been
applied to sex carnivals performed by insects as well
as birds. Not every spring, yet quite often, the wet
meadow in our back lots has been the mating place for
Bobolinks and Red-winged Blackbirds. The tumult and
din made by them the entire day sometimes becomes
nerve-racking. Under date of May 23, 1921, one of
my notebooks has this entry: "The grand ball—the
mating festival—the noisy dance caused by sex impulses, the same as in human creatures, that has made
a pandemonium of the west ravine for the past three
weeks seems to be about over, and the mated Redwings and Bobolinks are scattering to their breeding
grounds. The carnival of song and dance that has been
almost deafening down there has died away." Can anyone with the slightest knowledge of animal nature fail
to recognize the biological significance of dancing?
We are told that "Dancing practiced by both sexes
was first introduced into France in the reign of Louis
the Fourteenth." Yet 1700 years before that time
Cicero wrote, "No sober man dances, except a madman
or a fool." Dancing and dueling are common among
birds, even among some with so-called gentle disposi-

tions. The Dove as an emblem of peace must have been chosen by those who were unacquainted with the Mourning Dove's fighting qualities and the resounding blows that this so-called gentle bird can give a rival.

Thus far nothing has been said concerning the economic value of our birds; nothing of the tons of weedseed, or the millions and billions of noxious insects they eat. Much has already been published regarding the beneficial work done by birds, and I shall not cite the published records here, for the great value of their services is now pretty generally understood. Of the more than 360 species of birds that occur in Iowa, nearly all are more or less beneficial; all except a half dozen species deserve protection because of their aesthetic value as well as for the aid they give the farmer. On our own place we have seen 153 species, nearly one-half of the Iowa total, and a dozen more have been seen in the immediate neighborhood. We have found thirty-three species nesting on our place.

CHAPTER V

THE PHOEBE

Once, while spending a fortnight in Dutchess County, New York, I was told the story of a Phoebe's nest which had been built on the rocks back of a waterfall, and which was known to have been occupied annually for forty years. Neither the location of the nest nor the name of the observer who, as child and woman had watched the nest, could be learned. A large portion of the Phoebe (*Sayornis phoebe*) history here given is connected with a nest that was carefully watched for more than twenty years. It was an old nest when note-taking on it began. The barn in which it was located was fifty-five years old when the nest was destroyed. This afforded a chance for its age to have been forty or even fifty years. However, this narrative is limited to the quarter of a century during which daily notes were written in the months of Phoebe's summer residence.

The barn in which this lengthy nesting took place stood on our property. It possessed an alcove-like recess in which the nest was situated. It was built on a crossbeam nailed to 8-inch sleepers above and rested against the west face of the sleepers. The safety of the location was never challenged by anything save other birds and by insects, with the latter proving the more destructive.

The earliest date for a returning Phoebe has been March 19, but the average date is the 30th of that month. Sometimes a pair has come together, but it is more usual to see only the male for a few days. In few, if any, of our common species is mating effected so quietly. The matter of territory is settled with very little quarreling; on no more than three or four occasions has one Phoebe been seen to chase another. It would be interesting to know which Phoebe falls heir to the old nest. Of ten young birds that were launched safely from that nest in the preceding year, no two return to fight for it as do the Flickers in the same barn.

Very soon after her appearance Phoebe begins repairing the old nest. At the beginning of this century the walls of that nest measured from 3 to 4 inches in height. For twenty years the walls rose slowly; the annual increment amounting to about ⅛ inch; by the spring of 1921 they stood fully 5½ inches high. In the middle of April of that year a heavy snowfall drove Robins and Flickers to seek refuge in Phoebe's sheltered alcove. It is probable that one of these species attempted to climb upon the nest and in so doing overthrew approximately twenty-seven stories of the superstructure which measured 3½ inches. The portion remaining was considerably lower than the entire nest twenty years earlier. Nothing daunted, Phoebe built upon the old foundation, plastering with mud and moss the whole outside of the nest.

Another mishap swiftly befell the nest that had stood unharmed for so many years. In the spring following the first disaster, a Robin began her nest inside that of the Phoebe. An attempt to dislodge the Robin's nesting materials and mud caused the entire structure to fall to the ground, thus ending the existence of a nest that had cradled many a Phoebe and that held attachment for others besides birds.

On the site of the first nest Phoebe built a new one toward the end of May, 1922. She spent a portion

of three days in the work. Much swifter was the work
of another Phoebe that two years later built on top
of the corner post of the porch, where she worked one
forenoon and all the following day and had the nest
completed, with walls standing 1½ inches high. Material for this nest was gathered for the most part
within a distance of 10 to 20 feet. For the nest in the
barn the builder usually had to go a few feet farther
for her material.

If, in these twenty-five years, the Phoebes could have
been undisturbed and raised their two broods each
year in the barn nest, it would have been the natal
home of upward of 200 of this species. The actual
number was a little more than eighty. Several things
were contributory causes to this reduction. One year
Screech Owls nested in the barn above the entrance
to Phoebe's quarters; the birds were either caught by
the owls or were driven away by them. House Wrens
destroyed their eggs in several seasons, but their greatest enemies have been the lice with which the Phoebes
themselves have contaminated their nest. Apparently
it was by these vermin that the old birds were driven
from the nest a time or two after the eggs were laid,
and the young have been killed by them in five of the
barn nests and in one of the porch nests, in spite of
watchfulness and efforts toward proper sanitation. In
the board directly above the old nest in the barn an
auger-hole was bored. A teakettleful of boiling water
was poured through this hole in March and again in
June after the nest was vacated by the first brood.
Once in June a cupful of kerosene was used, which
may have deterred a second nesting. In addition to
the thorough scalding of the nest, I have climbed a
ladder when the young were a few days old and held
aside the nestlings while my sister poured a table-

spoonful of sulphur into the nest through the auger-hole above.

Many years ago Dr. Vernon L. Kellogg gave 264 as the number of species of lice known to infest birds; by this time his list may have been augmented by several new discoveries. Whatever the number, it sometimes seems as if Phoebe must be afflicted by all of them simultaneously. On two out of four occasions, when Phoebe has come to the porch post to build, a clean place seemed to be the inducement for the selection. We knew the date of her coming, also when the vermin began to appear; it was learned that about five weeks elapsed before the new generation of lice became dangerous to the nestlings. In the first nest the outbreak came early, overtaking the young Phoebes at the age of four days. As a precaution the nest had previously been treated with sulphur and commercial louse-killer. Daily the young had been taken from the nest for weighing and for observations on their growth, hence the presence of the enemy could hardly have escaped detection. On the second day after the vermin appeared and while their removal from the nestlings was under way, my sister picked 118 lice from one little Phoebe that weighed 161 grains and whose entire body scarcely equaled one-half the size of one's thumb. So heavy was the infestation that a meeting of the Board of Health for Phoebes was called immediately, and these suggestions of the doctor were acted upon without delay: the walls of the porch about the nest were thoroughly washed with a solution of corrosive sublimate and the nest well sopped with this solution. The doctor decided on the removal of the hair lining of the nest, which, after being washed in the solution, rinsed and dried with a warm flatiron, was returned to the nest. The young birds were restored to the care of their distracted parents. Thereafter for a week the young were daily hand-picked for vermin, the number on a single bird never exceeding a score. At nest-leaving time the young apparently were as clean as Phoebes ever are.

The material of this nest, together with that added by a pair of Barn Swallows, was carried away by treacherous House Wrens, and thirteen years passed before another Phoebe chose the porch post for her nest site. This was in the busy summer of 1918 when war work for everyone was paramount. A day or two after the eggs were hatched, and again several days later, the young were examined without the finding of any vermin on them. Therefore, when the young were twelve days old the behavior of the mother was startling. Coming to the nest with food, she made the rattling noise such as the male utters when calling his mate to a nest site. Investigations followed. The hand placed on the nestlings instantly felt as if on fire. The young birds were dead and their bodies were gray with lice, while the walls adjacent to the nest were covered with a seething mass of them. It was an emergency to be dealt with cautiously—with sleeves rolled high, with hands and arms well smeared with camphorated oil. With the aid of pinchers the dead were removed for burial.

Six more years passed in which the usual precautions had insured the lives of the broods in the barn. These were the years from 1918 to 1924. Meanwhile the ancient nest had been destroyed and the one in use in 1924 was but two years old. In it Phoebe laid four sets of eggs. The second clutch was thrown out of the nest by the House Wren, the shells together with their contents lying below the nest. The eggs of the first and third sets disappeared most mysteriously. I shall always believe that they were eaten by a pair of Robins that were raising a brood approximately four feet distant from the Phoebe's nest. In more than twenty years this was the first time Phoebe had been molested by any enemies except House Wrens and lice —two of the worst enemies any bird can have—and it was the first time a pair of Robins had nested in that place. To anyone objecting to my accusation on the ground that the Robin has never been seen to eat eggs, I would reply that long and intensive study of our commonest birds will reveal many things that never before were seen or suspected.

The fourth set of Phoebe's eggs in 1924 escaped destruction. The nest was treated with sulphur and was watched very closely, because at the same time there was in progress on top of the porch post the nest of a concubine of father Phoebe. Each time the eggs in the barn nest were destroyed, the male had a session of calling. After the destruction of the third clutch, his calls must have attracted an unmated female. She built her nest with unusual expedition, her eggs were laid on the same days as were those in the barn nest; that their period of incubation was a few hours longer than that of the others seemed due to the frequent and long disturbances caused the porch Phoebe by people about the house. This was the first convicted bigamist among our Phoebes, and in his case there was no doubt. For the most part he remained steadfast to wife No. 1. Three or four times when the porch Phoebe was greatly disturbed by too close inspection of her nest, her loud "tsips" brought a second Phoebe on the scene until her trouble was over; and on two or three occasions he came near the nest but did not visit it until after the death of his nestlings in the barn. He then came very timidly under the porch and brought a few meals to the young birds. Whether present or absent, the mother Phoebe showed no concern about him. If her actions spoke at all, they said: "Thus far

I have managed my nest alone, and alone I can carry it to the finish"—which she did.

Every possible effort was made to avert the tragedy that threatened the lives in the barn nest, which was so situated that the measures adopted to save the nest in 1905 could not be employed. Almost daily some sulphur was poured into the nest; nevertheless the scourge was not abated. When the young Phoebes were eleven days old the fiery inferno in which they were cradled became unendurable, and like sailors from a burning ship, these helpless little ones hurled themselves to almost certain death below. When replaced in the nest they again leaped from it. The situation had become desperate, while the desire to save their lives was unusually strong. With all the young out of the nest, one more thing remained to be tried: that was a teakettleful of boiling water to be poured through the nest. But unlooked-for results followed this proceeding: three-fourths of the nest toppled off. The young had been placed in the vacated nest of a Robin. This was refitted for them and was fastened on the beam near the wreck of their old nest. At least one parent brought food to them during the afternoon, but all were dead the next morning. The gruesome details of three vermin-infested nests, the occupants of only one of which were saved, serve to illustrate one difficulty in the way of Phoebe raising.

The nests built on top of the porch post could be seen from four rooms of the house. In several respects they afforded opportunities for study not furnished by the barn nest; in the barn nest the main advantage consisted in the easy view of it obtained through a wide crack in the floor above it. Numerous Phoebe nests have been found in the woods, these often built against the nearly vertical faces of rocks. Such nests have been visited at irregular intervals, which, if a week or so apart, gave small chance for real study. One such nest contained a Cowbird's egg, and when last seen the inevitable happened: the nest was filled with the large bulk of the parasitic nestling. Phoebe's reaction to a Cowbird's egg was tested in one of the porch nests. She was greatly disturbed by its presence; several times she came to the nest but sat in it only an instant; finally, before the eggs were cold, she remained for some time; the alien egg was then removed.

The porch post has afforded opportunities for watching Phoebe's manner of choosing a nest site. As is the case with most other species of our dooryard, the male leads the way and calls the attention of his mate to a place that he deems suitable; but the ultimate choice rests with the female, as it does with other species. Numerous times the male has tried to get his mate to accept the place on the porch and she has refused. One year his efforts continued through several weeks without avail. Perhaps not a season has passed without a male attempting to induce a female to build there. Notebook records make mention of such endeavors in more than half of the summers. Since never more than three Phoebes have been seen there at one time, and since a suspicion of bigamy was voiced in some of the records before the Phoebes of 1924 proved that there were two females to one male, it has been easy to believe that some of these efforts were made to attract a wandering female, though the male already had a mate in the barn nest. Such behavior seems queer when one recalls the summers when there were protracted wooings without any winnings. There was the entire season when a Phoebe called from the peak of an unoccupied barn. There was another summer when for weeks a Phoebe tried to get an occupant for the porch site, and still other summers when no female could be induced to use the barn nest. All things considered, one is inclined to the belief that, like the House Wren, a desirable nesting place may hold greater attractions for the female than does the male who is doing the wooing.

When the male Phoebe is calling attention to a nest site, he flies to it uttering his "pewit phoebe" notes, which may become shrilly strident if the female flies near it. If she comes to it and alights, he utters a rattling cry that is suggestive of the whirring sound made by a strong wire spring when released from tension. I have heard this note on only one other occasion. This was when the young were found dead in the nest. Simultaneously with the utterance of this rattling note, he seems to spring with joy from the prospective site and leaves it to his mate. Without distinctly predicating this bounding upward as a sign of joy when his mate alights, this behavior of Phoebe is peculiar to such occasions only. If she builds a nest on the spot and he helps feed the young therein, his leave-takings are always in a more conventional manner.

For six months Phoebe may be found with us. His arrivals and departures closely parallel those of the Northern Flicker; but he is more inclined to come into the old barn to roost as soon as he comes, than is the Flicker. In springtime it may be a mooted question how long he roosts in the old nest before nidification begins; but it is certain he occupies it in late summer after the female with her second brood has left. A sheltered place for roosting is quite to Phoebe's taste in early spring. One of them used a nail for a roosting place within one of the rooms of the barn for a few weeks. The porch nest has furnished some unquestionable data. In the case of wife No. 2 in 1924, she spent the night in the nest following the day in which she built most of it. Four nights intervened before egg-laying began, and on the second and third of these she was absent. A previous nest had a similar history for roosting. The hour for her retiring has been about 7:30 o'clock. After the nest is completed but before incubation begins, the Phoebes are not seen about the place. This is not so surprising as is the failure to find the male during the incubation period. This absence has been noted during so many nestings that it is thought to be his accustomed role. It certainly leaves the sitting bird with the problem of finding the entire food supply. When the eggs begin to hatch the male reappears and begins the work of feeding.

For a close study of the hours for egg deposition and the period of incubation, few nests can be situated more advantageously than those of Phoebe in porch and barn. Not every nest was studied as closely as it might have been, but enough data relating to the hours of laying have been collected to show that in common with others of our dooryard species, a little more than twenty-four hours intervene between the deposition of two of her eggs. In several instances her last egg has been laid after eight o'clock, two hours later than was the first; the interval of retardation evidently lengthens toward the last. Once it was learned that the time between the fourth and fifth eggs exceeded twenty-four hours and forty minutes. One spring, when rainy weather prevailed for three successive days, the nest did not receive an egg; the same omission happened for the Chimney Swift's nest, but below it a soft-shelled egg had been dropped. In two seasons the exact hour of deposition of an egg in the porch nest was determined: each time it was the fourth egg; for the first case it was at 7:58 a.m., and for the second, 7:20. On both occasions during ovipositing the bird stood in the nest for about three minutes.

As has been done for the other species studied, the period of incubation has been reckoned from the hour the last egg was laid. This period for the first nest in a season has varied from fifteen and a half to eighteen days, with an average of nearly seventeen whole days, while the incubation period of the second nest has varied from fourteen days plus several hours to sixteen days with an average of fifteen and a half days. These figures show that in two dozen nestings in the same nests, with probably the same birds for first and second nestings, with nothing whatsoever different except the temperature of the air to retard the early May incubation beyond that of the late June one, the lower temperature lengthened by one and a half days the period of incubation of the earlier nests. Other illustrations of the effects of low atmospheric temperature on the period of incubation were furnished by the unusually cold May of 1904, 1907 and 1923. These were the ones (and the only ones) in which the period reached eighteen days. A careful study of twenty-four of these nests shows a variation of nearly four days in the incubation period of some of them; it also shows that the very short period of fourteen days has occurred but twice.

CHAPTER VI

THE NEST LIFE OF THE
WESTERN HOUSE WREN *

The various incidents connected with the nest life
of the Western House Wren (*Troglodytes aedon
parkmani*) that are presented here, have been gathered
from numerous nestings about our home in northeastern Iowa. Many of the nests were made in boxes in
the yard. These boxes were provided with doors,
admitting of examination of the box contents, by which
nidification and the development of the young could be
watched. The exact number of nests can not be stated,
but it is not far from thirty. In recent years there
have frequently been three nests in progress at once—
five in a season—with one or two unmated males swel-
ling the chorus of wren music, while boxes in neighboring yards provided homes for several other pairs.

Much can be learned of wren home life from nestings
in boxes placed near the house, but far more intimate
knowledge has been obtained from nests in our barn.
These were watched through peep-holes, and the
domestic affairs of the birds were conducted at the
same distance from the eye that one holds a book or
newspaper when reading. In this barn are seven boxes
provided for the nesting and roosting of the Northern
Flicker, yet having served for Screech Owls, Sparrow
Hawks and Western House Wrens. Besides the peep-
holes in the tops, these boxes are furnished with doors

---

* This paper was read at the meeting of the American Association for
the Advancement of Science, Columbus, Ohio, December 29, 1915.

by means of which the boxes can be cleaned when necessary, and the young birds can be freely handled.

There has existed a general misconception among ornithologists relative to the amount of light the hole admits to the nest. They have been accustomed to dwell at considerable length upon the darkness and the hot, stifling conditions prevailing in the cavities inhabited by the hole-nesting species. One writer, worrying over the subject, and realizing that birds cannot count, stated his belief that darkness in the cavity prevents the female from seeing the size of the clutch of eggs. He arrived at this conclusion: that it is by the sense of touch that the female learns her set of eggs is large enough for the termination of her laying. He offers no explanation for the not infrequent instances of birds stopping with the fourth egg, when the average number for the species is seven or eight eggs; and he leaves us to suppose that should the female's sense of touch become benumbed, she would continue laying eggs *ad infinitum*.

It seems strange that these theorists have not applied a simple law of optics to their problem. Everyone realizes that the light admitted through a knot-hole does little to illuminate a large loft that is windowless; but let an uncovered box be placed back of such a hole, the rays of the light will be confined within the box; let there be a peep-hole in the top of the box for the examination of its interior, and it will be found that the illumination is ample; that the light that streams through a hole 2½ inches in diameter into a box 8 x 13 x 20 inches is sufficient for the reading of ordinary newspaper print lying on the bottom of the box; also that the same is true of the amount of light admitted by a 1¼-inch hole into a box 5 x 8 x 15 inches. Various tests such as these show us that the light in the cavities occupied by hole-nesting birds equals in intensity that usually admitted into our living-rooms. It was in boxes abundantly lighted for observation that the home life of the Western House Wren has been watched.

Could this wren discuss his own idiosyncrasies, no doubt he would pronounce himself tempermental. Certainly he has enough bad traits, queer traits, unexpected traits, to justify his use of so large a word. Very soon after his early-May arrival he may be seen flying through the orchard hotly pursued by a Bluebird, a Song Sparrow or some other bird neighbor even to the big Bronzed Grackle, for birds as well as men recognize in him a nest-despoiler. Others have caught him red-handed though I have not, yet have I frequently found incriminating evidences in the nests of various species, such as the Catbird, Phoebe or Chipping Sparrow, whose eggs have been pierced by a very slender bill, and I have seen this wren tear into pieces two nests of the Phoebe. This wren is a valiant fighter when his own domicile is threatened, and his vigorous, well-delivered blows on the back of an intrusive English Sparrow command admiration. When the door of his house is sufficiently narrow he bids defiance to the world of bird foes he has made, and his offspring suffer from very few enemies until they leave the nest. The perils then awaiting are many; chief among them are the dangers from cats, and from the Migrant Shrikes. I have seen a fledgling wren, after much hesitation at its doorway, finally make the fatal plunge into the outside world, quite as unmindful of a lurking foe as I was; and five minutes later I saw its lifeless form in the bill of a shrike.

In our wren the bump of curiosity is well developed, in proof of which the following incident is offered. The father of a brood being raised in a barn nest detected my presence beyond the peep-hole in the top

of the box. After vain attempts to identify the interloper from the inside of his nest, he came into the
barn through an open window which was located about
15 feet from the nest. This behavior was repeated on
a following day.

Our bird, in common with other species of wrens,
is possessed of great activity. Whereas the male Marsh
Wrens for their "busy work" build "cock-nests" which
are not lined, the male House Wrens amuse themselves
by carrying sticks into numerous boxes or into niches
or cavities suitable for nest sites. Not to speak too
positively on this point, it is believed that the work
of nest-lining with fine grasses or with grasses and
feathers is done solely by the female. The working
ability of our wren was illustrated by a pair that once
built in a Flicker hole in our barn. The depth of the
space below the hole was 11 inches and the other
dimensions were 16 by 6 inches. All the lightning
calculators in this audience have already estimated that
a space 11 x 16 x 6 inches contains nearly a half bushel.
The wrens did not fill this entire space with twigs, but
they carried in a peck or more, and half of the amount
was taken in on the first day, which was June 12.
Having begun early in the morning, they were still
at work at seven o'clock in the evening. A count during
eight minutes showed that they carried in eighteen
sticks. This rate of a stick a minute for each bird has
been outdone in another nest when a bird carried a
stick every half minute, going from 60 to 75 feet away
for the stick. Sometimes the male carried a twig to
the hole and passed it to the female within. The hole
was large and irregular in shape, but the wrens very
soon learned to carry long sticks through it, though
some were 9 and 10 inches in length by actual measurement. Many sticks were forked; a few of these caught
in the hole and were dropped outside. This nesting hap-

pened about a dozen years ago. Since then many nests have been watched, some that were made in small cavities through small holes. In no instance have the wrens been noted to carry sticks too long for the cavity, nor forked sticks such as they took through the large opening. Hence to the wren's list of traits there may be added that of speedy adaptability.

To activity and adaptability in nest building may be added another characteristic: the wren is not too fastidious in the choice of his foundation material, nor too proud to accept aid. To prove the latter point, I have repeatedly placed a handful of twigs on top of the wrens' box, and in every case they were used. This and other observations have led to the conclusion that the wrens usually avail themselves of the nearest supply of suitable material. But one exception to this has been discovered by Mr. A. H. Godard, who relates in May-June, 1915, *Bird-Lore* that he gave a wren dry sticks that were used, but green twigs substituted in place of the dry ones were not only rejected, but were carried away from the box and dropped.

As was pointed out a moment ago, the male wren assists in laying the nest foundation of dry twigs, which may be considered the bed-springs; also, it is believed the female alone places on top of these twigs the true nest of straw lined with feathers; but it is the male, working by himself, singing while he works, that casts out this nest almost as soon as vacated by the first brood—and what does he sing as he works? Methinks it is this: "Out with your old feather-bed. Out with your old straw-bed. Out with all your old insect-infested beds. Nothing but clean beds will do for my offspring!" Just here is the place to express the wish that *all men* would profit by this one good example set by the wren!

The duration of the nest, from the laying of the

first egg until the nest was deserted by the young, has varied from thirty to thirty-five days. The average duration for a series of nests has been thirty-two days. The eggs are deposited early in the morning, sometimes before five o'clock. Incubations, which have begun with the third or the fourth egg, have proved beyond question that the shortest time for the incubation of a wren's egg is thirteen days, and fourteen days may be regarded as the average time. Since some of the eggs hatch one, two and three days later than the others, there is that variation in the ages of the fledglings when they leave the nest. When disturbed unduly the wrens will fly out when only thirteen days old; they are hardly fit at fourteen days, but entirely so at seventeen days. The average age of the young wrens upon leaving these nests has been fifteen days. These figures are not based upon guesswork, but have been obtained from numerous nests, some of which were watched from the inside from start to finish—from the laying of the first foundation twigs to the departure of the last nestling through the door of the nest.

I shall take for the history of the home life of the wrens one barn nest that in most respects was fairly typical of all. It was built in a box 5 x 8 x 15 inches that was placed back of a Flicker-hole in the southwest corner of the barn. The hole was 17 feet from the ground. Just below the hole was a perch about a foot in length. Eight eggs were laid. Incubation began on the Fourth of July, after the third egg was deposited, and these three eggs were hatched on Friday, July 18, at the end of fourteen days. Thereafter an egg was hatched each day except Sunday when two were hatched, which showed that the sitting was closer after the laying of the fifth egg. It also showed an incubation period of fourteen days for the first five eggs, and thirteen days for the last three eggs.

Names for the nestlings proved a convenience in writing notes. The three Friday wrens and the Saturday baby were decidedly larger than the others and were named the Big Four. The two Sunday birds were sometimes called "the twins," and the other two were known as the Monday baby and the Tuesday baby. As soon as it could be done each of the six older wrens was marked by a colored string on one foot and later they were banded. The colors that marked the Big Four were red, brown, black, and white, respectively, and the twins were distinguished by gray and pink strings.

In the seventeen days of nest duration after the eggs began to hatch, notes were taken during forty-six hours and twenty-seven minutes. Barring the first and second of these days, there was no shorter watch than one hour and twelve minutes, and the longest watch was seven hours and forty minutes. The young were weighed for twelve days, which was as long as it was safe to handle them without danger of frightening them from the nest. In their rate of growth they were in the same class with the Phoebe and Red-winged Blackbird, which on their ninth day are ten times heavier than when hatched. The weight of one young one just from the shell was 15 grams. When six days old their eyes were beginning to open, and the pin-feathers on their wings were 3/16 to ¼ of an inch long; the sheaths of these wing-quills began to break when they were ten days old. On their seventh day they first showed fear. When eleven days of age one was seen for the first time outside of the nest proper, but still in the box. By the "nest proper" is meant the true nest of feathers and straw. In the remaining six days the Big Four showed daily increasing disposition to step out of the nest and prance around in the box, but the Sunday babies seldom left it. When food was brought all scurried back into the nest.

It has already been stated that it took five days for the eggs to hatch. In those days the male wren brought the greater part of the food. The female collected a small portion, probably about 20%. Contrary to many cases, this male did not bring the food into the box, but called his mate outside and gave her the food. At times she ate it after bringing it inside. Upon the seventh day the male brought 60% of the food, and a little less the next day. On the ninth day only 45% of it was brought by him, and for the following five days his percentage of the catch was 33, 34, 27, 6 and 12%. On the last three days of the nest he brought nothing, yet his record was unusually good for a wren father. In the hours that the nest was under observation, during the last eleven days 798 pieces of food were brought in, 113 by the male and 685 by the female, or in the ratio of 1 to 6. Grasshoppers constituted 63% of the whole.

In the early days of the nestlings the male gave the food to the female and she fed the young. He sometimes entered the box to gaze upon his offspring, but he was not seen to feed them until July 25, when the Big Four were a week old. After that he fed out about half of the food he brought, and cleaned the nest when it was necessary. The excrements were eaten by the female for the first six days; the last one that was seen to be eaten was on the eighth day. In the later days of nest occupation it was cleaned about once each hour for each nestling, or more exactly once for each six feedings; while the average feedings for each nestling were five per hour. But in the earlier days of the nest each young one was fed not oftener than once an hour, and all of them showed signs of underfeeding.

Continual restlessness was a leading evidence that they were underfed. When the Big Four were five and six days old they were taken from the nest and fed while remaining in an artificial nest for several hours. At such times, when they were well fed, their constant squirming ceased and they remained quiet as they did later when given five meals per hour. The reason they were taken from the nest and fed by me was because the Monday and Tuesday babies were dying from starvation. Monday weighed 15 grains when hatched. The next day its weight was but 16 grains when it should have been 30, while that of the largest wren was 90 grains. By this time the Tuesday baby was hatched and weighed only 13 grains. Small chance had these mites among the husky, robust wrens. As they lay in the nest they suggested human babies in bed with six other children, the larger ones being strapping, long-legged, active imps, weighing from 70 to 90 pounds. These big fellows obtained the lion's share of the scant supply of food, notwithstanding that the little ones opened wide their mouths and might have received nourishment had the food been of suitable size.

Some years ago I described the starving to death of a newly-hatched Flicker. In that case it was jostled to one side by the larger nestlings which obtained the food. Nothing like this happened with the wrens. All eight mouths were opened at once and the mother had choice of any one of them. The food proved too large for the throat of the youngest to swallow and was given to another. It has been very interesting to watch the feeding of very young birds—for example, the Catbirds in the nests they have built only two feet beyond the window-pane. At first they brought nothing but small measuring worms, but larger forms of larvae were brought as soon as they could be swallowed. So it was with the wren, for as soon as his Big Four could swallow grasshoppers he ceased to bring "small deer" and brought grasshoppers. As a consequence the Tuesday baby died when a day old. Monday was kept alive until its fourth day. In this way its life was prolonged: all the young wrens except this one were removed from the nest; the mother brought in a large larva, almost as large as her nestling; next she brought a grasshopper, then the father brought a grasshopper. At the end of an hour of fruitless attempts to feed big game, the mother brought some insect small enough for Monday's throat. Meanwhile the six other nestlings, kept in the artificial nest, were stuffed with canned salmon until they slept quietly. No amount of clicking or chirruping on my part would induce one to open its mouth, but the instant the father twittered outside all six sprang to their feet and stretched wide their mouths, then the canned salmon was popped in. Not until near death did the two starvelings fail to respond with the others when father sang. If mother was brooding, their springing up raised her in the nest, but usually she dashed out instantly. Sometimes his call sent her out when he brought no food. This was the case also in another nest where there were but three young ones and the father was never seen to bring any food.

Let us consider for a moment some other nests. In the one just mentioned, though the father brought no food, he frequently came in, cocked his head on one side then on the other, while he surveyed his brood, then he flew out and sang. His song to my ears was this: "Go on. Jane, go on! You are doing all right!" And Jane did go on bearing all the burdens of the nest alone. Take another nest—one built in a box near one of the house-windows. When the nest had progressed somewhat beyond the hatching period, with a

parting shout to old Jane to go on, the father departed.
It might have been one of those mysterious disappear-
ances of which we sometimes hear, if the little rascal
had gone far. But out under the cedars he was singing his sweetest to a new Jennie, while helping her to
build a nest in another box. The villianous little bigamist had not gone so far away with his new Jennie
but that old Jane, his grass-widow, could hear every
note of his refrain as she toiled all day in the hot sun
to rear her large brood. After he left it he was never
seen to come near his first nest. A similar case happened last summer in the yard of a neighbor.

In another summer, about the same box near the
window, was studied the behavior of a wren that was
a grass-widower. On or about June 9 an accident befell
Jennie's eggs and she left. The male wren remained
true to his box and held it against all comers for the
rest of the summer. For two months, through the
fierce heat of the summer, he sang from its roof without securing a new mate. On July 17 his singing was
timed. It was found that his song occupied about two
seconds, and that he rested three seconds; that he
averaged ten songs in a minute. He rarely sang upon
his box top for more than three minutes without leaving it for a brief vacation. There were other singing
wrens in the yard, making it impossible to learn if he
sang when away from his box. The singing of a wren
that has a mate, is not so frequent. Near the nest of
the Big Four, while the eggs were hatching, the
father was noted to sing forty-five times in forty-seven
minutes.

I have given only fragments taken here and there
from the home life of the Western House Wren.
Mention of two more points will be made. We frequently read of some one's witnessing the coaxing of
the fledglings from the nest by the old birds. Such

observers must possess far better eyesight than mine, to say nothing of reasoning powers. I have watched many broods leave the nest, representatives from a dozen or more species, and have seen nothing that in the remotest degree resembled coaxing. In fact, in the case of a Barn Swallow the reaction of nest-visiting persisted after the young had flown, and twice the mother carried food to the empty nest. Some broods are weaker than others of the same species and remain considerably longer in the nest than the average time. A coaxing bird parent should know this and make due allowances. When the eggs are four or five days in hatching the young usually go out in the order they were hatched. This order the coaxing bird parent must be able to keep in mind by aid of notebook or Bible records; and it must be able to count and reckon. Granting all this, then we can easily imagine what takes place. The Catbird with a nice, ripe berry in its bill sits afar off and says in Catbird language: "Eleven days is the average length for the nest-life of a Catbird. Come, Kitty, this is your day to leave, and tomorrow Tom must be ready." Or perhaps a Flicker is under observation, clinging to a nearby limb, trying hard to regurgitate the food in his throat, while he calls out: "Today White-foot, Black-foot, Pink and Blue are twenty-six days old. I want to see every one of you out of the nest this very day; but Red-foot, being a day younger, may stay until tomorrow." Or, once more, it may be a Sparrow Hawk, dangling a freshly-skinned ground squirrel in her beak, as she shrilly screams to her first-born who has his head out of the hole: "Hello, Jeremiah! You are now of age—nest-leaving age— twenty-seven days. Come out and get this fine squirrel! And Jezebel, if she contines to be extremely ugly, shall have a luscious meadow mouse all by herself day after tomorrow, which will be her coming-out day." None of these birds, nor many others, that have been marked, named and watched daily from hatching to nest-leaving, have shown any of these signs of being coaxed from the nest. Instead, the young Catbird has tramped around the rim of its nest far a day or two, strengthening its legs; and the young Phoebe has flown up from the nest a few inches while stretching its wings until the physiological impulse comes to leave the nest, then leave it after much shrinking and hesitation.

The family of wrens, which consisted of the Big Four and the Sunday babies, left the nest on August 3. In the last six days the older nestlings left the true nest frequently, skipped about the box, pecked one anothers' bills and the foundation twigs of the nest. Red, the heaviest young wren, was the leader in all activities, the "smarty" of the family—the first to leave the nest proper, the first to go from the box to the perch outside, the first to fly from the nest home. During the last morning Red went out to the perch often, and was soon joined in this pastime by Brown and Black.

The watching of the nest on its last day began at 8:56 a.m. and ended at 4:36 p.m.—seven hours and forty minutes without pause for food or drink, yet every minute had its reward. The notebook entry for 9 o'clock and 17 minutes reads: "Black has been running about, flies to the hole then runs around and around. This running is very smile-provoking. The wrens suggest brown-clad children proceeding with their play by many quick hops." There was much wing-shaking. Sometimes three would sit in the hole together, then again four would be there, chattering, preening and shaking their wings. At times all slept in the nest. At three minutes past noon the mother came in with two grasshoppers. She turned this way and that with her prizes, but could find no takers. She went to the hole, then returned to the nest; she awakened a sleeping fledgling that took one grasshopper, and she ate the other. Then she rested in the hole for five minutes. Thus the little play went on for five hours. At 1:35 p.m. Red went out for the last time. In a half hour White followed, then Brown.

With three still in the nest this note was written at 2:43 p.m.: "All have been stuffed until they can eat no more." And five minutes later this note: "It was with difficulty that the mother could serve a worm." Until about noon the Sunday babies had seldom left the nest proper. But the excitement of nest-leaving appeared to become contagious and the younger wrens joined in the commotion. One of them left before Black, which followed a minute later.

That left Pink, the smallest wren, alone, and it uttered excited cries. Then it tried to climb. After thirteen minutes of effort it reached the hole for the first time. In the hour and a half of its solitary occupancy of the nest it went to the hole seven times. It slept sixteen minutes in the nest. Food was brought to it eight times, but three of the meals it was forced to decline, and the mother carried the food out. This does not savor much of starving the youngster out.

Pink certainly was poorly developed for outside roosting that night. One wonders where such immature wrens spend the night! Once I frightened out young wrens prematurely. That evening one alighted on the window-sill. The window was opened, the wren walked in and was kept in a box over-night. Last July a neighbor saw a wren carry food into an untenanted box, which had sparrow nesting materials in it and had lost a narrow board from its back. My neighbor crept up to it and found a brood of wrens snuggled down for the night. They had recently left their home in a nearby box. Who can now say that something like this may not be a common occurrence?

An observation made in 1918: At the same wren box where I made the observation on the grass-widower, mentioned in a previous paragraph, I witnessed an unusual episode in May. A mated pair of wrens had been nest-building for more than a week when an interloper came on the scene — evidently another female wanted the box together with its incumbent male! All the morning one wren had chased another until 8:50 o'clock, when the two rival females were clinched in what appeared to be deadly combat. For a quarter of an hour they struggled and rolled over and over. While they fought the male sometimes sang from the box top, and sometimes he flew to the ground where the fight was in progress, but he made no attempt at intervention. There was an armistice of five minutes. One female was in the grass directly in front of a window, when the other female, crouching like a beast of prey, crept stealthily upon her. The fight was resumed for a few minutes, though the struggle was much more feeble than before. Then the combatants disappeared. During the forenoon the male now and then carried in a stick and sang at intervals, and a female twice came to the box for very brief visits. My notes for the following day read: "Today but one female comes about the box and its lordly owner. She sits in the currant bush or on an apple bough and flutters her wings, but he appears to look askance on her and to turn a cold shoulder. He occasionally carries in a twig or sings a little, but I can see no indications that he looks upon her as a mate, from which I conclude that she is the interloper." When a week or more after this the nest activities were resumed, it was impossible to tell whether or not the interloper had won the unusual contest.

CHAPTER VII

THE CUCKOOS

The Cuckoos have been very aptly called "Birds of Mystery." A mysterious anomaly in the distribution of Yellow-billed and the Black-billed Cuckoos challenges to an investigation. In an attempt to solve the problem ornithological books and magazines are brought out and searched with resultant information that proves still more puzzling: the Yellow-billed Cuckoo is found to winter as far south as Brazil and Argentina. Its breeding range extends from the West Indies to southern Canada, and westward nearly to the Rocky Mountains. Observers in the Gulf states report it as a fairly common summer resident, but most of them fail to see the Black-billed Cuckoo as it migrates. The most southerly nesting places of the latter, as located and reported, have been in South Carolina and southern Kansas. In the northern portion of its range and in the cooler altitudes of mountains it outnumbers in places its Yellow-billed cousin. Clearly it is a bird of the Transition Zone, and this would seem to explain its superior numbers in the Mississippi River region of northern Iowa, Wisconsin and Minnesota, until we learn that in western Iowa in the Missouri River valley the Yellow-billed Cuckoo is the commoner form. The theory has worked imperfectly: in respect to their locally uneven distribution, the birds of mystery remain mysterious still.

About my home the Yellow-billed Cuckoo (*Coccyzus americanus americanus*) is far less common than the Black-bill. It has been known to nest only once on our place. An individual of this species was noted carrying nesting materials on August 21, and very likely it was a bird whose previous nesting attempts had resulted in failure. I was sitting in the top story of the Chimney Swift tower, drawing the background of a bird portrait, while watching the feedings of young Chimney Swifts at long intervals. My position commanded a view of the treetops below the window without revealing my presence to the cuckoo. She was watched on that and on subsequent days and her behavior was the same at all times. She never was seen to visit the ground where suitable sticks were exceedingly plentiful, but on the first day her quest for material was confined to the tops of some dwarf plum trees, which she searched for dead twigs that she could break off. After much tugging and pulling she was forced to abandon the struggle for some of them, but when successful, she carried the captured stick to her nest site, which was about 25 feet above the ground in a Norway spruce tree. In choosing so lofty a situation she showed taste quite at variance with that of her Black-billed relatives, which have built in brushy plum trees in places that are at no greater height than 8 feet. Two days later she still gathered twigs, but this time from cedar trees near her nest.

Individuals of this species were seen on about half of the following days until September 19. The temperature for this month was unusually cool; this taken together with autumnal rain may have caused the desertion of the nest. In the following year a Yellow-billed Cuckoo stayed until October 8. Its visits to the same pine tree in a neighboring yard lent color to a suspicion that its migration may have been delayed by a late nesting.

At intervals for a dozen years the Black-billed Cuckoo (*Coccyzus erythropthalmus*) has nested in our dooryard. Two, and probably three, of the nestings had successful outcomes. In another year, soon after the egg-laying began the nest was deserted. On the ground nearby lay the shell of a cuckoo egg showing signs which suggested the House Wren as the despoiler.

Only in the woods have I seen the cuckoo courtship. It seemed a rather spirited affair for birds so characteristically shy. Not only are the birds evidently mated before they come to us, but the late date of their coming suggests the failure elsewhere of a first attempt at nesting. Once I found nidification began in late June; at other times it has not commenced until well into July.

For a week or two after the advent of the cuckoos, their night song or calling is heard. After this the call is seldom heard except when given as a warning upon the appearance of a person out of doors. Great care has been exercised to prevent disturbance of these birds, in consequence of which their nests have not been studied as closely as they might have been. Once, before the location of a nest was known, I began cutting some tall weeds growing in front of the nest. Three had fallen before the cuckoo was frightened from her nest. She flew to the ground, feigning a broken wing and uttering most distressing cries, which sounded like the squalls of a cat in great agony. Two weeks later, when the young were out of the nest, there was an uproar that seemed to bring all the birds in the neighborhood to a tree in which there was a Robin's nest. Investigation showed that the piteous wail came from a young cuckoo, which had lit in the tree and was being punished by the old Robin. These instances made plain that the usually silent cuckoo can make plenty of noise upon provocation.

The testimony of others upon the tendency of cuckoos to desert their nests if disturbed, may have caused too great caution to be exercised in our home yard. This, coupled with nest sites that could not be seen from windows, has left many' questions unanswered. One morning two young Black-billed Cuckoos were out of the nest. By standing on a box placed on a chair we could see an unfledged nestling still occupying the nest. Both of us took a hasty look and left very speedily without touching the nest or its occupant. Without further growth the little cuckoo died in the nest, and ever since there has been the vexed question: did we create a disturbance?

When the time comes that a nest of this species has been studied intensively by an observer hidden from the bird, I suspect that it will be announced that both parents take part in the incubation and brooding of the young. This surmise is based on the fact that almost never have I found the nest of a cuckoo unoccupied, which corresponds to the nesting behavior of the Mourning Dove, Northern Flicker and Brown Thrasher. In all these species both birds share alike in these duties.

The living conditions of the two young cuckoos, whose younger brother perished in the nest, were under observation for three weeks after they left the nest. The publicity of their family life for the first ten days was equal to that of most birds and far greater than that of many, while for the first four days it could be excelled by none. Considering the elusive habits of cuckoos in general, this seemed rather remarkable. For the most part, the young birds sat in full view, usually in a row of young trees standing a short distance from their nest-tree. The going and coming of the parent bird was without concealment. At no time was more than one parent seen. The non-appearance of the other parent, taken together with the death of the nestling, was suggestive of a double tragedy.

My vantage place for watching was from the window of the "opera box" in the tower, where I was about 100 feet from the young birds. Even with the aid of good binoculars the character of the food put into their pink-lined mouths could not be determined. The pink color of their mouths could be plainly seen. Hairy caterpillars and grasshoppers were the only items of food that I could identify, when carried by a cuckoo to its young. On the first day after leaving the nest, the fledglings were fed seventeen times in an hour; on the second and third days the average time between meals was seven minutes. The feedings were noted during watches of one and two hours duration after nine o'clock in the morning.

The books frequently speak of the cuckoo's preference for low, damp locations for its nesting places. When ecological studies of life are carried further, it will probably be found that low grounds are the natural habitats of certain insects especially acceptable to the cuckoo's palate. I have seen it collect a light yellow, hairy caterpillar from such places. The flight of the parent to and from its young was low, generally no more than two or three feet from the ground. This low flying tended to render the bird less conspicuous and is a marked characteristic of many of the marsh-haunting species. The row of low trees in which the young birds perched grew close to the house-yard fence on the west. North and west of the trees was open space. The parent, after having delivered a meal, flew north a few rods and usually lit on the wire house-yard fence 2 or 2½ feet above the ground. Occasionally a capture was made there, but as a rule it flew over grass-land for 80 or more yards to another fence, which stood on the edge of a ravine (or wet meadow) covered with wild grass. Here the fence was of boards and the bird's alighting place was about the same distance from the ground. After surveying the grass below, it would run along the top of the board for about 10 feet before pausing. In this way it once moved over eight panels of fence — 64 feet — before it made a capture. Now and then it alighted on the top of a fencepost or the top of the fence. It was noted that it hardly paused among the grass-tops when making a plunge for its victim. Only twice have I seen a cuckoo on the ground: once a young Black-bill stayed as long as five minutes on the ground in the grass; the other time was when I frightened the sitting bird from the nest.

The young cuckoos grew apace as do all well-fed young birds. When ten days from the nest their length was estimated to equal that of an adult Robin. It was mainly in length of tail that their size appeared inferior to their parents'. The last time either of them was seen was on August 30, when their age was five weeks or thereabout. They then showed no signs of red on the eye-lids. At later dates I have seen young migrating Black-bills whose eye-lids showed no red. It would be interesting to know at what age this color appears.

CHAPTER VIII

HABITS OF THE
SHORT-BILLED MARSH WREN *

This study covers a period of twenty-six years. At the outset an apology should be offered because the period is not sixty-six years instead of twenty-six. Fifty and sixty years ago natural conditions had not been so radically altered that a satisfactory study of the life history of the Short-billed Marsh Wren (*Cistothorus stellaris*) could not have been made. Even twenty-five years ago conditions were far different from those at present. Various phases of this wren's behavior have been made manifest gradually and the study of them has been as careful, as diligent and as constantly sustained as I have been capable of making it. I did my best, but another might have done better.

One fact that ornithological literature has made tolerably clear is that my field of study in northeastern Iowa must be near the center of the most populous portion of this wren's summer range. The topography of my study field is rolling prairie, which being near the Mississippi River "rolls rapidly," or in other words, it is very much up hill and down dale. The dales, or ravines as they are called locally, grow narrower and their streams cut deep channels as they recede from the water-sheds. But these streams for a half mile to a mile from their sources spread out over the depressions, forming marshy places or wet

---

* Read at the Forty-ninth meeting of the American Ornithologists' Union, Detroit, Michigan, October 20, 1931.

meadows, sometimes upward of 10 rods in width. These swampy spots, until quite recently, have retained the native wild grasses and other plants characteristic of such locations. In them grew slough grass, two species of rushes, rice cutgrass, sedge, manna grass, red-top and swamp milkweed. It is believed that when ecological studies have progressed further it will be found that this lowland vegetation is the favored habitat of certain insects that these Marsh Wrens prefer for food.

Cistothorus stellaris is the Marsh Wren of my neighborhood, its long-billed relative, the Prairie Marsh Wren (*Telmatodytes palustris dissaeptus*) having been seen by me three times only in the past thirty years. As a spring migrant the appearance of the Short-billed Marsh Wren has been decidedly rare: only on seven days in all, which were on May 9 and 12, in 1907; on May 9, 1908; and on May 17, 19, 21, and 22, 1916. It is surmised that the same bird was seen on the two spring days of 1907, likewise that the same thing was true for the four May days of 1916 for the bird found on those days in a brush-pile refuge in a swampy place. None other of these wrens was seen until July; for the three years just mentioned as well as for fifteen other summers the wrens arrived on some July date ranging from the 1st to the 30th; for three years their arrival dates were in August; for two in September; and for three years there were no records.

That for eighteen summers the first appearance of a bird species should be in July is not surprising, but because thereafter it remained within certain territorial limits until time for fall departure, that it sang, built nests and sometimes laid eggs in those nests, are peculiar habits that call for diligent investigation. The dates of their arrivals suggest that they had nested elsewhere; also that the wrens coming early may have had their nests destroyed, while those coming later had probably raised a brood.

Since my observations were not begun sixty-six years ago, it was desirable to question men of eighty years or upward, who were familiar with farming operations of long ago. I began none too soon, since now all my informants are dead. Some most gratifying reminiscences were called forth. Among them were those of William C. McNiel, who had been my teacher in public school sixty-seven years ago. To the questions: "Did you mow with a scythe the slough grass in your youth?" "Did you find there bird nests made of grass, round like a ball?" he replied: "Yes, lots and lots of such nests. They were along the edge of the wild grass, not in the middle of the slough. We cut the tame grass with the mower, but had to use the scythe to cut the wet ravines. The nests were on the outer edge of the wild grass. The eggs were white and the birds were gray." Of equal clearness was the memory of another man who said: "Some of the nests held white eggs and others brown eggs." Evidently he had cut down nests belonging to the Prairie Marsh Wrens. All the men were agreed that they cut the ravines about the first of July, the same time it is done at present.

Having obtained adequate testimony regarding the former abundance of the Short-billed Marsh Wren in my locality; having for eighteen summers recorded its arrival in July, followed by its halts of longer or shorter durations in several of which there may have been nestings; having found it of rather frequent occurrence in fall migrations—a query naturally arose as to the reason of its scarcity in the spring migrations. In autumn this wren's choice of plant associations seemed to suggest the correct answer. No longer partial to the wild grasses of the ravines in the fall, it more often was found in plants of coarser growth, such as meadow sunflower, Spanish needles, ragweed, blue vervain, asters, jewel-weed, sandbar willows and in other small willows growing near the roadside. When moving northward might it not keep to the underbrush of woodlands bordering the Mississippi River and its tributaries? This supposition was changed to confidence upon the rereading of two items in *The Auk* of 1908. At the time these items were published they were not memorized because then the spring migration routes of these wrens made no problem calling to me for solution. In the April, 1908, number of *The Auk,* E. Seymour Woodruff said: "On May 14 [1907] I secured a female Short-billed Marsh Wren in some witch-hazel bushes in the dry creek-bed of Spring Valley, Shannon Co., [Missouri]. Considering the fact that this was a dry, heavily-wooded and mountainous region with no marshes within many miles, this record is very surprising." In the October number of the same magazine for the same year Aretas A. Saunders in his article, 'Some Birds of Central Alabama,' stated: "On May 3 I was much surprised to find a male bird of this species, along a little alder-lined creek at Hollins." Then to make assurance doubly sure there has been in spring the finding by Oscar P. Allert of these wrens in similar brushy situations in the woods only six or seven miles from their former breeding grounds in prairie marshes. This has happened in several seasons when I failed to find a single wren on the prairies. The foregoing records have come as gratifying confirmations of my hypothesis.

When investigating the habits of a bird we are prone to search ornithological literature. Information concerning the Short-billed Marsh Wren is scant. Ten years ago in the copies of three ornithological magazines for twenty years, equivalent to sixty years for one publication, there were found about two-score mentions of this wren. Probably the records for the succeeding ten years would be similar. By far the best article I have found is that of La Rue K. Holmes in the 1904 number of *Cassinia*. A research article by Fred J. Rogers recently appeared in *Bird-Lore*. Both of these authors mention the nesting in July of this wren. Ira N. Gabrielson, in the *Wilson Bulletin* (June, 1914), records the finding in Iowa of a Short-bill's nest on July 28, 1910. The nest contained six eggs and was found in a hayfield. Richard C. Harlow, in *The Auk* (April, 1918), relates that on August 4, 1913, he found two nests, containing four and five eggs respectively, and on the same day another nest containing five young birds. The first and second authors named mentioned the presence of these Marsh Wrens in spring on the territory having July nests. But no one except myself has testified regarding their nesting in July soon after their first arrival in that month.

One nest containing eggs was found. In five other summers it was believed that there were nests. Some one may ask if I did not look for them. I did. My notebook for 1907 shows that, on July 23, for two hours and twenty minutes, in the broiling heat of midday, I waded in mud and water, in grass head-high, looking for a nest; and the search was resumed on later dates. I did not then know that the edge of the wild grass was the place to look for nests. Another thing was learned as the years passed: that *Cistothorus stellaris* brooks ill any invasion of its territory, and will desert it when disturbed.

The summer of 1916 was very hot and dry, but the wrens remained undisturbed in their chosen places. In one ravine was a very friendly singer with a silent companion. Apparently they were a nesting pair. By

August 19 it was deemed late enough to look for the nest. The sun shone fiercely hot soon after noon when came two boys hired to help me. With sticks in hand to move the cutting blades of grass, we searched back and forth across the ravine. The exploration of the suspected area had hardly begun when one boy said that in this very place a few days previously his father "had seen a great, big snake as big 'round as father's arm." His father, being a husky, corpulent farmer, fancy could easily picture a snake somewhat below the size of an adult boa-constrictor. Up to that time his companion had worked pluckily for a ten-year-old; but thereafter the search languished, and very soon was postponed to another day, which never came. Soon afterward I met his father and in the interests of natural history (since garter snakes only are found in our ravines) I asked him for a description of the snake. He replied that he had seen no snake. This story illustrates one difficulty in the study, although adding nothing to the Marsh Wren's history.

The one nest, that was found, was on our land. We had felt compassion for two pastureless calves and they had been admitted to a 2-acre lot, a small portion of which is marshy. The nest was found on August 30, 1909. It contained one whole egg and the broken shells of others, but the wrens had gone. It established the fact of the nesting of Short-billed Marsh Wrens that did not arrive until mid-summer. The first one was observed on July 18.

The hardships and uncertainties connected with the lives of these wrens are many. These pertain not only to the experiences of the birds themselves, but also to the work of their observers. My farmer neighbors follow rather closely the plan of a three-year rotation of crops. If their hillsides, adjoining a ravine, have been planted to corn and if the season has been a wet

one, it has been pretty certain that the wild grass uncut
would await the July coming of the Short-billed Marsh
Wren, and that their delightful presence could be
enjoyed for the rest of the season. When the adjacent
hillsides have borne crops of oats or barley, the grain
from them is threshed by the third week of August at
the latest, after which the farmers turn their livestock
on this land and the wrens soon leave. During the
breeding season undisturbed surroundings for them
seem requisite. However, when pastures have been
large for the number of animals in them, sometimes
these wrens have been found there, but not often, nor
for long periods. On the other hand, wrens located in
an unfrequented ravine have been known to hold most
tenaciously to their grassy cover even after a mower
began its work. Once I watched one that sang while
clinging to almost the last stems that fell before the
sickle-bar. In another summer after the mowing a
wren stayed for five days in a small triangular patch
of standing grass that covered no more than the 30th
part of an acre. The amount of our own swampy land
is small. In some of it the grass has been left for the
Marsh Wrens, but they failed to come to it.

Fortunately for the prosecution of my study of this
species my home is near the source of a small stream,
the course of which lay through our village (when it
was a village). The Short-billed Marsh Wren became
a summer resident of several backyards near us.
People sometimes asked, "What bird is it that sings
all night?" I have heard its song until late hours of
the night, and people who have not slept because of
sickness in the family or their own illness, have assured
me that they have heard the wren's song throughout
the entire night.

By the 10th of August the volume of his song has
decreased perceptibly, and a week later his singing is

still more infrequent. This corresponds closely with the subsidence of the House Wren's singing. But the Marsh Wren does not abandon entirely his role of musician. As late as the 6th of September, beginning at 6:30 in the morning, one sang for an hour in the willows near my bird-blind. It was to this place that I went for several September mornings at sunrise, or a little before, to watch the first appearance of birds that had spent the night there. Along with the Short-billed Marsh Wren were Soras, Virginia Rails and Song Sparrows. The wren stepped out from the thick growth of young willows, where it must have roosted. After it began to sing it stayed from a half hour to an hour among the willow sprouts before moving to the marsh grass.

It chanced to be the 10th of August, when once I timed the singing of one of these wrens. Soon after I was seated beside a roadside fence, approximately 40 to 50 feet from his favorite haunt, he flew toward me and the fence, alighting on the third wire, then moving soon to a flat-topped fencepost, which was a favorite singing-place of his. He sang for seven minutes, averaging from eleven to twelve songs per minute, each song occupying about two seconds, and the interval between songs lasting from three to four seconds. A passing motor car did not interrupt his musical exercise.

At almost any date, except late in the season, a proper greeting of him may call forth a snatch of a song or merely a "tsip." He may be depended upon to say something. To call him from his retirement into view has sometimes been done by clapping my hands, but more frequently by a "clicking" sound, an oft-repeated click similar to that addressed to a horse. There is apparent willingness on the part of this wren to sing from a variety of locations: from a grass-stem,

the top of sedge, rush, or swamp milkweek, or even
from the branches of a willow, 8 or 10 feet above the
ground, but the top of a wooden fencepost is a common choice. Likewise flying toward me is a common
habit. By gradual stages the bird approaches, usually
encouraged by a "clicking" call. Once one came within
3 feet of me. It was a fall migrant and we were utter
strangers, never having met before that hour. It flew
to the fence and lit 8 feet away. I advanced a couple
of steps, whereupon it reduced the space between us
to 3 feet. Several times a Marsh Wren has approached
within 5 or 6 feet, and on innumerable occasions some
of them have come within 7 or 10 feet or the longer
distance of 20 feet or thereabout. This is one of the
species so very often described as "skulking," "shy,"
"evasive," "secretive," and as having similar characteristics, while everyone knows some "tame" birds
upon which a hand has been laid during incubation, or
birds that have perched upon the hand for food. Barring the LeConte Sparrow, sometimes found in the
same swamps with these wrens, I know of no other
species exhibiting such bold confidence in humanity.
As might be expected, there is a great difference in
individuals in respect to this tameness or boldness.

Another person giving close study to these wrens
has not had success in calling them to close proximity,
such as I have described, but it may be worth while for
others to test the "shyness" of these birds that come
into sight and approach the observer at the same hour
that neighboring sparrows, the Song, Lincoln's and
Swamp, are refusing to stay in sight long enough for
identification.

I have hundreds of proofs that the singing of this
species is not always an expression of unalloyed, soul-
felt joy; that sometimes it appears that the song may
be a warning or it may be a sign of irritation, when

delivered in answer to my calling. That it expresses recognition of a human presence has been illustrated very many times. Tests often were made while I worked in my garden, hidden by a row of trees, from the wrens in their habitat only 200 to 300 feet distant: for an hour or more no singing had been heard, but the moment I stepped into sight of them the singing began. Again, while ascending the hillside toward my bird-blind a wren song has not been heard until I appeared within range of his vision. He would sing until I entered the blind where I stayed upward of a half hour or more; the instant I stepped out he began singing again. More frequently and for a greater number of years have been the experiences while approaching a Short-billed Marsh Wren habitat a quarter of a mile away. In a cut in the roadway there would be a pause to be sure that no wren was singing, then as soon as I came into sight the singing began. A like test was made upon Killdeers, with a brood of young that began giving the warning cry as soon as the disturber of their peace appeared in sight.

Once I spent an hour beside our west fence, watching the building of a dummy or cock nest, distant about a dozen feet. The builder collected his dead grass in a spot about a rod from his nest. Each time upon emerging from his nest he began to sing and never missed a song until back in his nest with an additional grass-blade. Now and then a silent wren appeared on grass-tops a few yards away; this was supposed to be his mate. Her nest was not found, but it is believed that this singer was the bird that has been described as giving his matutinal song in the willows five weeks later.

This was in 1908, and the following year the nest with eggs was found quite near the location occupied by the wrens just mentioned. In 1910 two wrens appeared to have chosen the marsh grass by the roadside for their nest-site, in a location easy for study. The location was also easy for grass-mowing, and the road-master, selecting the easy tasks only, cut that grass.

In 1915 a pair of Short-billed Marsh Wrens appeared to have located for a nesting, but livestock soon was turned into their domain and they left. In 1916 several of the species were present and the attempt to locate the nest of a pair has already been related. More than in any year of this study were the numbers of this wren present in 1919. They came in July, settled in territorial spaces in four different spots, where they were found daily; they sang, and some of them carried dead grasses as if for nest-building, but their stay was too short for raising a brood. In the twelve years since then their numbers have gradually decreased. For three or four seasons the July halts, when occurring, have been brief. Friendly association with these wrens has been confined to the autumn migration.

Upon farming operations must fall the blame for the disappearance of a most interesting species. Farmers, who have never seen these birds, who are unaware of their existence, have driven them from their marshy acres. On many farms these acres have been fenced into permanent pastures, on other farms the swine, cattle and horses are pastured on such land a part of every year. In the wet or damp soil their hoofs cut out the wild grass in long muddy stretches where noxious weeds replace the original growth. To these alienating influences must be added the intolerance of the Short-billed Marsh Wren of disturbances by man or beast in its chosen habitat.

To this gloomy picture of present conditions on the prairie may be added a brighter bit that I am permitted to relate: 6 miles to the northeast, on land formerly covered by heavy forest, which has been entirely

cleared away, the Short-billed Marsh Wren is sometimes found. In 1930 Oscar P. Allert found there
four pairs of wrens, one of which for several weeks
kept to a peculiar location. It was near farm buildings,
on a hilltop, in a growth of timothy. There the male
wren delighted the land owner with its night singing and
its friendly behavior. For all of us who have lived
in close companionship with this species of bird, its
absence causes keen regret. That it may not perish
utterly from the earth we would join those ornithologists who are urging reservations of marshy lands for
the conservation of birds choosing them for habitats.

CHAPTER IX

NOTES ON THE RAILS

There has been no exact record kept of the length of time that I spent daily with the Rail family, but an estimate coming near to accuracy has been made, giving resultant figures of 200 to 300 hours—a period that for a Labor Union workman would mean more than thirty days of occupational employment. This period is an extremely small fragment of time when compared with the hours that I have spent beside the nests of each of several hole-nesting species, viz: the Screech Owl, Sparrow Hawk, Flicker, Chimney Swift and House Wren. When the hours spent by other people with the Rails are compared with mine, there is the suggestion that few persons, if any, have spent half as many hours with these entertaining birds.

When speaking of my hours spent with the Rails, it should be mentioned at the outset that every year I meet a few Soras (*Porzana carolina*) feeding by the brooksides, but the Virginia Rail and the King Rail have not been regular annual visitors. Their occurrence is, quite likely, smiliar to the casual meetings of them enjoyed by many bird students. There may be no more than a fleeting glimpse of the Rail as it hurries out of sight within the vegetation growing near. But in one wet spring a long call was made by a King Rail (*Rallus elegans elegans*) that was seen to wander from the muddy highway into our dooryard, where it spent several hours. In the garden it walked back and forth as fearlessly as a chicken would have done. The size and behavior of this rail often suggests its resemblance to the domestic hen.

For me the golden era for rail study was embraced in the years 1907, 1908 and 1909. That these years proved fruitful for other observers is suggested by the many reports, given in the bird magazines, which focus about this period. There was a succession of wet seasons, when the swampy lands retained more than the usual amount of water; this apparently favored the successful nestings of these birds.

In my neighborhood there were conditions far surpassing any others that have been furnished in a lifetime. The chosen haunts of the rails were not more than 300 feet from our house in about a fourth of an acre of the swampy ravine that lies on the western border of our lots, giving us a width of 30 to 40 feet of marsh land on the east side of a division fence, close to which grows a row of willow trees. There the water of a brook was augmented by that of a spring which had not ceased to flow in those days. The land on the west side of the fence for more than fifty years had been utilized for live stock which ate all vegetation close to the ground. This use of the land had been abandoned a few years before the period of this study. The ravine in the summers under consideration was too wet for the mowing of the grass, hence for the only time in seventy years there was provided a suitable habitat for rails in this nearby spot.

On the eastern margin of the marshy ground in the autumn of 1907 I had built a small wooden blind, measuring 46 inches square, having the door on its east side and a window on each of the other sides. It is a rude affair, but for twenty years it has afforded shelter in inclement weather and a rare treat for observation. From its windows have been seen 110 species of birds, among them the only Blue-gray Gnatcatcher observed on our place, also the Rock Wren, which moved eastward by fully 200 miles the eastern limit of the range of this species. Inside of the blind was watched for the first time the nest life of the Screech Owl, and in later years that of the Sparrow Hawk. Better views of the rails could be secured because the posts on which the blind was built raised its floor about 2½ feet above the ground.

From the concealment of the blind it was possible to watch the natural activities of the rails and to become convinced that the members of this family possess dual forms of behavior: the one seemingly best known to a majority of writers and superficial observers calls forth such adjectives as furtive, sly, skulking, secretive, and suspicious, and is the startled manner of conduct displayed on sudden meetings; the other is the behavior of normal life and is seen only by the patient observer, sitting quietly on the edge of a bog. That for such a student a blind is not absolutely necessary was proved on many a day before mine was built. As I sat in the open, watching their ways of life, they did not rush out of sight, when on several occasions a friend passing by, stopped to view them and to talk about them.

For a few days one spring two King Rails were to be seen on the old assembly grounds, when none of the rail cousins were present. At another time this species was there along with both Virginia Rails and Soras, but their association together was too brief for any study of their actions toward one another. However, everything seen of the King Rail has been confirmatory of the characterizations of those ornithologists who have found the species "very tame," and "one of the most bold, shrewd, and fearless of water fowls."

There were times when Virginia Rails (*Rallus limicola limicola*) were with us and no Soras were to be seen, and many more days when Soras were seen but none of the former species. Out of sixty-one days when both species undoubtedly were present, on only forty of them were both kinds of rails seen together. Two hours daily is not a large estimate for the time spent with these birds. This makes approximately eighty hours for observations on their behavior toward each other. It did not take long to see that, although smaller, the Sora beyond doubt was the master bird; that it seemed to take delight in dashing at his handsomer cousin and putting him to rout. It may be because of aeons of living in fens and boggy places with this domineering relative, the Virginia Rail acquired the startled, grotesque gait he takes, when after standing in dignified attitudes for several minutes he suddenly rushes off, as if he had seen a frightful apparition.

Among themselves the young Soras are quite playful, but still more sportive are the Virginia Rails. With a cry two or three of them would bound into the open space under the willows, suggesting the advent of clowns upon the stage, and would chase one another about, shaking their wings and flying from the ground for a foot or two in a very amusing manner. That they are something of acrobats, too, was proved now and then by one mounting to the top of a fencepost or to the branch of a willow tree until 5 feet or more from the ground. Such activities on the part of the rails have been denied by certain writers whose observations were entirely too limited to warrant their conclusions.

In the open spot on the east side of the willows both of these species spent much time sunning themselves and preening their feathers, though feeding was their chief activity. The food apparently was all picked from the surface of the running water and consisted of seeds and insect life. Ready access to the grassy refuge on the west side of the fence seems largely to have influenced the choice of this spot, since it is well known that neither species is averse to seeking food on the border of a marsh, and sometimes they are found some distance from wet ground.

It was frequently noted that the numbers of both species of rails were augmented on mornings following rainy or foggy nights. Similar observations, made by others, indicate that this sort of weather is preferred for migration.

Although the nest of the Sora is often found and studies have been made of its situation, its construction and its contents, yet several ornithologists have spoken of the nesting behavior of this species as a mystery. Much less seems to be known of it than that of either the King or the Virginia Rail. In view of the fact that 1909 gave me my first and last chance to study the nest life of the Sora it is especially deplorable that this year was overcrowded with work, death and disasters. It was in 1909 that one, very likely two pairs of Soras nested in our little marsh. It was on June 5 that a Sora was seen carrying dead grass as if in the act of nest building. The location to which it was carried was not more than 40 feet from my place of observation. Later there came proofs that a nest was built; doubtless it was cosily roofed over and contained a handsome set of eggs never viewed by me.

On June 6 there was witnessed some play of the Soras which must have been courting antics. It resembled the game of leap-frog as played by boys. As one Sora stood motionless another one jumped over it; the jumping bird then stood while the other Sora leaped over it and took its place about 18 inches in advance of its partner while another jump was made. I had the impression that the dangling feet of the jumper, as it went over, brushed the back of the standing bird. It was a very amusing performance.

The presence of adult Soras was revealed on July 4, 7 and 11 when visits were made to their habitat, but no young came into view until the 16th of that month, when several appeared. On the following day five of the young ones were seen, of which four were black, downy, little fellows, while the fifth one was quite well feathered, an indication that it belonged to an earlier brood. All the downy young were of different sizes—a pretty sure sign that there was a difference in their ages. (This calls to mind the nest found by Aretas A. Saunders in Montana that contained eighteen Sora eggs, some of which were fresh and others well advanced in incubation.) Although occasionally three or four young ones were in sight at the same time, none of them loitered long in the open space. A few days after one of them was caught by a cat, all of them disappeared, and it is hoped they found a safe place elsewhere. Even then hot and dry weather was fast drying up the water in our ravine, and no succeeding year has been wet enough to induce the rails to tarry with us for very long.

CHAPTER X

ELEVEN DAYS IN THE
LIFE OF A CATBIRD

This is the twenty-second day of September, the day upon which I am two months old. Night before last there was a slight frost, but this afternoon a soft breeze blows from the south. I feel it drawing me toward the land of its birth, and very soon, when the cold north winds begin to chill us, I shall fly away to some summer land; but before I go allow me to tell you the story of my first eleven days.

This thicket in which we are sitting has been a nesting place for Catbirds for generations; but my parents selected that dwarf plum tree just below one of the west windows for their recent nest site, never dreaming that prying eyes behind the blinds would detect their secret. The discovery was made on the morning the first egg was laid. The beautiful blue egg in which I was being incubated for thirteen days was the last one of a set of three to be deposited in the nest. This occurred on the morning of July 9th some time later than half past six o'clock.

After the three eggs were laid my mother became constant in her sitting. If my father assisted in the work of incubation, he was never found on the nest, nor was he seen to bring food to her. Regularly at the end of twenty, or thirty minutes, she left the nest for a period of about ten minutes to stretch her wings and legs, and to find food. Even with this frequent change she must have found the half hours tedious, for she often yawned, displaying the bluish-pink lining of her mouth. Almost constantly she watched the window for prying eyes behind the blinds; but she was a brave bird, and would not leave her eggs when she heard the window-sash raised; not until the blinds began to swing upon their hinges did she fly away to the limb of a neighboring tree, where sat my father. Together they made the welkin ring with their cries of disapproval, bringing all the birds in our vicinity as witnesses to the outrage on the sanctity of our home; for when I was half incubated, my egg was taken from the nest and weighed. I was not hurt thereby, and my mother did not mind the blotch of ink on my shell, but returned at once to her sitting as soon as the blinds were closed.

On the morning of July 21st a wonderful change had occurred in the nest, and only one egg remained. I in my shell was weighed again. Six days before my weight had been 57 grains, now it was 53 grains, and my brother born a few hours earlier, now nearly bursting with worms, weighed 60 grains. There remained but one bird and one egg. The fate of the other nestling was a mystery whose solution was eagerly sought. Pauline Pry thought best to search the ground beneath the nest. On hands and knees in the wet grass, with the thorns tearing her hair, she searched until she found a tiny birdling nearly covered with ants, and with the skin torn from his right thigh. She thought my little brother was dead, but very soon the warmth of her hand and of the sun, revived him so that he feebly opened his mouth. The Doctor was called to look at him; she, too, thought the little sufferer would die. As soon as the stricken baby could be weighed, he was returned to the nest. Probably he died soon, since he was never seen to move thereafter. Before any arrangements to bury him were made, my mother was seen eating something yellow from the nest. After swallowing several bits, she lifted the remains of the dead baby in her bill, and flew away with it.

For the greater part of that day my mother sat in the nest. Five minutes before noon she came with a green worm in her bill, and took her accustomed place. Several times she raised herself slightly, and as the clock was striking twelve, she stood and fed the worm to my brother Tom. In her absence he frequently lifted his head, opening his mouth for food, but if it was not raised upon her return, she would settle herself in the nest with the worm in her bill.

The next morning I was out of my shell, and there were two mouths to fill. In ten hours on the previous day Tom had gained 13 grains. I had been fed several times before I was weighed, and it was thought that my 51 grains of weight were an excess of 4 or 5 grains above that at my birth, while Brother Tom tipped the scales at 78 grains. One glance at us would have convinced any person that one day had given him a great start ahead of me. His head was much larger than mine. His big mouth was open so often, and his neck was so strong that he could reach far above me, and secure many more worms.

During the six hours that our nest was under constant observation fifty-two meals were served to us, consisting chiefly of those tender, slender, juicy, green worms, that people call inch-worms, varied by an occasional bug or miller. Seventeen of these pieces of game were brought to us by our mother, and the remaining thirty-five by our father. The task of brooding us kept mother in the nest at least half of the time. If she were there when father came, he gave the food to her and she fed us. If she were absent he came shyly to feed us and clean the nest. This latter duty was performed ten times, six of them by my father. Both parents ate the excrements. I fear most people think this very shocking, but it is the habit of all altricial birds I know, when their nestlings are quite young. My parents continued to do it until we were five days old.

Although the average time between the meals for each of us was but fourteen minutes, we were not fed with that regularity. Sometimes father and mother arrived together at the nest with food; or perhaps one of them brought two worms at once. Hungry we always were, yet occasionally we could not swallow what was given us, until two or three times the worm had been lifted out and thrust back into our yawning throats. When you were a blind, naked little baby, too weak to hold up your head for more than an instant, did you ever starve for twenty-seven seemingly endless minutes? It is a terrible experience. The rustling of the leaves in the wind, or the swaying of the nest-cradle constantly startled you into the belief that some one was bringing food. Up went your head, and the full depth of your pale lemon-colored throat was disclosed. But your slender neck was too weak for supporting long so great a weight, and your head sank to the bottom of the nest, and you slept to be wakened soon, fruitlessly. The minutes dragged along. Your father came with two worms and Tom got them both. The wind rocked the nest; the leaves flickered in the sunlight; the torturing seconds seemed interminable, until he came once more with a fat bug which Tom's long neck and large mouth enabled him to get. At length your mother came, and you were fed. She comforted you with the warmth of her breast, yet the desire for food was ever present. Thus in eating and sleeping passed your first day, and the second day was like unto the first. If such were your experiences, they were akin to mine.

When I had completed two whole days, and Tom had started upon his fourth day, we were considered strong enough to sit for our first portraits. It was not a trying ordeal to lie for a few minutes in a warm hand, my neck stretched comfortably over the mount of Apollo, while my distended abdomen rested in the hollow of the hand. At the end of a half hour I was back again in the nest, receiving all the food, while Tom had his portrait drawn life-size. His pin-feathers were beginning to show beneath the skin, but mine were discernible only through a magnifying glass. We were in the downy stage, naked, except for little tufts of down upon our heads, and along the middles of our backs. Our voices were scarcely audible to the human ear in the faint peeps we uttered, when taken from our nest.

You have heard that one day gave Tom a great advantage over me in his ability to secure the food brought to us. You will better realize this when I tell you that at the end of twelve hours in my first day I had grown to the size of 79 grains, while Tom weighed 123 grains. Two days later our respective weights were 165, and 229 grains. You would have noticed a great change in the size of our food. At first we were served with worms scarcely one-sixteenth of an inch in diameter, but on my third day those with many scratching legs, immense, fat fellows, as thick as an earth-worm, were thrust down our throat. The people behind the blinds thought such appropriateness in the selection of food, suited to the dimension of our throats, showed a wonderful instinct in our parents.

Upon my sixth day we posed again for our portraits. We were in the pin-feather stage at this time. Life had been one long continued feast: we grew rapidly, but like all other little birds we were not fat; we were merely immensely distended abdomens with insignificant appendages in the shape of legs and wings. Tom posed for his picture during an hour and a quarter. He was weighed "before" and "after," and it was found that after deducting the weight of his excrements he had lost 2 grains. By this time we could propel our bodies along the hand for an inch or more by a wiggling motion. Our eyes were no longer such prominent protuberances beneath the skin; they were open just a little crack and we could see, but we did not seem to care to keep them open much of the time.

With the coming of sight a new world was opened to us. We could see that our nest was as good as any little Catbirds need desire, built in a suitable crotch; it was composed of strong grasses below and upon the outside; within were fine rootlets with a few horsehairs for an extra lining. My mother is a very nervous bird and would not sit for her portrait while the blinds were open; therefore, in drawing her it was necessary to peek between the shutters. This work was done the day before Tom was born, when it was essential for her to keep closely to the nest. Of my father there is no picture except that which may be drawn from my description of him. He was a very good father to us: few people can boast of a better one among the human kind. He did everything he could when we were babies except brood us, and, no doubt, he would have done that had it been required of him. He brought fully two-thirds of our food, but he is such a shy fellow that he would dart away if he discovered any of the prying eyes behind the blinds. His eyesight is so keen it is remarkable how often he detected those onlookers. He was ever faithful as a guard near the nest, and his alarm-note was sounded whenever there was the least appearance of danger. This alarm-note is disagreeable to people, and they appear to hate him for it, forgetting what a faithful father and beautiful singer he is; and they write about him such things as this: "The Catbird has certainly a good deal to contend with. His name has a flippant sound without agreeable suggestiveness. His voice is vehement without strength, unpleasant in its explosive qualities. His dress is positively ridiculous,—who could hope to rise in life wearing a pepper and salt jacket, a velvet skull cap and a large red patch on the seat of his pantaloons."

Our family is very fond of currants. When the house-people gathered their season's crop they said there were only twenty-two ripe currants left for them. Later, when they saw all the worms that were brought to us from the bushes, they decided that had they worked as faithfully over them as our parents did, there might have been currants for all. When we were large enough to eat fruit, blackberries were ripe, and we were served occasionally with them. Once mother brought a small ripe gooseberry, which thrice she tried to thrust down a throat before there was apparent success. A quarter of an hour later an observer saw a nestling disgorge a small gooseberry that answered to the description of the one that had disappeared.

I have related how large a part my father took as the bearer of food to his nestlings. To a stranger mother appeared to be shirking, because she spent so much time in brooding us. But the house-people had occasion to reverse their opinion of her one evening when a strong northern breeze was blowing, and mother had been absent about a half hour enjoying her evening meal. As we were lifted from the nest for our daily weighing, we were found to feel quite cool to the hand. Our normal temperature being several degrees higher than that of mankind our need of sheltering wings became very obvious. As we grew larger less of her time was devoted to that ministration, yet other demands arose that required her attention. I must confess with chagrin to an accident —one that sometimes befalls the children of other respectable parents—we became lousy. I suspect we caught these plagues from those pestiferous young English Sparrows that were swarming in our tree. Not very far away was a ripening oat-field, and hosts of these sparrows rested in our yard on their way to that field. I have heard that these birds are covered with vermin. I have heard, also, that respectable people may catch vermin, but will not keep it. That is the reason my mother spent so much time searching us and our nest for obnoxious insects. She was a pretty sight as she sat on the edge of the nest, tilting her head this way and that, as she watched over our welfare. Generally her approach was from a different direction from that of my father. Both flew to lower limbs of the tree, then up, up they came hopping, father appearing on the left edge of the nest, and mother on the right. In our early days both stood on the edge of the nest while they fed us, but when we could climb up its side, they stood upon twigs four or five inches above us.

We began these attempts at climbing when about seven days old. Three points of interest center about that period of our existence: our pin-feathers were about to burst their sheaths; we showed the first signs of fear; and we ceased for a few days to increase in weight, in fact, we decreased a little. Pauline Pry, who had weighed daily the fledglings of several other species, said that she had remarked the simultaneous occurrence of these phenomena in the other young birds. However, it was not a problem that troubled me. As long as an abundance of food came to the nest my attention was given to obtaining my share.

For exercise we often stood in the nest, and we stretched ourselves thoroughly; we made vigorous dives for the spots where the vermin annoyed us, and we preened our pin-feathers. An odd thing is the instinct of a tiny nestling that guides it in the finding of the oil, and its application to its sprouting plumage.

Other broods of young Catbirds had been known to leave their nest when ten days old. Tom had reached that age on the morning of July 31st. Henceforth we were watched with untiring interest. No one ventured to open the windows lest he frighten us from our home. Sometimes Tom would mount to the brim of the nest and tramp half way around it, and when he settled back into his accustomed place you might have heard a sigh of relief from the on-lookers. When food was brought we scrambled to the top of the nest and stretched our scraggy necks. Almost incredible was the change from the rough attire of that day to the handsome juvenile dress we were to wear on the morrow.

The next morning every leaf, every blade of grass was drenched with dew, but we were up early, and out of the nest. I was sitting comfortably upon a little twig above a bed of catnip, when some one seized me. I did not have a fit, but I opened wide my mouth, and shrieked at the top of my voice. My parents were greatly distressed, and followed us as we went toward the door. Arriving inside the house I became calm. As was always the custom when taken in-doors, I was weighed. My fluffy plumage made me look much larger than hitherto, but the scales said I could balance only 386 grains, which was less by 24 grains than my weight three days before. All that morning I posed for portraits; sometimes I sat upon a broken stick, then again in a warm hand, but I was always homesick for my mother. I kept calling for her, and the house-people thought to quiet me with food. At first I would not open my mouth unless they whistled to me. Their big fingers bungled badly in putting the food into my mouth, until the Doctor brought down some forceps, after which the feeding was more successful. There was an abundance of food, blackberries, grasshoppers and earth-worms. Care was taken to have the worms served just right; they were washed in a basin of water, and I heard a care-taker say, that she was sure she had removed their heads, since she had cut off both ends. In time I appeared to lose my relish for these viands, and I cried very often for my parents, whom I could hear calling to me. It seemed at the end of many, many hours, yet it was really only noon, when I was brought out to this thicket, and placed upon that limb that over-hangs a thick mass of foliage.

The sun was nearing the horizon, and the air was growing chilly, when I saw Pauline Pry coming up through the orchard with a pailful of berries. She stopped at the thicket, and looked for me, but I never turned my head, nor gave any pleasant sign of recognition. She went to the house, but was back again in a trice with her drawing-board. When the sun passed out of sight, she was still at work on a portrait of me. And the morning and the evening of my eleventh day were ended.

CHAPTER XI

THE STRANGE FLYCATCHER *

Once upon a time, a long, long time ago, our great naturalist, John J. Audubon, discovered a flycatcher new to science in the woods along the prairie lands of the Arkansas River. He named it Traill's Flycatcher for his friend, Dr. Thomas S. Traill, of Edinburgh. Having a name should have in no way affected the life or happiness of the little bird whose harmless, unobtrusive ways would not have turned man into an enemy had not this bird possessed two cousins resembling it so closely that it was difficult to distinguish it in the field. At first this did not matter much, for few people cared about which flycatcher they saw; but as the years passed and the number of scientists grew, the bird was shot and its poor little skin was submitted to some expert for identification. In this way the ranges of the Acadian, Traill's and Least Flycatcher were agreed upon. The range of the Traill's was granted to be continent wide. For more than a century people were allowed to see the Traill's Flycatcher from Maine to Oregon without their word being questioned. An evil hour for the flycatcher arrived in the last quarter of the nineteenth century, when after a general overhauling and dusting of old bird skins the Alder Flycatcher (*Empidonax trailli alnorum*) was recognized as a subspecies in 1895. Genuine trouble

---

* The breeding form of flycatcher to which this chapter refers and which is found in the northern Mississippi Valley is *Empidonax trailli trailli*, now called Alder Flycatcher. The common name was Traill's Flycatcher at the time Miss Sherman wrote this chapter. — Ed.

was now in store for our little bird. Nowhere was its life safe from the ornithologist with a gun. But its life seemed safer than that of its cousin, the Alder. It was scared out of Ohio, or it evaded the man with the gun most successfully.

It was farther west in the Mississippi Valley, where both the Alder and the Traill's were said to occur, that one's veracity became endangered. No longer in safety dare he say that he saw a Traill's Flycatcher. If anyone was so rash, another bird student was sure to deny it with the statement that all his skins had been pronounced Alders by Dr. Oberholser.

In 1921 a strange flycatcher came to our dooryard. It was in the last of May. From the topmost dead twigs of the plum trees he sang all day long; surely he must be of a breeding species. True enough; in a few days his mate was seen building her nest. The spot chosen was in a small elderberry bush, on the south side of the bush, at a height of 44 inches from the ground. A loose bunch of material hung below the nest, which was rather loosely constructed, and placed in a fork of a small branch of the bush. On the morning of June 14 the first egg was found, and one was added on each successive morning until there were four. The body color was a rich cream mottled with reddish brown spots.

From the time of its first appearance, much time was given to the study of the bird; it was carefully compared with other flycatchers. In outline he bore a strong resemblance to the Wood Pewee. This was emphasized by the lack of any eye-ring. This lack of eye-ring has always been a puzzle because some ornithologists say that all the small flycatchers have conspicuous eye-rings. But this stranger had no eye-ring, neither did his wife nor his children, nor his children's children have any. None of the species that have returned to us in the succeeding years has had an eye-ring. Nothing in ornithological literature that I have examined throws any light on this point, except in Dawson's 'Birds of Washington' is this statement concerning Traill's Flycatcher: "a faint eye-ring pale olive-gray." Perhaps our bird has a pale olive-gray eye-ring but I have been unable to detect it. In the second year of the era of the strange flycatcher Dr. Lynds Jones called, with his class in ecology enroute for California. The strange flycatcher was heard but not seen. Dr. Jones, familiar with the notes of the Traill's Flycatcher, said he heard a bird singing the notes of that species, and added that the habitat was such as is chosen by Traill's. That ought to be conclusive. Yet how dare we decide anything definite about a bird with which fate has played such shuttle-cock concerning its history? In a few years the fly-catcher's name may be thrown into the discard, or a collector of birds taking flycatchers along Carpenter Hollow, Sny Magill, Bloody Run, or even on the banks of the Turkey or Yellow Rivers, will find his birds all belong to some other speies, and will say I could not have had nesting Traill's Flycatchers. Then let there be no risks. Our bird did well without other designation than "the strange flycatcher," and under that title may his tribe increase!

His song ought to identify him. It or they (for he has two very different songs) have two syllables. I spell the song more frequently heard as *"quit-yer,"* and the other as *"took-hay,"* but seldom do two people agree on the spelling of bird notes. Until incubation has started our bird sings pretty constantly, a little less so in the middle of the day. He begins early and is the last to be heard as darkness thickens in the evening.

CHAPTER XII

THE NEST LIFE OF THE
SPARROW HAWK *

The nesting of a species new to our place always is an event of great interest, and doubly so when the birds are of the hole-nesting sort, whose home life at very close range has never been exhibited (so far as is known) to mortal eye; but when the species is one of the Raptores interest heightens and feelings become indescribably mixed; there is the anxiety to watch the nest life mingled with fear for our harmless, little feathered friends, that trustingly have returned to their summer home; hence on April 4, 1912, it was with a perturbed mind that a pair of Sparrow Hawks (*Falco sparverius sparverius*) that had arrived the day before, were watched while they inspected the nest box occupied by Screech Owls two years previously.

Never before in our immediate neighborhood — National, Iowa—had Sparrow Hawks nested, yet for years man and nature had been at work preparing the way for them. Four years prior to this lightning had smitten the tallest and fairest willow of a group of these trees, and its dead branches invited the Hawks to rest; there the home-seeking pair found facing them, 80 feet away, a hole in my bird blind that gave entrance to a nesting box whose bottom surface, 8 by 12 inches in dimensions, was deeply covered with sawdust and excelsior. This place seemed to satisfy them for several days until they ventured to the barn, where they found

---

* From 'The Auk', Vol. 30, No. 3, July, 1913.

eight other boxes similarly furnished for nesting and roosting places for Flickers. During the next two weeks they visited the various boxes and scratched in the excelsior, their choice of a nesting place seemingly pointing toward the barn, but in this they were not encouraged. Toward the end of April they again frequented the dead willow and the box in the blind became their final choice.

There the first egg was deposited on April 28 before eleven o'clock in the morning, and an egg was laid on each alternate day until the sixth, and last, on May 8. That the hour for laying was later than that of many common species appears from the fact that on April 30 the second egg had not been laid at half past nine in the morning, but was in the nest by four o'clock in the afternoon, when the nest was again visited and the female found at home. Each egg was weighed upon the day it was laid, and their weights in the order of laying were 212, 227, 220, 225, 228 and 204 grains respectively. Four of these salmon-colored eggs were very similar in appearance, bearing large blotches of a chocolate brown, the sixth egg was finely speckled instead of blotched, while the fifth was strikingly different from the others having large unmarked spaces of the ground color through the center, and some blotches on the ends. The bird that came from it was as marked in its disposition as the egg-shell was in its coloring.

Incubation was performed mainly by the female, only once was the male found in the nest, which he did not leave until the blind had been noisily entered, since by the female sitting on her favorite perch we had been led to think that the nest was unoccupied. On the other hand the female was accustomed to fly from the nest the instant the key touched the lock of the door, if she had not already flown upon hearing human footsteps or voices. Sometimes it was noted that the eggs were left uncovered nearly or quite an hour, while both birds sat in their tree preening themselves, an exercise in which they spent a vast amount of time.

The first egg proved infertile, the third one, taken to reduce the number of hawks, also as a souvenir, contained a living embryo. Of the remaining eggs the second and fourth hatched on June 4, the bird from the former egg was still wet at 7:45 o'clock in the morning, and weighed 154 grains. The following morning at a quarter of eleven o'clock the hawklet from the fifth egg was found not thoroughly dry, weighing 166 grains, and showing that it had been fed. The bird from the sixth egg still wet, and weighing 139 grains, was found at half past eight o'clock on the morning of June 6. These data plainly show that the period of incubation must have been thirty days for the fifth egg, and twenty-nine days for the sixth egg.

Very soon after hatching the young would bite vigorously at a finger that touched their bills, opening their eyes for an instant as they did so, but not until they were two or three days old did they keep their eyes open longer than a few seconds at a time. From their first day they uttered a faint cry, when expecting food, that suggested the scream of the mature Sparrow Hawk, also peeps similar to a chicken but more mournful. This peeping was continuous while they were out of the nest. There was a third cry, difficult to describe, which they uttered when fed.

On June 13 the first manifestations of fear were detected, when the hawklets flattened themselves on the bottom of the nest, but such signs were rare for a few days thereafter. It was on the following day that for the first time they were seen ranged against the sides of the nest their backs to the wall; this arrangement appeared to be the normal one, thus the center of the nest was given to the one that was eating, or to the mother, when she came to feed them. When two weeks old they could run quite well; when placed on the floor of the blind they ran to the inner angles formed by the studdings and the walls, where with backs well braced they faced the foe, and a few days later met with savage claws an approaching hand.

At a very early age their alert bearing together with their bright eyes and snow-white plumage made a picture long to be remembered. By June 10, the down, or more correctly the neossoptiles, began to look dirty and the next day pinfeathers showed in this covering. By the 13th, the pinfeathers had pushed these neossoptiles away from the body to such an extent that the nestling looked half clothed. At sixteen days of age the barbs of their remiges showed sufficiently for one to be positive concerning the sex of the hawklets, and it was learned that eggs Nos. 2 and 6 had contained males, and Nos. 4 and 5 females. It was the shell of the fifth egg that bore unusual markings. Could oologists (or the clutchers of eggs) have studied the life of the bird that came from this egg, it is believed that all would have been convinced that "what is in the egg" is of greater importance than the lifeless shell. Numerous visitors came to see the young Sparrow Hawks and a nestful of Flickers that were being reared in the barn. Two of these friends from a distance named the young hawks, bestowing on the older male the name of Jeremiah, and his younger brother, because of his extreme meekness, was called Moses; the females were named Ruth and Jezebel. The last mentioned was an extremely wicked little wretch. When but sixteen days old she began to fight. Upon the opening of the nest door that day the rest of the brood stood back against the side of the

nest and opened their mouths, a feeding response probably, but with a threatening mien Jezebel stretched
herself to her utmost height, some 7 or 8 inches, then
struck at my hand repeatedly with her claws. From
that day onward a marked difference was observed in
behavior of the males and of the females. When a
finger or a stick was pointed into the nest all opened
their mouths; the males did little more than this as
they hugged the farthest side of the nest, but the
females, springing to the center of the nest, every
feather on their heads standing out seemingly at right
angles, wings spread, mouths open and squawking,
were ready to claw and bite, Jezebel being the fiercer
of the pair. When taken from the nest the rapidity
with which she would whirl round, when a finger was
circled above her, was remarkable especially at the
early age of eighteen days. Sometimes clawing was
done by Jerry, but Moses usually was as gentle as a
dove. The record of their daily weights shows, that
after the mother ceased to feed them, the females
appropriated more than their share of food, in fact
on June 22 it was noted that Moses, one day younger
than Jezebel, was five days behind her in weight, and
three days in development of plumage. No strife over
their food was ever witnessed. This yielding of their
lawful share of food by the males may have had its
origin in their disposition in mature life to give the
food they bring to their mates. Ruth was found eating
more frequently than the others.

Viewing of the nest when the mother bird was at
home was eagerly sought. The blind in which the nest
was located is a rude structure, 45 inches square, built
for shelter while watching Rails and migrating birds.
In preparation for observing the nest while Mother
Sparrow Hawk was at home the windows were completely darkened. Some cracks in the walls let in a

little light, also a little fresh air, which in the latter days of the nest proved an appreciated blessing. Protection from the faint rays of light that penetrated through the cracks was afforded by the depths of a sun-bonnet. The keenness of vision of a hawk is proverbial, that these precautions were sufficient was proved when for a half hour undetected, I, 16 inches away, looked through a peep-hole into the mother hawk's eye, and watched her as she brooded. This was not achieved upon the first attempt, when two hours were spent in fruitless waiting for her coming. After that, except near the close of the nest period when both parents were absent hunting, all attempts to watch the nest during the mother's visits were made after visitors to the blind had left me there alone. At first standing noiselessly upon a box with head scraping the roof of the blind for one hour, or for two hours, was not an easy task, later it became almost insupportable with the heat of an afternoon sun beating upon the blind, and with the stench from a nest, whose walls were thickly incrusted with excrements. But consummation was near at hand when hawk screams were heard from without, that called forth anticipatory peeps from the young after they were old enough to note the screams. When the mother came in there was little clamor and no struggling for food on the part of the nestlings. In their earlier days they merely braced themselves in the circle where they lay, later they stood in an orderly row against the side of the nest. With great rapidity the mother tore the flesh and bending her head almost at right angle with the bill of the young one she gave it the morsel. Her motions in this act were very dainty and graceful; this bending of her head was apparently necessitated by the hooked beaks of both. Sometimes the pieces served were so large that they were swallowed with difficulty.

No more than five minutes were occupied in these feed-ings. At first the food served was "dressed meat," and the remainders of the feast were carried out by the mother, and eaten by her in the dead willow. On June 17, she brought in the body of a half-grown ground squirrel with the skin still on, probably I frightened her out permaturely, since she left the rem-nant of the squirrel. It was not until a week later that she began regularly to leave the quarry for the hawk-lets to feed themselves. Thereafter she entered the nest with the food, but remained inside less than a minute, sometimes no more than twenty seconds.

Experiments were made with the nestlings to see if they would eat living animals. When quite young a blow-fly was given, and some days later newly hatched English Sparrows were put into their mouths, but all were rejected. On June 30, thirty-three English Spar-row nestlings and eggs were given them, among them were two live fledglings nearly ready to leave the nest. The eggs and the dead Sparrows were eaten, but the five Sparrows remained all day in the hawk nest uninjured. It appeared to be a case not of the "lion and the lamb" but of the Sparrow and the Sparrow Hawk lying down together. This escape from the eye of the mother bird must have been due to her very brief visits.

In the spring while the question: 'Shall or shall not the Sparrow Hawks be allowed to remain and increase their kind?' was pending, all available ornithological literature was searched to learn if possible the degree of danger from these Falcons, that was threatening our birds. Besides one writer's statement that to a family of Sparrow Hawks twelve small birds were brought in one day, there was the reliable data fur-nished by the examination of stomachs of this species. The figures given by Dr. Fisher show that eighteen per cent of the stomachs contained the remains of birds. This is the same percentage that was found for Screech Owls. In previous years we had harbored these predaceous little villains, and some small birds had survived, therefore it was decided to give the Sparrow Hawks a trial at the same time to watch closely their relations with other birds. The first birds disturbed by them were the Phoebes; when the Hawks frequented the barn the Phoebes disappeared, but when the Hawks were frightened away Phoebe resumed her task of refitting the very old nest that had cradled so many generations of her species; and later two broods were raised there in safety. The Flickers were driven away from the barn, but returned there to nest after the Sparrow Hawks chose the blind for their nest site. The Flickers, more expeditious than the Hawks in incubation, hatched out their brood on June 6—the first egg having been laid on May 21—, this hatching chanced to be on the birthday of Moses, and a comparison of development of Flickers and Sparrow Hawks made an interesting study. The Flickers gained in weight a trifle faster, but were homely, whining, helpless little creatures after the Hawks were well feathered and active. Both species left their nest on the same dates.

After the female Hawk began incubation English Sparrows built a nest in another box in the blind not 4 feet distant, and there raised their brood. Next to these the species that nested nearest was the Red-headed Woodpecker. A pair of these birds began their nest on May 29, in the dead willow about half way to the top. They brought out but one offspring. It is impossible to say that any of their young were taken by the Hawks. The only time a disturbance was witnessed was on June 28, directly after the Redheads had changed places in the nest. The female Sparrow

Hawk left her perch a few feet away, went to the Red-head's hole and looked in; the departing Redhead returned and drove her away. Exactly 46 feet from the trunk of the dead willow, and 50 feet or thereabout from a favorite perch of the female Hawk a pair of Mourning Doves raised a brood. Their young were flying about in the willows on June 20. Probably it was this pair that built its second nest in a cedar tree a few rods distant, and its third nest on the site of the second, where a Dove was sitting until September 8, after which she deserted her eggs, containing well developed embryos. This is considered worthy of mention because all the other Mourning Doves of the neighborhood had left before that date. Another pair of Mourning Doves raised two broods in the house yard. From a plum tree nest conspicuously in sight of the Sparrow Hawks a pair of Brown Thrashers brought out four young, which fully grown were following their parents, and begging for food when the latter were building their second nest. Another pair of Brown Thrashers built their nests in gooseberry bushes, their first nest being 105 feet from the hawk tree, the second 200 feet from it. In both cases the young left their nest, but it is impossible to say that all escaped afterward.

Enough cases have been cited to show that these Sparrow Hawks were not nest robbers like the Blue Jays, neither did they take any of the chickens, numbering fully 150, that were brought out in a yard 20 rods from their tree. As far as my observations extended, their avian victims were fledglings not long out of the nest; also that the Hawks were crafty enough not to prey to any great extent upon the birds in the immediate vicinity of their nest among which they were in bad repute. They were frequently mobbed by Bronzed Grackles, that made vicious passes at them, especially if one were eating, whereupon it raised its wings and screamed, perhaps screamed for mercy. A dash of the Kingbirds sent the Hawks squawking from their tree. Once a pair of Baltimore Orioles followed one of them to the tree and for some time acted as if they had a score to settle. At another time Meadowlarks raised a tumult and followed the Hawks. It was feared that the victim that time was the little Meadowlark, that with a Cowbird nest-mate had been watched and weighed from the day of their hatching, and had but recently left the nest. The Cowbird, seen at intervals later, was known to have escaped.

When the hawklets required the largest supply of food the greater part of four days, beginning June 26, was given to uninterrupted study of the home life of the Hawks. Various places were chosen from which to watch, until an upper window in the house was found the best. It was 300 feet from the nest, but nearly twice that distance was traveled to reach the blind every time food was delivered in the nest. These trips were for verifying the identifications of the quarry, and in case it was a bird to secure its tarsi. The top of the willow was about level with my window from which with the aid of 8-power binoculars the behavior of the Hawks was easily seen. The male did the greater part of the hunting, but there were a few times when the female brought food of her own catching. The average length of the intervals between the bringing of the quarry was two hours and twenty-five minutes, the longest interval being three hours and forty-three minutes, and the shortest twenty-three minutes. This refers to food that was brought into the tree, not to the nest, for the female frequently ate the game brought in. For example on June 28, she ate three birds, and was absent five times, which altogether amounted in duration to two hours and twenty minutes, when she may have eaten several other birds. The notes for that day show that the prey was: in the forenoon at 8:15 o'clock, a bird, which was eaten by the mother Hawk, as likewise was the bird brought at 10:07; at 11:30, a bird, taken to the nest, and in the afternoon at 3:01 o'clock, a meadow mouse, taken to the nest; at 4:00, a bird, eaten by the mother; at 6:55, a meadow mouse, which was taken to the nest as was the sparrow brought in at 7:17 o'clock. It is most likely that the father Hawk brought a piece of game early in the morning, and another piece about one o'clock in the afternoon, when for an hour observations were suspended. At noon that day the aggregate weight of the four hawklets was 7648 grains, and it was 8166 grains at half past seven in the evening, a difference of 518 grains, the known supply of food having been two meadow mice and one small sparrow. In the forenoon of June 25 there was brought to the young three half-grown ground squirrels and a bird.

At different times the character of the game varied; for a time nothing but ground squirrels was seen, followed by two days and a half when, excepting one squirrel, birds only were brought in, and this was succeeded by a similar period when only meadow mice were seen. It would appear from this that the male Hawk found a brood of young birds or mammals and hunted their neighborhood until he had exterminated the whole brood. Confirmatory of this was a succession of four birds about equal in size, whose bodies resembled in shape those of young Brown Thrashers or Robins just out of the nest. After June 14 the identified quarry consisted of seventeen birds and nineteen mammals; of the latter eight were meadow mice and the rest ground squirrels. Besides these there were nine unidentified pieces, several of them apparently insects, that were fed the young after they left the nest. The tarsi of the eight bird victims found in the nest were sent to Washington, D. C., where Mr. E. R. Kalmbach and Mr. H. C. Oberholser very kindly identified them for me. Six of the eight were pronounced to belong to sparrows.

According to the economy of these Hawks incubation, the brooding and the feeding of the young, and the guarding of the nest was the part of the female, while the male hunted for the family; only once was he seen in or near the nest. A few times he circled overhead and joined in the screaming, when I was near the nest, his notes sounding thinner and in a higher key than those of his mate. At such times the female made a great commotion with her screaming and flying at me, notwithstanding all her noise and bluster she was an arrant coward, never coming nearer than 4 or 5 feet of my head. With a hundredth part of the provocation a Red-winged Blackbird or a Brown Thrasher would have hit, perhaps hurt a trespasser on its domain. After a time the female recognized me and began to scream, while I was still distant and nearly hidden by trees. The neighbors said that they knew when I appeared out of doors from the screaming of the Hawk. Other people, men, women, and children daily frequented the enclosure in which stands the bird blind, but her screams were reserved for me alone. To guard the nest she sat in the dead willow. In April both of the pair sat in the top of the tree, during incubation and the earlier days of the young the branches extending from the middle of the tree were used, and during the last ten days of the nest the top branches were again occupied.

Hunting was done for the most part to the southwest, the land there being devoted to farming, while the buildings of our decadent hamlet are situated in the other directions. Immediately to the southwest of the hawk tree lay an 80 acre cornfield abounding in ground squirrels. Not a tree nor a bush intervenes between this tree and the nearest farm yard a half mile away. Sitting on her lofty perch the female often spied her mate while he was still afar off, and with much screaming flew to meet him, and secure the prey he bore in his talons. Sometimes the meeting was no more than two or three hundred feet from the tree, but it was impossible to see her manner of seizing the quarry. Sometimes the male, still holding the prey, dashed by her to the tree, where still screaming she secured it. Once a ground squirrel retaining its head was brought in, all others were beheaded ones. The birds, headless, tailless, and wingless, were well plucked, yet the mother bird appeared to find some work to do on them before she delivered them to the nest with scarcely the smallest feather remaining on them. Sometimes she skinned the ground squirrels, the nestlings ate the skins when she omitted the operation. The meadow mice were not skinned, but she always spent several minutes plucking out the hair, nevertheless much remained when taken to the nest. After she had snatched the prey from her mate, she usually uttered whine-like screams for two or three minutes before beginning her work on it. Crotches or peeling bark on the tree afforded her three or four places suitable for her flaying. In moving from place to place she sometimes carried the prey in her talons, but generally in her beak, and always thus when she flew from tree to nest. This flight she never made directly from her skinning places, but always descended to the lower branches of the willow by a series of short flights before starting for the nest; this she never did so long as she saw herself watched.

More vociferous screams than usual greeted my first appearance on the morning of June 28, awakening suspicions which were confirmed by a visit to the nest, and finding there that Moses had his head out of the entrance hole. After that hour one fledgling or another sat in the hole most of the time, shutting out the light and the fresh air. The weather was very hot, and the nest exceedingly filthy, yet that it was still "home, sweet home," to the hawklets was attested by the alacrity with which they hopped into it when held before the door. Jeremiah, the first born, marked by a red string on his foot, left the nest in the forenoon of June 30, some time between a quarter past eight o'clock and noon; and Ruth followed early the next morning. Frantic screams of the mother attended my search for Ruth. Very unlike the crouching, bustling, menacing creature of the previous evening was the very erect and slim little bird found perching in a willow sapling about 50 feet from the nest; and it was a gentle, farewell nibble that she gave the extended finger. Moses left the nest early in the morning of July 2, and Jezebel between five o'clock and half past that hour of the succeeding morning.

For a week the Hawks, old and young, stayed about their tree. On the morning of July 11, the other birds sang a halleluiah chorus in the dead willow, that had been held by the Hawks for ninety-nine days; and no one could help wishing that the last had been seen of the Sparrow Hawks, but they were not so obliging. During the next two weeks occasionally one or two of them came to the old tree. Not infrequently until the last of September three of them together were seen elsewhere. In the case of some other species it has been noted that sometimes the brood was divided, the father bird taking part of them some distance from the place in which the mother cared for the others. It remains for future investigations to decide whether the father Sparrow Hawks takes the males under his guidance, and the mother Hawk the females; whether the advocates of the system of segregation of sexes in education can claim a praise-worthy precedent in the practices of the Sparrow Hawks.

In the two months they remained in the neighborhood after leaving our place the Hawks were seen most frequently about the nearest farm yard to the northwest, about the county fair grounds, and on the public school grounds. At the last named place on several occasions they were seen to perch on the brackets of the cornice of the schoolhouse. Twice the days were rainy, and the birds may have returned for shelter to their accustomed roosting places.

CHAPTER XIII

NEST LIFE OF THE SCREECH OWL *

In large boxes put up for the accommodation of woodpeckers lived the Screech Owls from whose nest lives these studies were made. It was in one of these soap-boxes, nailed against the trunk of a willow tree that the first of these Owls was seen on March 24, 1909; evidently it had been there in January of that year, as the feathers of a luckless Bohemian Waxwing remained to prove. A Screech Owl was seen to spend the day there again on March 30 and on April 2 and 18. On the morning of April 5 a rufous feather fluttering from the entrance hole of the west flicker-box in the barn betrayed the nesting place. The bottom of the box was covered with excelsior in which the female had scratched a hollow in the corner farthest from the entrance, where she was sitting on four fresh eggs. For six days the nest was closely watched and the following facts were ascertained. The meat-offerings brought by her mate and dropped through the hole for his divinity within consisted of a white-footed mouse on two of the mornings, and a Junco on two of them, while on the remaining two mornings nothing was there. On two evenings the female went out early before the nest watch began; on other two she went out after dark alone, and on two evenings her mate

---

* Read at the annual meeting of the American Ornithologists' Union, Washington, D. C., November 15, 1910.
From 'The Auk', Vol. 28, No. 2, April, 1911.

came after dark to the hole and called her with a very low cry, which once was answered by a low sharp note from the female, who on both evenings, almost immediately went out to join him in the search for refreshments. This little incident may be of interest to two classes of people, the sentimentalist and the evolutionist, who may be seeking the missing link between the Screech Owl and the young man who calls to take his lady-love out for ice-cream.

The evening of April 10 was one of those upon which the female had gone out early before the nest was visited. A watch of more than two hours was maintained in order to learn the length of her absence from her eggs. In the meantime a violent wind storm sprang up, that continued all night and the following day, wrecking wind-mills and some buildings. Once the scratching of the bird's claws against the barn was heard, but she failed to come in, probably the fury of the storm prevented her making the home port; however it may have been, she did not return to her eggs, and the history of this nest was closed.

In the following June a nest-box was built into one corner of my blind in the hopes that it might serve an anxious pair of Flickers that were house-hunting. At the same time the future needs of the Screech Owls were kept in mind, as this new nest is just 85 feet from the box on the willow in which the male Owl had his headquarters. The nest in the blind has a depth of 20 inches and a bottom area of 8 by 12 inches. The bottom was covered with a thick layer of sawdust over which was spread a deep bed of excelsior. Very unfortunately for the most satisfactory sort of observations, the top of the nest comes to the roof of the blind so that the two peep-holes from necessity were made in the sides. There is a hand-hole also, which is covered by a door.

In 1910 the Owls were not seen until the sixteenth day of March, when the male sat in his box on the willow, and the female with a mouse beside her in the nest in the blind, where the first egg was laid on March 27. Until that time came these birds were seen in their respective boxes on but four days. Meanwhile the box in the blind and the nest box in the barn showed signs of nocturnal visits by the scratched up condition of the excelsior in them.

The first egg was found in the nest on the morning of March 27, and was still alone on the evening of the 29th. The following day the nest was not visited, the only day in two months and a half, when visits were omitted. No doubt the second egg was laid some time on the 30th of March; the third one was deposited on April 1, but two days intervening between the laying of the second and third eggs, while three or more days were the period between the other layings. The fourth egg was in the nest at half past four o'clock in the afternoon of April 4, but was not there at eight o'clock on the previous evening. This shows that it took from eight to nine days to complete the clutch of four eggs. Whether the Owl laid in the night, or in the morning as other birds do, was not ascertained.

The blind, intended as a shelter while watching migrating birds, was built upon posts on a tiny plot of nearly solid earth in a small quagmire. In an air line it stands 300 feet from the house, and nearly that distance back from the street. When the young Owls were almost ready to leave the nest they were freely exhibited to the neighbors, but previous to that time the existence of the nest was revealed to only a half dozen friends, who proved that six women could keep a secret. In its outside dimensions the blind is but 45 inches square, hence when four of us entered it, the audience in the ceremony of viewing the Owls,

like that of the Greek Orthodox Church, remained
standing.

Such were the quarters and surroundings in which
the study of the nest was conducted. It was generally
visited several times during the day and at least once
every evening; the time for the evening visits was
usually an hour or two after dusk. Besides them there
were two night watches that extended through the
greater part of the night, one to half past two, and the
other to three o'clock in the morning; and still another,
begun after midnight, lasted over an hour. Once a
lamp was burned for a few hours, during the rest of
the long watches the time was spent in darkness. When
an examination of the nest was desired it was illumined
by a flash-light lantern. All pictures of these night
watches must from necessity be silhouettes, easily
drawn by the imagination of anyone. The only really
exciting time was the evening of April 5, when
a thunderstorm was raging; the rain beat hard upon
the roof and sides of the blind, and the wind blew
great gusts, which momentarily seemed to threaten
the overthrow of my frail shelter. If there should be
a fifth egg it was imperative that the fourth one should
be marked that night, so for more than an hour the
going out of the female was tremulously awaited.

The Owl of 1909 went out every evening and such
procedure was expected of this one without fulfillment.
Constant incubation appears to have begun on the
first day of April after which she was frightened out
on two evenings, one of them being the stormy night
just mentioned. In order to count the eggs she was
pried up with a stick thrust through a peep-hole. Out
she would not go although her exit was anxiously
awaited night after night until the thirteenth of the
month, when once more she was frightened out in
order that the eggs might be weighed. Then 248 grains

was the weight of egg No. 1; 250 grains that of No. 2; 236 grains of No. 3, and 219 grains of No. 4. When fresh probably they weighed about the same as the eggs of the previous year, viz: 252, 253, 255 and 261 grains, these figures being arranged in the order of their sizes. Just before it hatched egg No. 3 weighed 199 grains and No. 4 weighed 193 grains. The owlet from the last egg tipped the scales at 153 grains as it came from the shell. Eggs No. 1 and No. 2 were found to have hatched on April 27; No. 3 hatched the following night, and No. 4 about five o'clock in the afternoon of April 29, showing that the period of their incubation was about twenty-six days.

Unlike many other young birds, newly hatched Screech Owls are in one of their most attractive guises. Covered to the tips of their toes with a thick white down, they appealed strongly to the hearts of the human mothers who saw them, and as one of them remarked the little owls "looked as if they had white socks on." As they tumbled about in their nest they very forcibly suggested human babies in fleecy white cloaks that are learning to creep. Held in the hand with their beaks downward and out of sight they looked like diminutive blind kittens; perhaps the most noticeable thing about them at that age was their large heads. But this winning aspect of the nestlings was of short duration. In a few days the pin-feathers began to show in the white down which soon turned to a dirty gray color. By the time they were twelve days old they had become most repulsive, exceedingly filthy to handle with an appearance that was decidedly repellant. Perfect miniatures were they of a doddering, half-witted old man: the blue beak was prominent and suggested a large hooked nose, while the down below it took the shape of a full gray beard, and that on the top of the head looked like the gray hair that covers a low, imbecile forehead: the eyes not fully open were bluish in color, and had a bleared and half-blind appearance. This loathsome semblance lasted no longer than ten days by which time the eyes were full and bright and yellow, the bird was covered with a thick gray down, and looked as if a fac-simile of it could very easily be made from a bunch of gray wool devoid of any anatomy. After this its aspect steadily improved as its feathery covering developed. All the young were of the red phase, as were both of the parents, the male being a deeper rufous.

A friend, a Southern lady, well known because of her writings on negro folk-lore, has written me that the negroes call this species of owl the Shivering Owl. Some ornithologists have suggested that this common name may have reference to the shivering quality of the bird's call-notes. It seems possible that ornithologists may have overlooked a characteristic of this species apparently familiar to many a pickaninny as well as to some bird-nesting boys of a lighter color, and that this owl may have been called the Shivering Owl, because it shivers. It certainly shivers, that it screeches may be a question for dispute. This peculiarity is one of the early things to be observed in the life of these nestlings; but the shivering does not become very pronounced until the bird is two days old, and continues until it is about two weeks old, at which time the young owl is well covered with thick down: therefore it seems quite possible that it shivers because it is cold. To this argument two facts lend weight, one is that the trembling diminishes gradually as the down grows thicker, and the other that the quivering bird sitting on the palm of one hand becomes quiet when well covered by the other hand.

The power of locomotion seems to be very good in young owlets; when one was but a day old it was placed on the floor of the blind where it moved the distance of a foot or more in a very few minutes. As soon as their eyes were fairly open they moved about freely in the nest. On May 3 the oldest owlets kept their eyes open a narrow crack, their lids were red giving the appearance of sore eyes: five days later they looked around as if "taking notice," this was the day upon which they first showed fear. When about three weeks old their manner of winking became a noticeable feature; catching a glimpse through the peep-hole of a human eye a youngster would stare as if lost in the deepest study, then close one eye in a deliberate long-drawn wink that was exceedingly droll, or in the same manner it would wink both eyes simultaneously which was not so amusing.

The light in the nest was about as bright as that in an ordinary room, that which entered through the three windows of the blind was greater than usually illumines house rooms. In neither place did the young show signs that the light was too powerful for their eyes. Only when carried into bright sunshine was there a blinking: most human eyes are similarly affected. The male Screech Owl often spent nearly the entire day with his head out of his box, in the full rays of the sun, his actions indicating that he quickly noted any unwonted movements. Unfortunately the hole of the female's box could be seen from exposed positions mainly, and not from the house. Twice only was she seen with her head out of her box, then I was more than a hundred yards away in the back yard of a neighbor; as I advanced toward the street into plainer view, she quickly scuttled out of sight. Several times during the day-time she accidentally was frightened from her nest, the directness with which she flew to a tree, then into the box of her mate showed no indications of poor vision. By day both she and her young were able to discover an observing eye when the peep-hole was closed all but the merest crack. A flash-light lantern was used nightly, its rays entering by one peep-hole while observations were made through the other; sometimes the lantern was introduced through the hand-hole and flashed within an inch or two of the mother's face. None of this appeared to excite fear, the light was utterly disregarded, but she at once would commence to sway and to peer at the human eye she detected in the gloom beyond. These things lead me to think that the eyes of this species are similar to those of the cat, capable of seeing well by day, also at night.

Except when disturbed the mother at all times appeared stupid, yet the young were as alert as most nestlings during the day. Until the shivering period was past they sought the warmth found under the mother's wings; after this as one would naturally suspect, they as do other young birds, continued to sleep much, standing in a bunch with their heads pressed together; they preened themselves but not so much as do some nestlings; frequently they yawned, monstrous, big-mouthed yawns. Stretching was the favorite exercise; during it the birds seemed to be made of india-rubber. On May 16 the height to which one stretched itself was 7 inches by actual measurement. Sometimes they ate if food was before them, and always they exhibited a wide-awake interest in any eye that they espied looking at them through a peep-hole, even when the mother paid no attention to it. They would stare quietly at it for a time, then stare while their bodies swayed from side to side: this swinging motion would slowly come to an end, the performers would grow drowsy, two pressing against each other would lean their heads together and drop off to sleep. This pose was a favorite one a few years ago among photographers of human subjects. It may be needless to say that, it is much more artistic and charming when assumed by owls.

During their nest life but three varieties of cries were heard from them, the first, beginning as soon as they were out of the shell, had some resemblance to the peep of a chicken, and was uttered by them when out from under the mother's wings, seemingly a cry for shelter and for food: this ceased when they were about three weeks old. At this age a second cry was heard for the first time, which had a decidedly squeaking sound and was made when they were squabbling for the warmest place in the family circle. The remaining cry, a sort of chatter, appeared to be the tone for a dinner discussion, friendly enough in quality, for they were never seen to quarrel at meals. Besides these there was the snapping of the bill which commenced the day they began to show fear, and a hissing sound made when they were frightened.

The owlets were marked with different colored strings, and were weighed every evening about twilight, when an hour or more was spent in the weighing and in observations of them outside the nest. While removing them from the box a struggle generally occurred with signs of fear and the use of claws defensively, but not until three days before they left the nest did one make an offensive clawing attack upon my hand. While out of the nest aside from an occasional snapping of the bill they seldom showed signs of fight or fear, but allowed themselves to be patted and handled freely. Once one of them having exercised until tired turned its head to one side, laid it flat on the palm of my hand and went to sleep. For inspection they were placed on a stool over whose edges they frequently walked, but often saved themselves from falling by catching hold upon the edge with their hooked bills. Sometimes they arranged themselves along the edge of the stool, looking solemn and wise, then one would begin to sway, the others would join in the exercise, which was continued with the precision of a class in calisthenics. As soon as they could climb by using claws and bill, a three-cornered shelf was the favorite perch for one of them; there immovably as a stuffed owl it stood until forcibly displaced.

The female Screech Owl calls to mind the village loafer who in describing his life occupation said that "sometimes he sat and thought, and sometimes he jest sot." In the case of this owl she "jest sot." During one of the long vigils—the one that lasted until half past two in the morning—there was a noise three or four times as of the eggs rattling against each other, and once she snapped her bill. This was all. Verily, a sitting Screech Owl is not a lively companion for the still watches of the night. After incubation began on only four occasions was the nest seen without her, two of these have been mentioned, the evenings on which she was driven out for the purpose of marking and weighing the eggs: on the other two she left voluntarily as the blind door was opened.

Her disposition was unreliable and created much trepidation and uncertainty as to the limit of inspection she would bear. One illustration of this was given on March 28 when she left her nest while her visitors were at the distance of 6 rods or more from the blind; again on May 1 there was another instance. Up to this time she had suffered the removal of her young from under her both in the daytime and in the evening, then it was the tossing of a common shrew into the nest that scared her out. This was at one o'clock in the afternoon, three hours later her young were stiffening with cold, but warmth furnished by the flame of a lamp and by the sun saved the nestlings' lives.

The mother expressed disapproval of the examina-

tion of her nest by the snapping of her bill, the laying
back of her ear-tufts, and the glare of her eyes, but
never did she offer to bite nor to claw the hand. Once
her leg was seized by mistake for a nestling, and she
uttered a cry of distress heard at no other time. Quietly
she sat brooding her young for the first ten or twelve
days, after which the order was reversed and they stood
upon her. Day by day she shrank more and more from
view until only an ear-tuft could be seen, then came a
day when nothing could be seen of her, but she did
not desert the nestlings in the daytime until May 26,
three days before they left the nest. Those days she
probably spent in the box of her mate where she was
seen to take refuge when frightened from her nest.

It was impossible to learn how many of the days
the male owl occupied his box, but from the date of
the first egg to that upon which the young left the
nest, sixty-four days, he was seen there on twenty-seven
of them. Sometimes he did not show himself until
evening: sometimes an unusual noise about the blind
brought him into view. On other days he kept his head
out of the hole almost all the time, going to sleep if
all were quiet in the blind. When nest duties were not
pressing his mate was seen to thrust her head out of
her nest, as the holes of the two boxes faced each other
many a Romeo and Juliet scene of an owlish character
may have been enacted, and winks were exchanged
beyond doubt. A few days before they left the nest
the owlets began to sit in the hole and there seemed
to be little time day or night when the hole was not
occupied by one of them.

The male Screech Owl appears to have been the
general purveyor for the family. In the first fortnight
of incubation there were nine mornings when an excess
of food lay beside his mate; of this she rarely ate
during the day, but there were times when she did so.

On the remaining days of incubation she had food beside her twice, but as soon as the eggs commenced to hatch there was a superabundance provided. An example of this was furnished on April 29 when there lay in store four meadow mice weighing about two-fifths of a pound altogether. This excessive provision lasted only a few days, the supply decreased daily, and none was seen after May 15. Nine o'clock, half past nine, and ten o'clock were hours upon which he was known to have brought food to the nest, eight o'clock in the evening being the earliest time. Twenty minutes before that hour he uttered his first call, after which were two other calls before his claws were heard on the roof overhead followed by continued calling; a sound like the mewing of young kittens was judged to be the answering voice of his mate.

On a few of their earliest days the owlets were weighed in the morning and at night, their increase in weight showing that they were well fed during the day. When the bird from the fourth egg was just hatched, its down being still wet, it was lifted from the nest. It opened its mouth for food and cried; at that time and afterward it was noticed that the young did not open wide their mouths nor throw their heads backward as do the nestlings into whose throats the food is poked, but while begging for food they thrust at the hand with a nuzzling motion very similar to that made by young kittens when searching for dinner. Bits of flesh clipped from meadow mice in store, that were placed in the mouth of a nestling, were swallowed with some difficulty and no apparent relish. Their beaks were stained upon the outside with bloody matter, and as they grew older they would nibble at the mother's bill as if teasing for food. All these things led to a belief that in their earlier days they were fed predigested or partially predigested food, which they pulled from the beak of the mother. After May 10 on only three mornings was any food found in the nest; from that date the mother sat with her bill in one corner of the nest, while the nestlings stood on her back, her wings and her tail. It was surmised that she sought this position to free herself from the teasing of her young. On the tenth an owlet was seen for the first time pulling at food (the body of a frog), as if eating it. The next morning during observations the mother lifted her head from the corner and appeared to eject something from her mouth; at once the owlets scrambled to the spot and seemed to eat for a few minutes. At that time a chance to view the nest from the top would have been most fortunate.

Although Father Owl failed on forty-one out of sixty-four days of nest life to provide a store of food for daytime use, it does not follow that the nest was unserved. The food given to the sitting Screech Owl, and later to her young, consisted of moles, house mice, one white-footed mouse, two jumping mice, pocket gophers, ground squirrels, beef both raw and cooked, canned salmon, English Sparrows' eggs and their young, all of which was eaten or at least it disappeared. On May 13 the nestlings were seen eating eggs of the English Sparrow: two days later the oldest owlet was seen to eat portions of a gopher leg; holding the meat with one foot it tore off and ate a mouthful, then rested four or five minutes before eating again. On May 28 the youngest fledgling was watched while it ate the front leg of a gopher. Twice it tried to swallow the piece and was obliged to disgorge and tear off bits of the flesh, on the third trial the leg disappeared bone and all, the whole performance occupying upwards of twenty minutes. That fore leg had not been weighed, but its mate remained and was found to weigh 203 grains: the weight of the owlet that night was 1904

grains. To use a well-worn illustration, it was equivalent to a boy weighing 95 pounds eating at one meal
a 10 pound leg of mutton. The young Owls could not
be induced to eat when outside of their nest. One evening while in the house they would not touch young
English Sparrows offered them, but ate them the moment they were returned to the nest.

Pellets ejected by the young were found for the first
time on May 10; it may be well to note that this was
the first date upon which they were seen eating the
food that lay in the nest. A pellet disgorged on May
27 weighed 62 grains, which was one-thirtieth of the
weight of the bird that ejected it. No pellets from the
mother's throat were found in the nest, yet once she
was known to have remained there continuously for
twenty-one hours. She seemed to have well defined
ideas of house-keeping. Not always did the food
dropped into the nest by her mate fall close to the wall
beneath the hole, and the contributions to her larder
that were pushed in through a peep-hole never fell
there, but soon all was piled up in orderly shape against
the north wall beneath the entrance-hole, which seemed
to be the normal arrangement until she was disturbed
by the frequent opening of the hand-hole; she then
changed her location to the north side of the nest and
piled the game on the south side. One day the temperature rose to mid-summer heat, and some of the excessive supply of food became exceedingly gamy and
over-ripe. Discontinuance of the nest study was
threatened, but in the night there was a clearing out
of objectionable matter and such conditions did not
recur. Nor did the plumage of the young become
soiled. Their natural position in the nest seems to have
been a standing one, this taken with the fact that the
nest was made above a deep bed of sawdust may
account for this cleanliness.

After the very sudden and unexpected going out of the mother bird on the first day of May, she was not seen to leave the nest until the seventh evening of the month: from that date onward for a week she sometimes stayed in the nest until part of the weighing was done, or if out, she came in and remained with her nestlings. On the 17th of May she did not go out when the owlets were removed from the nest although two of us were in the blind engaged in conversation, but she uttered a mournful, tremulous cry two or three times. After that in the evening she left the nest when the blind was visited. At times one parent would come to the windows, which at night were covered with heavy pasteboard shades, where it would cling calling to the young that were out of their nest. On a few nights a sound was made that resembled the chattering of human teeth. After the 18th of the month the expression of displeasure, displayed by the parents, grew more emphatic evening after evening. At first the demonstrations, made at a distance, were limited to snappings of the bill and a noise resembling the yelp of a dog: gradually feigned attacks on the person of the enemy increased in number and came nearer. The bird from some perch in a tree would describe an elliptical path in the air, coming with savage snappings until overhead and about 10 feet up, it would utter one weird *eh-hue* cry before it swung back to its tree. In this long-drawn *eh-hue* note it was not so much what the owl said as the tone of voice in which it was said that engendered *cutis anserina* popularly known as "goose-flesh."

It was a keen disappointment that there were not more opportunities for the study of the food habits of the Screech Owls. In the forty pieces of game found in the nest there were eight birds, three frogs, one common shrew, and twenty-eight mice: the last named were chiefly meadow mice with two or three house mice. Enough of the meadow mice were weighed to ascertain their average weight to be upward of 600 grains. After leaving their nest on May 29, the oldest ones being thirty-two days old, the owlets were caught and kept in captivity several days. Their food was weighed and it was learned that when fed to satiety each one consumed meat equal in weight to one meadow mouse. This estimate may fairly indicate that the forty pieces mentioned were nearly one-eighth of the amount eaten by the entire family during the nest season. On this basis of reckoning sixty-four birds fell victims to these night terrors; as but one of the eight birds seen was an English Sparrow, little credit belongs to the owls on that score; four were Song Sparrows and three Juncos. After the Juncos had passed northward there were numerous reddish feathers in the nest indicating that Swamp Sparrows often appeared on the bill of fare.

The very large proportion of Song Sparrows and Juncos slain invites investigation. During some part of the nest period fully thirty species of small birds were present, of which Goldfinches, Vesper, Savannah, White-throated, Tree, Chipping, Field and Swamp Sparrows were as numerous at times as the Song Sparrows, or more plentiful, for in time all Song Sparrows disappeared. In three places on our grounds this species had been accustomed to nest, but as the days went by one voice after another was missed from the bird chorus. The fact that Juncos and Song Sparrows more frequently than their numerous congeners fell victims to these rapacious birds, suggests the thought that probably they flush at night more readily. Usually the head, wings and tail of a bird were torn off before it was dropped into the nest, only once was a whole one brought in. At times the food was marked; from this it was made certain that the body of a Song

Sparrow lay untouched for two days, thereby showing that a mouse diet was preferred.

Out of forty pieces of game eight were birds or 20 percent of the whole. Dr. Fisher's investigation of the food habits of this species shows that of 212 Screech Owls whose stomachs contained food, 38 of them had eaten birds or 18 percent of the whole. This indicates that our owls were but 2 percent worse than the species in general, yet their ravages were so great that it was decided if we desired a little bird paradise where all good birds were welcome through the summer time there Screech Owls could not be encouraged to remain, therefore the captive owlets were sent to a neighboring village, a pair of them to two invalid little boys in a hospital, the others to a friend in the same place. Soon all of them gained their freedom and with it the chance to prey upon all the little birds about them.

CHAPTER XIV

DOWN WITH THE
HOUSE WREN BOXES *

If, when a felon is on trial for high crimes and mis-
demeanors he is confronted by numerous eye-witnesses,
who are trustworthy and fully competent to testify,
if by their evidence it is proved that for upward of
twenty-five years he has been seen committing the most
flagrant crimes against his neighbors; if the depositions
of these expert witnesses have been spread upon the
public records and printed in volumes accessible to
every one, it would appear that the public ought to
demand for the good of our country that the felon be
sentenced, and that the sentence be executed without
dangerous delay.

In the case of the people of North America versus
the House Wren together with his subspecies the
Western House Wren, the eye-witnesses of his crimes
are numerous, trustworthy, and exceedingly competent;
among them are men, who rank with our most eminent
ornithologists: men whose professional business during
many years has been the careful study of birds. Besides
these there are many other men and women less famous, but equally trustworthy as witnesses, who from
the Atlantic seaboard to the Pacific coast and from the
Gulf states to the farthest north range of the House
Wren in Canada have made numerous statements regarding this species. Their observations cover a period
of more than a quarter of a century and have been pub-

---

* From 'The Wilson Bulletin', Vol. 37, No. 1, March, 1925.

lished in various ornithological books and magazines, which are open to the examination of all.

In this prosecution the public must be jury, judge and executioner and, most unfortunately, a large part of the public is unfitted to act in any of these capacities: as jurymen, because they have already formed an opinion; this opinion is not based on any real knowledge on the subject, either first-hand or otherwise, but having a wren-box on their narrow village lot they refuse to listen to the warnings of those who have seen the House Wren at his nefarious work. They are fond of *their* bird and are angry when the truth is spoken about it; they act precisely like the parents of vicious children, refusing to believe the evil things their darlings do. They did not see the rattlesnake strike its fangs into the tender flesh of the little child that died last summer, yet the dying child was found and the rattlesnake near it: good enough circumstantial evidence for them was this, but the testimony of most trustworthy and competent witnesses of the evil done by the House Wren they flout and vilify. Neither are they fitted to act as judges. A judge in law must have knowledge of the literature of law, but with little or no knowledge of ornithological literature many people feel themselves supreme judges of this Wren; they will not take the bird magazines wherein they could find much convincing testimony.

It is a relief to turn from the ignorant and narrow-minded to those of more open minds: to those for whom the opinions and testimony of eminent scientists may have weight, and to remind them that among those who have borne most damaging testimony against the bad character of the House Wren may be found Messrs. Robert Ridgway, Otto Widmann, J. A. Munro, P. A. Taverner, Dr. Arthur A. Allen and Major Allan Brooks. For the presentation of this case to the open-minded a vast amount of data might be quoted: if desirable there can be given the names of the observers, together with the date and name of each magazine, also the page in it upon which the incriminating evidences against the House Wren have been published. In collecting these data a careful search has been made through 552 copies of bird magazines in which several hundred people have had something to say about the House Wren and its subspecies the Western House Wren; for convenience at this time the name House Wren will include both the species and its subspecies.

Of all the magazines *Bird-Lore* has published the largest array of evidence relating to the criminal character of the House Wren. In its January-February, 1905 issue, two veteran ornithologists spoke without shouting, yet most emphatically, regarding the danger from the House Wren, which attends the placing of bird houses. Any policeman will tell you that in a time of peril a gentle admonition will turn some people into a path of safety, but that on others he must use his club. It must be confessed that in connection with the danger here discussed, there is scarcely one of us who has not deserved the club. It is now a full score of years since Mr. Otto Widmann wrote the following gentle warning: "I would also say to those who put up bird houses of any kind to keep a watchful eye on the House Wren. He is as great a nuisance as the English Sparrow. He enters homes in the absence of the owners, ruins their nests, pierces and throws out eggs and can do enough mischief in one season to threaten the existence of a whole colony of martins. Nor are his attentions confined to bird houses either; open nests also suffer from his sneaking visits, and much of the damage laid at the English Sparrow's door may be traced to the innocent-looking Jennie Wren."

In the same number of *Bird-Lore* Mr. Robert Ridgway gave similar testimony. In speaking of his bird houses he said: "These nesting-places are occupied solely by House Wrens, for they will not allow any other bird to use them. Each spring a pair of Carolina Chickadees build their nest in one of them and have begun incubation by the time the House Wrens arrive, but that is as far as the poor Chickadees get, for the wrens immediately oust them and destroy their eggs." Again in the same magazine ten years later he writes: "The House Wren is equally tyrannical, and no small bird can nest in its vicinity. Several pairs of Carolina Chickadees and Tufted Titmice, and a pair of Bewick's Wrens, that had been with us all winter, and would have nested in boxes near the house but for the rascally House Wrens, who, though possessing boxes of their own, drove the other birds away." Farther on he speaks of this destructive little demon, saying: "The first House Wren ever seen or heard by me in southeastern Illinois was noted in the vicinity of Olney some time near the year 1870. . . . Bewick's Wren was THE 'House Wren' of the entire region. . . . In the vicinity of Olney, the House Wren is now by far the more numerous of the two, especially in the town itself; and, wherever it has chosen a home, Bewick's Wren is forced out, for Troglodytes will not brook the presence of any species, Wren, Chickadee, Titmouse, or Nuthatch, which requires similar nesting-sites. Thryomanes on the other hand is exceedingly tolerant of other species, and therefore is far the more desirable, especially since it is equally tame and a far better songster. . . ."

A half decade passed and again Mr. Ridgway spoke, this time in the *Illinois Audubon Bulletin,* (1920). The deposition is similar to that given above, and this is the heart-breaking part of it: that spring after spring it is the same old story for a score of years, even for fifty years, except that the story grows worse as the years advance; this is true not only at Olney, Illinois, but wherever the placing of boxes has contributed to an undue increase in the numbers of this species. It is neither desirable nor practical to quote all the evidence that has been recorded. In a rapid trans-continental survey only a few records can be mentioned. In Litchfield, Connecticut, more than twenty-five years ago the House Wren was denounced as a despoiler: "not a robber but a spoiler. He does not take other birds' eggs and eat them. He pierces them with his sharp little bill and throws them out of the nest. My direct knowledge of this fact comes from his treatment of the Chipping Sparrow. I have seen the wren throw the eggs of the latter out of the nest." From Saint Johnsbury, Vermont, came the message, "We have seen them drop the Bluebirds' eggs from the house door and take possession; which is more than the English Sparrow has done!" Similar offenses against the Bluebird were reported from Bristol, Connecticut; Hackettstown, New Jersey; Troy and Collins, New York, to mention only a few. In the magazines have been reported instances of his destruction of the eggs of the English Sparrow from Canton, Pennsylvania; of the Flicker and Robin from London, Ontario; of the Cardinal from Noblesville, Indiana, and from La Grange, Missouri; of the Texas Bewick's Wren from Wichita, Kansas; and of his usurpation of the boxes of Tree Swallow and Bluebird from Okanagan Landing, British Columbia.

Many people have seen him throwing from the nest the eggs of his own species. In fact, egg-throwing throughout the summer seems to be his main diversion. Egg-shells will answer if the whole eggs are wanting. An instance of this kind happened in my building erected to support a chimney for Chimney Swift occupants. Birds are excluded from its lower portion in which are stored various things, among them a Shrike's nest, containing the shells of eggs that had been blown. By accident a House Wren gained entrance to this room and was found there. Every shell of the Shrike's eggs had been carried from the nest and thrown to the floor. Some of the shells were not badly broken and all were returned to the nest. A few days later the wren again entered, again was found there, and again the egg-shells were scattered over the floor. The gentle Phoebe not infrequently is a victim of the wren's viciousness: her eggs are pierced and thrown out and her nests are torn down. One of her nests, not in use, built on top of a porch post was completely destroyed by a House Wren. He carried off the material but made no use of it. In a similar manner has he been seen tearing to pieces the nest of an English Sparrow, also to enter one of these nests and steal the feathers of its lining.

Mr. Widmann laid stress on the destruction of open nests by this wren, and Mr. Ridgway has given an account of the great decrease of several small species of birds, such as the Baltimore Oriole, Yellow Warbler and Warbling Vireo in his neighborhood. He does not say that two minus two leaves nothing, but I have the hardihood to say that it does: that two birds minus their two eggs leaves nothing for annual increase or replacement; that this loss repeated year after year soon brings a species to the verge of extinction. One has but to recall how soon the English Sparrow has nearly wiped out the Cliff Swallows and the Barn Swallows in places where formerly they were exceedingly numerous. He does not declare, as does Mr. Widmann, that much of this damage can be traced to the door of Jennie Wren, but I have the boldness to declare that I know it to be the truth. The state of things about

Olney, Illinois, parallels so closely that of a deserted village, that something other than a coincident must be the explanation for it. This decadent hamlet twenty-five years ago, before the coming of the House Wrens, was a paradise for many birds; Baltimore Orioles and Warbling Vireos swung their nests in the trees, Chipping Sparrows built in the bushes, and the Maryland Yellowthroat nested in the dooryards. Gradually people moved away, taking with them their cats and their bad boys; for eight summers not a Blue Jay was seen; chicken yards having been abandoned the English Sparrow went off to the farms; no doubt, all would have continued well with the little birds if the House Wren had not arrived; he took possession of the boxes placed for Chickadees and Bluebirds as well as numerous holes in old buildings; he flourished mightily, and as his tribe increased the other little birds decreased as summer residents, until very few of them could be found. In solving a problem of this sort it is well to have a large workable acreage under observation and to study it intensively. No person can witness the despoliation of every nest by the House Wren, yet by the process of elimination taken together with a knowledge of his character the correct answer can be found.

That the gentle admonitions of Mr. Ridgway have influenced the editor of one Audubon publication is attested by his magazine, which has ceased to advocate the placing of wren-boxes; but most of us seem to have needed the club. Speaking for myself, it must be confessed that I may have sinned against my small bird neighbors, when for purposes of study, there has been tolerance, years ago, of two nestings each of Screech Owls and Sparrow Hawks. But there is only one sin that causes constant mourning in sackcloth and ashes, that causes me to lie awake nights visioning the future condition of our country with its bird population con-

sisting mainly of those undesirable aliens, the Starling
and the English Sparrow, together with Screech Owls,
Bronzed Grackles, and House Wrens: that sin was
the putting up of bird houses and allowing them to be
occupied by House Wrens. It may comfort some
people to learn that for this sin full punishment is
being meted out in this world: except the Traill's Flycatcher, whose vigilance and pugnacity protects his
nest, and the Goldfinch, whose nesting comes after
the wren's frenzy has abated, can any other little birds
hatch their eggs, since the House Wrens became numerous; the successful breeding here of small species is
ended, they are becoming scarce as has been reported
from Olney, Illinois.

The cheerful twitterings of the Wren are pleasing,
but no more so than the songs of the Warbling Vireo,
the Yellow Warbler, the Maryland Yellowthroat, and
other small birds that he has robbed and routed. Some
of these by second trials in more remote spots are still
perpetuating their species, but in greatly diminishing
numbers, wherever the House Wren has largely increased. For corroboration of this statement the
regional lists of birds given in the ornithological magazines are cited. Some of the reports give the Chipping
Sparrow as now rare where formerly it was abundant.
To be sure the species has other enemies; in some
places the Blue Jay as well as the Bronzed Grackle,
the latter a bird that, most unfortunately, is increasing
in many places. Bad as it is it does not sneak through
all the small bushes and into bird houses. As for
injury done by the English Sparrow one would do
better to choose twenty of these rather than one
House Wren.

Again the ornithological magazines are the authority
for the statement that the House Wren is extending
its range. Reports of its recent appearance on Cape

Cod and in the vicinity of Quebec have been given. In the *Wilson Bulletin* for December, 1919, the late Dr. N. Hollister wrote of bird life about Delavan, Wisconsin, compared with what he had known there twenty to thirty years earlier. In speaking of former years he said, "House Wrens were reported by ornithologists as breeding now and then in other portions of the state and some few may have been present in my region, but as a summer resident the bird was certainly rare in the vicinity of Delavan. Now I found it, in July, one of the most conspicuous and generally distributed of town birds." With only one change, that of the town, this would read true of every place in the Upper Mississippi Valley it is confidently believed. When a nesting area becomes over-crowded with certain species, as for example the Flicker or the Brown Thrasher, they fight among themselves (each within the circle of its own species), and break up nests by destroying the eggs. This sort of race suicide may be continued for several seasons until over-crowding ceases and normal life once more holds sway. No such happy adjustment happens among the House Wrens. In this species it is the females that fight until one is killed, thus leaving an excess of males. Among a dozen of the species it has been found that there are two to four males that can not find mates. Never has it been discovered that these were the more destructive of the two classes of males, it may be the other way about; that the evil spirit is stirred in them by the presence of the unmated males ready to take away their partners. Whatever is the true explanation it is a matter of belief that the destructive habit has increased disproportionately with the increase of the species.

The reason for this great increase must be clear to every one. It is the result of the campaign for erecting boxes for wrens; boxes with small openings that protected the wrens from their natural enemies and enabled them to breed in undue numbers. That the species needs no such protection, but survives in plentiful numbers in the remote portions of its breeding range is another fact proved by the regional lists printed in the bird magazines. How many persons have searched for such records? Those who have done so, have read of the House Wren having been found breeding "abundantly" in the wild portions of Pennsylvania and of West Virginia, in the mountains of Virginia, in the northern woods of Michigan and Wisconsin, in South Dakota, Saskatchewan, Alberta, British Columbia, Washington, Montana, Colorado, and in the higher altitudes of New Mexico and Arizona. Certainly enough instances to prove that this bird needs no special protection.

This protection has been given by some unwittingly, by others obstinately, those who refused to believe the emphatic warnings of Robert Ridgway and Otto Widmann spoken twenty years ago. An example of one open-minded searcher for truth was afforded by a conscientious and learned ornithologist, who could not quite accept the words of Mr. Widmann, hence set the men of his state to seeking proof. How long they sought was not stated, but it was considerably less than seven years. It calls up the picture of a woman bent on vindicating her wren, who takes her tatting, sits in the shade of her apple tree in sight of her wren-box, and while she tats an entire afternoon she sees no eggs destroyed, consequently declares that there is nothing but malicious lies in the whole story. Such zeal on the part of one investigator might provoke a smile if the subject were not so serious; but those of us who for twenty to fifty years have studied thoroughly and carefully the life of the House Wren know the difficulty of catching him red-handed. More often than otherwise the detection comes accidentally. Fingerprints are deemed trustworthy evidence against the human criminal. One "fingerprint" of this wren is the dropping of the egg, its contents uneaten, outside the nest; but this evidence is lacking at times. It may be said, in brief, that the collecting of evidence is not rapid work; it takes years, yes, *years*. A man who begins this work today, possibly, may know as much a score of years hence as does the man who began twenty years ago, but no more. However, it is very doubtful if he will know as much, since he begins in a world crowded with House Wrens, whereas the other man had a nearly wrenless background. And will the word of the beginner of today be any more reliable than the words of the eminent men who have spoken erstwhile?

The word of a truthful, competent, observant man can be trusted *seemingly* about most things, but not about the destruction done by the House Wren. He may tell of a dozen or more things seen in this wren's life that very few besides himself have ever witnessed, and all his statement will be accepted if he does not mention the menace of the wren to other bird life; on this subject he can not be trusted. It is not because the menace is a new idea to them nor because its workings have not been seen by them that they are obstinate, for they readily accept new truths about things that they have not seen, such as statements about vitamins, endocrine imbalance, sex-linked inheritance, chromosomes, the atomic world, and relativity.

Were a criminal belonging to the human race on trial, had his trial dragged along for many years during which he had time and again been confronted by the testimony of witnesses who were expert, competent, and veracious, it is certain that public sentiment would demand that a verdict be given and a sentence be passed. In the case of the felonious House Wren have not numerous jurymen pronounced him guilty? Capital punishment has not been demanded, though if no steps are taken to stop his unrestricted breeding it is safe to predict that the time will come when all true bird lovers will wring his neck as cheerfully as they now wring the neck of the pestiferous English Sparrow. By no means is it asked that the death penalty be exacted; instead of that drastic measure a mild sentence is urged—merely that the wren-boxes be taken down, thereby returning this wren to the place in nature that he occupied before man's interference destroyed the natural balance. In order that this restoration be not short-lived it is hoped there may come a true appreciation of his disposition, so that no one will suffer a breeding House Wren on his premises any sooner than he would tolerate vermin on his person.

Bird-Lore has a splendid motto: "A bird in the bush is worth two in the hand." But if we are to have that bird in the bush in future years, and if it is to be any other than a House Wren, then we need the slogan, "Down with the House Wren Boxes." The stand we take on this question will affect more than present interests, and each one should so act that a kind Providence need not protect his memory from the just execrations of future generations.

CHAPTER XV

THE OLD ORNITHOLOGY
AND THE NEW *

It seems necessary at the outset to define the two schools of ornithology to be discussed in this paper. The old school deals with ornithology: "That branch of natural science which investigates and treats of the form, structure, and habits of birds." Its members respect the derivation of the word, meaning to discourse about a bird, and call themselves "ornithologists." They abide by the definition quoted which states that ornithology is a science and that it investigates or studies birds; in other words, they do scientific work, following the rules for scientific research.

Various writers have been busy defining science in our scientific magazines, even in some newspapers. None of them get far beyond the dictionary's definition: that science is concerned with knowledge, with truth; meaning true knowledge, not mistaken notions, that all too often pass for knowledge and truth. In this connection may be quoted the words of Dr. Theodore W. Richards, our first native American to receive the Nobel prize in science. He wrote, "First and foremost I should emphasize the overwhelming importance of perfect sincerity and truth." To this he added, "And then patience, patience! Only by unremitting, persistent labour can a lasting outcome be reached." Clearly

* Read at the Des Moines meeting of the Wilson Ornithological Club, December 28, 1929.
From 'The Wilson Bulletin', Vol. 42, No. 1, March, 1930.

then truth and hard work are the exactions of science. Conformity to this requirement is the role for ornithologists of the old school. Their work is research, the spirit of their gatherings can be told in the words of Paul by the substitution of a single word: "For all the Athenians and the strangers which were there spent their time in nothing else, but either to tell, or to hear some new thing." ("About birds," are two words to be added). The old school may be divided into two classes, the professionals and the amateurs. Of the latter class William Brewster is a notable example.

The followers of the new school of ornithology far outnumber the members of the old school. They shy from using the word "ornithologists" (perhaps it is too hard for them to pronounce), and call themselves "bird lovers"; and again they shy away from "ornithology," naming their twaddle "bird talks." They do no research work themselves, and have so slight regard for the truth about birds, that they neglect, sometimes positively refuse, to read the truths published by others. They will not take the bird magazines nor buy worthy books. One sentence fully describes them. They dabble a little in bird lore in order to gabble about birds.

The members of the new school also may be divided into two classes, the professionals and the amateurs. The professional class comprises those who are striving for fame or gain, or both; those who are panting for publicity, who imagine that they are on the road to world-wide fame by giving their "bird talks" before Women's Clubs or at gatherings of Community Clubs. As examples illustrative of this class will be taken two cases chosen from my own observations. The first place will be given to the man, who, when passing a singing bird on a telephone wire, expressed his very high appreciation of the Song Sparrow's music. When questioned, he admitted that he referred to the song of the bird on the telephone wire, and was told that it was a Dickcissel. His counterpart is found in a woman. Her story has been told once, but it so fitly illustrates this class of fame seekers that its repetition, possibly, may be pardoned. We met, and, as can readily be believed, I soon spoke of the exceedingly evil habits of the House Wren. She said, "I never heard of the House Wren." Following a brief description of the bird she exclaimed: "Oh, I know now what you mean! *You* call it a House Wren; I never knew that *anyone ever* called it a House Wren; *I* always call it a Jenny Wren." She is only one of the many instructors about birds who refuse to take bird magazines, who refuse also to learn the most elementary facts about birds. There are thousands of babblers like her, and how they do love to babble about birds! They are the teachers of the amateur class in the new school.

Passing now to the class who for gain lay defiling hands on the birds, quotations will be given from their writings, published in the highest class of popular magazines. The first example given was published in 1909, when magazines were paying twenty-five cents per line for poetry. One gem entitled "The Shipwrecked Sailor," reads:

> "Yet he smiled
> Abandoning hope and drowning unaware,
> Til a great sea-bird, tern or ptarmigan
> Caught by the whiteness of his lonely face
> Swooped low exultantly; huge swish of wings
> Measuring his body, as he struck him once.
> Thud of ribbed beak, like the call to arms
> Stirred the wounded soldier. . . ."

Since 1909, when these lines won two dollars for the author, there have been the terrible shipwrecks of the Titanic and of the Vestris from which some of the victims escaped with their lives. None of them told of suffering blood-curdling attacks from ribbed-beaked birds, either tern or ptarmigan, hence we must conclude that this was a rare case of the man-eating ptarmigan going to sea.

On account of the high cost of living, poetry prices mounted to a dollar per line in 1929. The quality of the outpourings seems to be about the same. Here is a sample from a poem entitled "Home":

"There shall be towels as fresh as the clover
Stored on the cedar-wood shelves down the hall,
A kitchen as white as the eggs of the plover,
And candlestick lights for the library wall."

Between the lines one may read a romance: The author, contemplating matrimony, plans a home; he is a modern youth and travels; he goes to Great Britain; he samples everything; he eats; he calls for plovers' eggs and is served with the eggs of a Bantam hen. Moreover, he is served rightly.

In sharp contrast with these nature fakes there come to mind, whenever the October leaves are falling, the lines of one who must have sat at the feet of Nature, perhaps in her very lap. They were found in a scientific magazine without a taint of money about them. Quite likely the author was a college professor who did not work for money. Except a little tautology, what fault is there in them?

"The autumn leaves are falling,
Falling, falling, everywhere.
Some are falling through the atmosphere,
And some are falling through the air."

Again wonder thrills us upon reading some of the prose effusions about nature that have been accepted and published by the highest class of popular magazines. Some of these look like a big yellow cotton patch on a blue silk dress. Now and then they contain some remarkable statements relating to ornithology which may be quoted. When snow was lying deep on the ground in Vermont a writer said she saw a Rose-breasted Grosbeak on March 12. The same magazine published the story of a November blizzard in Michigan. In it we are told that in the thickness of the storm water fowl were rushing south and among them "Swallows twittered and swept low across the water." A well-known British writer tells a story that, as a story, is an erotic, neurotic, idiotic mess, but when he lays his defaming hands on the birds it is time for us to protest. His heroine is "twenty and loverless." She knew all the birds, she watched for the spring arrivals of cuckoo, swallow, sedge warbler, and kestrel; as they came she scattered millet for them. Her bounty halted these solely insectivorous, or flesh-eating birds, and as they ate her millet they hopped through the lilacs and sang to her. Late one afternoon she wandered forth and met a stranger. Cupid smote both of them with his famous darts. As night deepened they sat beneath the boughs of a tree, "they heard a tiny commotion in the tree overhead; it was like the breaking of most fragile glass. He pointed through the branches to a nest. She knew what he meant; a new-born traveller was fighting his way out of the shell into the wind-swept world." What marvelous acuity of hearing had these love-lorn creatures! But their British creator evidently had failed to read Professor C. O. Whitman and to note his statement that birds' eggs do not hatch in the night, and rarely after three o'clock in the afternoon, even though the shells may be pipped; that the hatching bird has its time for sleep and like its parents it sleeps in the night.

The Reverend Dean Inge has said, "Perhaps the great struggle of the future will be between science and sentimentalism, and it is by no means certain that the right side will win." It may be that the great struggle is now taking place in regard to the birds and that the ignorant sentimentalists will seal the fate of the few birds now left to us. They comprise the vast mass of people who belong to the new school of ornithology. They are the amateurs who in their own language *"just love the birds."* They refuse to study, even to read the truth that days, months, and years of hard delving by the disciples of the old school have brought to light. To them the words, even the names, of the great leaders in ornithological science have no more meaning than they would have if quoted to a Bushman or a Hottentot. Moreover, they refuse to believe these same words, when told of them orally. By them all birds are to be loved and protected, even though they are the birds that are destroying other birds at an alarming rate.

A prolific source of information (perhaps the only source) for these amateurs of the new school seems to be the newspapers. If some of the men who supply the columns of these papers with their stories of bird life, containing "facts" unknown to scientists, have any true knowledge of birds they fail to demonstrate it. One marvels over the announcements of the results of some of their original research investigations. Among them may be mentioned the statement that Catbirds and Brown Thrashers use mud in the construction of their nests. One of these men declares that in north-eastern Iowa there has been a "ruthless slaughter of blackbirds," and he adds: "A peculiarity of this species is that the male bird comes north in the spring two weeks in advance of the female, after mating in the southland. How they find each other is one of the mysteries of bird instinct." True, indeed, the "mystery" is sufficient to hold one spellbound! But this research student of the new school of ornithology failed to tell us the name of the blackbird of his remarkable discovery, whether it is the amorous, polygamous Cowbird or that sweet singer, the Bronzed Grackle. You may be sure he emphasized the insectivorous habits of his song bird, yet he gave no hint that the "ruthless slaughter," whether of Cowbird or Bronzed Grackle, might be the means of saving hundreds of other and better insectivorous birds. There are other things besides food habits to be considered in the evaluation of birds. Some such consideration ought to have saved our birds from the introduction of their pestiferous foes, the English Sparrow and the Starling. Many years ago the Encyclopaedia Britannica under the heading "Birds" made the statement that the Starling "constantly dispossesses the Green Woodpecker." Its habits remain the same after its transplanting to America. It usurps the homes of our native woodpeckers, yet seldom is a voice raised against it. That 4,000 Starlings in Washington, D. C., and 600 in Ohio were banded, *then released,* is an offense against our woodpeckers that scarcely can be understood or forgiven.

Returning again to the choice excerpts from popular magazines, for several months one of them offered numerous things new to science. The bold young man who writes these things begins by telling us about the Brown Creeper "who is a true warbler according to ornithologists," he confidently asserts. This statement was published in April, 1923. In February, 1926, another of our leading magazines shows an excellent picture of a Brown Creeper, bearing beneath it this legend, "Little Willie Woodpecker," and the text that accompanies the picture implies that under the *alias* of Willie Woodpecker the Brown Creeper is a beneficial bird. Thus it may be seen that in the short space of thirty-four months the changeling creeper metamorphosed from a warbler into a woodpecker.

Turning once more to the magazine of the bold young man, we may read of his trip taken through southern Ohio in July. He says of it: "The most conspicuous bird seen in the Ohio region was a male butcher bird or great northern shrike, along a roadside, industriously feeding a voracious young bird of the same species." Where were all the southern Ohio ornithologists of the old school, that the noteworthy breeding of Northern Shrikes in their very midst should be left to the discovery of this young tourist? The same young man is no less interesting when he wanders into the realms of history and mammalogy. He invades my own home neighborhood, when attempting to give the origin of the name of Prairie du Chien, Wisconsin. People, having knowledge of Upper Mississippi Valley history, recall that the early French explorers found an Indian called "The Dog" living on the prairie at the mouth of the Wisconsin River and they called the locality Prairie du Chien, a name it has borne ever since. All those, having the least bit of knowledge of the prairie dog, know that the eastern boundary of its range is several hundred miles west of the Mississippi River. But our bold young man has this to say about it: "Many similar and rather absurd instances might easily be cited; notably the 'prairie dog,' which, of course, isn't a 'dog' at all, but a member of the *rat* family. For that particular misnomer we probably have to thank the French settlers who so named 'Prairie du Chien' because the locality was full of 'prairie dogs' whose outward resemblance to a dog happened to be that they had four legs and a *tail,* which latter they wagged vigorously."

Time is lacking for tarrying longer with the many delightful things published by the new school of ornithology. Those quoted are treasures garnered while reading a very limited range of popular magazines. Doubtlessly wider reading would disclose thousands like them. No space for their like has ever been found in the bird magazines. Yet every week the *Literary Digest* can fill a page and the *Journal of the American Medical Association* does fill three columns with the gems that sparkle in their own special fields of knowledge.

There is no implication in the preceding pages that ornithologists of the old school never make mistakes. They would be more than supermen, if that were true. But their mistakes are not delightful and joy-giving, on the other hand they are painfully saddening. Since ornithology is a science; since the purpose of science is knowledge, truth, perfect truth, the aims of most ornithologists are to contribute to truthful, exact knowledge as far as in them lies. The purposes of science are not attained by copying old, time-worn errors, nor in neglecting to read the many truths that research workers are constantly bringing to light. The case of Professor Tweezers amply illustrates this point. He decided to publish a life history of the birds of his state, to repeat once more the many things already told in various state histories, which have appeared in ponderous forms of one to four volumes. Since it is utterly impossible for one man to have thorough, first-hand knowledge of the habits of all the birds of one state he was obliged to draw very largely from previous publications. But to make his book salable and to give it an appearance of original research he invited aid from his neighbors, from the Sam Smiths of Hazelbush

Hollow, and the Mary Joneses of Metropolisville, whose observations as quoted are no better than scores of similar ones already published. All this is according to custom and quite justifiable. It is when Tweezers publishes ancient errors, adds some of his own, and refuses to read numerous life histories, that others have published, that he becomes reprehensible. Well might he be arrested for "cruelty to animals" when he hustles callow Purple Martins out of their nest, when the duration of the nest period is but half completed, when the quills of their wing-feathers have not yet burst. His untruths about this species might more readily be pardoned if Dr. Brownesque and several others had not given him the correct data.

Professor Tweezers is not alone in his bookmaking projects, there are several other members of his family. Some of these Tweezers would refuse to change the figures you have placed on a bank check, but they do not hesitate to mutilate the correct figures you have given in a bird history. There is a certain Tweezers who showed his masculine strength by slashing off a half day from the incubation period given for one bird. It is strange that he did not show his superiority in a bolder, braver, more heroic way by slashing off a whole day. So far as respect for truth is concerned, five or ten days might have been cut off with equal reason. If science seeks knowledge and truth, there ought to be protest against those Tweezers who seize upon the outcome of days, weeks, or months of hard work done by others, only to mutilate it or to turn and twist it to suit their own ignorance or prejudice.

To emphasize the injustice they do both to truth and to bird students I take one example selected from my own experience. I had made as careful a study of nesting Sparrow Hawks as I could and it was published in the *Auk*. It seemed to please one of the Tweezers, the reason soon became apparent: he needed it to use in his book. He used it, giving my name and paraphrasing the whole nest history. To that no one could object, if he had not inserted a downright, inexcusable falsehood. He said that I wrote that these hawks fed their nestlings "insects." And there that lie will stand as long as the writings of this particular Tweezers shall endure. To some people this may appear a small matter. It is not. Besides being a gratuitous untruth, it suggests a habit that is beyond credibility. Besides never seeing it done, two seasons of close study of nesting Sparrow Hawks lead me to believe that no mother hawk of this species would be willing to approach the nest carrying insect food.

The case just cited calls to mind another class of people that may be mentioned: They are "half-castes" or hybrids between the old school and the new school of ornithology. With a smattering knowledge of a few birds they are busy trying to whitewash the reputations of certain birds proved to be bad. While they deify a bird they are at great pains to damn the characters of the people who have made known its evil habits. They forget that time is long; that after them will come bird students and ornithologists who will recognize the truth and forcibly denounce the errors and untruths in which these mongrel "half-castes" delight to revel.

CHAPTER XVI

EXPERIMENTS IN FEEDING
HUMMINGBIRDS DURING
SEVEN SUMMERS *

The experiments herein described were begun without intending them to bear upon the question of the
food naturally sought by the Ruby-throated Hummingbird (*Archilochus colubris*); the original aim of the
feeding was to attract the Hummingbirds about the
yard in the hope that sometime they would remain to
nest there. The experiments have been conducted on
independent lines without knowledge of any similar
work that was being done by others until the autumn
of 1912, except in one instance, where special acknowl-
edgements are due Miss Caroline G. Soule of Brook-
line, Mass., who in *Bird-Lore* for October, 1900,
described her success in feeding Hummingbirds from
a vial, which she had placed in the heart of an artificial
trumpet-flower made from Whatman paper and
painted with water-colors. This suggestion of using
artificial flowers was taken, but more durable ones were
made from white oil-cloth, their edges were stiffened
with one strand of wire taken from picture cord, and
they were carefully painted with oil colors, the first to
represent a nasturtium, and the second a tiger-lily.

In August of 1907, upon the appearance of a Hummingbird about our flowers, the artificial nasturtium,

---

* Read at the 31st Annual Congress of the American Ornithologists'
Union, New York City, Nov. 11, 1913.
From 'The Wilson Bulletin', Vol. 25, No. 4, December, 1913.

tacked to a stick, was placed near a clump of blooming phlox, and its bottle was filled with a syrup made of granulated sugar dissolved in water. The next day a female Ruby-throat was seen searching the depth of tiger-lilies that grew north of the house; as she flew to the east of the house she was instantly followed, and was seen drinking from the artificial flower for the space of about a minute, after which she flew to a rose-bush, wiped her bill and rested a brief time before flying away. This was about noon. She returned at intervals of about a half hour for the next three hours, then at 3:10 o'clock she came back to search quite thoroughly the phlox blossoms, this being the first time she had paid any attention to them after finding the syrup. Ten minutes later she drank deeply from the bottle, and was seen no more that day.

In this way began the feeding of the Ruby-throated Hummingbirds, which has been continued each summer since 1907 with a varying number of birds. The first season it appeared that but a single bird found the bottled sweets. Perhaps it was the same bird that came the following summer, and was not joined by a second Hummingbird until the latter part of August. In 1909 the number was gradually augmented until seven of these birds were present together. The following year there were days when again seven came at one time; since then four have been the largest number seen together.

The days and weeks are calm and quiet ones when a single bird has the bottles to herself. More or less fighting ensues as soon as another bird comes on the scene, and the tumult of battle increases with each new arrival until the presence of six or seven of these tiny belligerents makes the front yard appear like the staging of a ballet. With clashing sounds and continuous squeaking cries they chase each other about, often swinging back and forth in an arc of a circle with a sort of pendulum-like motion. Sometimes they clinch and fall to the earth where the struggle is continued for many seconds. So jealous are they lest others share the syrup that they seem more anxious to fight than to drink. When seven are present they are very difficult to count, and appear to be three-fold that number. We have read accounts of forty or a hundred Hummingbirds hovering about a tree or bush. Clearly these numbers must have been estimates, probably large ones, too, any one must believe, who has made sure that only seven birds have created the maze of wonderful and beautiful motion in which there seemed to be a dozen or a score of participants.

The number of bottles in use has been sufficient on most days to satisfy the needs of all the Hummingbirds present. Each new bottle has been added by way of an experiment. The first one was placed in an artificial flower painted to imitate a nasturtium, mainly yellow in color; the second flower in form and color closely resembled a tiger-lily. The experiment with the yellow and the red flowers was to test a supposedly erroneous theory which had been published to the effect that Hummingbirds show a preference for red flowers. In further proof of the fallacy of this statement the third flower, shaped like the nasturtium, was painted green, and was placed in a bed of green plants which at that time bore no blossoms. It was pronounced by other people to be "exactly the color of the surrounding foliage." It was staked out and filled on August 5, 1909, when no Hummingbird was in sight, but in about ten minutes some of the species had come, and fifteen minutes later one was drinking from the bottle in this green flower.

It was then suggested by my sister, Dr. E. Amelia Sherman, that I try a bottle without an encircling flower. The problem of supporting a bottle without an artificial flower was solved in this way: The bottle was encased in a piece of unbleached muslin, enough of the cloth extending beyond the bottom of the bottle to allow the tacking of it to a stick. The support of the bottle in a position slightly up from the horizontal was furnished by a piece of leather with a hole in it through which the bottle was thrust, and the leather was then nailed to the stick. In this arrangement the most vivid imagination can find no suggestion of a flower. It was put out on August 8, and in forty-three minutes a Hummingbird was drinking from it. The bottle was then moved from proximity to the artificial nasturtium and tiger-lily, and a Hummingbird found it and in its new location in thirty-two minutes. This place about 8 feet from the artificial flowers has been its position in the four succeeding summers. In July, 1911, two more flowerless bottles were added to the group, making six in all. For convenience in referring to them the flowerless bottles will be called by numbers 4, 5 and 6.

Bottle No. 4 had not been long in use before it was noted that the Hummingbirds showed preference for it, while the nasturtium was sought least of all. This seemed due to the deep insetting of the bottle in the flower, which caused the birds to brush against its lower leaves, an unpleasant experience when sticky syrup adhered to it. For this reason the filling of the nasturtium was sometimes omitted for several days whereupon the Hummingbirds soon ceased to visit it, although drinking regularly from the tiger-lily a few inches away. When the filling was resumed the birds returned to it as they had been accustomed.

In the fourth season of experiments the bottle held by the green flower was put out when the others were, but was not filled for six weeks. During that time

Hummingbirds were present and drinking on twenty-three days. It is safe to say that they were seen drinking fully 400 times from the other bottles, but never once were they seen to approach the green flower. The first morning it was filled four of them were about the yard and one drank from this flower two minutes after the filling. The following year (1911) after dark on July 14 the green-flower bottle was set in its bed of green and was left empty for a few days. About noon on the 17th one of the Ruby-throats visited it, thrusting in her bill; the bottle was then filled for the first time that year, and in a half minute a bird was drinking from it. To this is added a transcript from my journal bearing date of July 17, 1912; "About 9 a.m. before I had put out any syrup a Hummingbird was dashing from bottle to bottle and tried the green flower one. It was bent over in the green foliage, and certainly has had no syrup in it for six weeks or longer. I filled it after I saw the bird visit it, and she came again to drink."

The new bottles No. 5 and No. 6 covered like No. 4 with white muslin and nailed to a weather-beaten fence picket were put out after dark on July 23, 1911, but neither was filled for one week. The next morning about eight o'clock a Hummingbird was searching one of these bottles for suspected sweets; four such visits were noted in one day and on several other occasions. At the end of the week the filling of No. 5 began but no syrup was put in No. 6 for two years. During these years a record was kept of each time a Hummingbird was seen to visit and search this unfilled bottle, and the total number was fifteen in addition to those visits already mentioned.

Thus far this writing has been confined to a description of the things seen; no theories have been advanced, no deductions have been made, no hypotheses have

been carried to their logical conclusion. The first deduction offered is, that at the beginning of the experiments
in 1907 the artificial nasturtium may have led the
Hummingbird to explore its depths, and finding its
contents to her taste, she returned to it. Other birds
may have found the syrup there in the same way, yet
it seems more likely that most of them were led to
the bottles by seeing another drinking. This probably
was the case with the Catbirds that have drunk from
the bottles on several occasions, although they have
found it an inconvenient performance. The same may
be true of a pair of Chickadees that drank as long as
they remained with us. They clung to the stiff leaves
of the tiger-lily and found no difficulty in the way of
drinking. Only one Hummingbird learned to perch on
this flower and drink from it while standing. From the
earlier experiments it was suspected that the Hummingbirds found the syrup through some sense, rather than
stumbling upon it by chance or through imitation, but
several things disprove such a supposition. The principal one is that migrants passing through the yard in
the spring, but more especially in the fall, fail to find
the syrup. That these migrants can be recognized as
such by their behavior will be shown further on.

The twenty-five or more visits paid to bottles No. 5
and No. 6 before they were filled for the first time
show that the birds recognized them as receptacles for
their food, though they were new bottles occupying
new locations. To make sure that the birds should not
be attracted to them by seeing me stake the pickets out,
this work was done after dark. The first summer that
No. 6 was out frequent pretenses of filling it were
made in sight of the birds, but no response followed.
The next summer no such pretenses were made, yet a
Hummingbird was seen to search this unfilled bottle

on May 12 and 31, twice on June 1, on July 21 and 26, on August 4, 7, 12, 23 and 26.

One is led to wonder if the Homeric gods on high Olympus were more deeply stirred by the appearance among them of the youthful Ganymedes bearing cups of nectar, than are the Hummingbirds at sight of their cup-bearer. When several of them are present the wildest confusion reigns. Possibly not one of them is in sight when the door is passed, yet instantly the air seems filled with them: some swinging back and forth in the air, squeaking and fighting, or darting from bottle to bottle thrusting in their bills as they pass, while an over-bold one will buzz about my head, sometimes coming under the porch in her zeal for the meeting; but the timorous ones fly from their perches into sight over the bottles then back into a bush. Some one of these types of behavior marks the bird boarder from the migrant. The latter pays no attention to cup-bearer or bottle but diligently searches each bunch of blossoms. For two or three weeks after the drinking birds have left, there is occasionally a migrant among the natural flowers. The bottles are full of syrup but it passes them unheedfully.

Habits seem to change when steady drinking is practiced, but in the case of the birds the habit does not appear to be a harmful one. At once she ceases to search the flowers and, like the typical summer boarder, she sits and waits for the food to be served. Each bird appears to have her favorite perch, a dead twig of syringa or lilac bushes on the north, or on the south in one of the snow-ball bushes; the telephone wires on either side of the street offer acceptable waiting-places at times. Not infrequently I have been intent upon other duties about the yard and looking up have found a Ruby-throat perched directly over-head, her bright eyes seeming to say "I want to be fed." So complete appears the cessation of the search for other food that it led to the keeping of a full record for the past three years of every time one of these birds has been seen catching insects or searching the natural flowers for food. Most of these instances noted were, if the whole truth could be learned, probably, cases of strangers just arrived within our gates, that had not yet acquired the drinking habit.

In 1911 the drinking birds were about our place on forty-three days. During that time on only four occasions was a Hummingbird seen catching insects or probing the flowers. A large number of plants called "Star of Bethlehem" had been raised, these flowers in previous summers having proved a great attraction to the Ruby-throat in the yard of a friend living two miles distant; but our drinking birds were never seen to visit these flowers. After their departure strange Hummingbirds searched them thoroughly as well as the phlox, tiger-lilies, sweet peas, nasturtiums and clover. These strangers were present on twelve days. In 1912 the drinkers were with us on seventy-seven days, and were seen but ten times seeking other food than syrup. In 1913 for forty-nine days the drinking birds imbibed, and on nine occasions a Hummingbird was seen gathering food elsewhere. In the 169 days that make the grand total for the three summers, the Ruby-throats were seen drinking syrup between one and two thousand times, they were seen collecting food away from the bottles twenty-three times, but one cannot be positive that insect food was always taken then. Never for an instant was one of these birds in captivity, and there was the utmost freedom for it in choice of food.

This choice of a sugar diet together with the large amount consumed caused surprise and soon called forth the estimate that a Hummingbird would eat a teaspoonful of sugar in one day. Some method of testing

this estimate was sought, resulting in a plan for putting
the bottles beyond the reach of the ants that swarmed
about them: The stick that supported the artificial
nasturtium and tiger-lily was nailed to a block of wood
which was submerged in a flower-pot filled with water.
For a short time this arrangement served very well
until leaves and flower petals fell in forming rafts upon
which the ants were able to cross. No myrmecologist
was at hand to suggest a remedy, but at last ants' aver-
sion to kerosene was recalled and the water was
covered with a film of kerosene, which effectually de-
barred them. Nevertheless one day the ants were
found taking the syrup as of old; an examination of
existing conditions showed that a grass stem had lodged
against the supporting stick, forming a bridge over
which these wise little creatures were busily passing to
and fro. Except when the bottles were isolated in this
manner, ants of various sizes and different colors fed
constantly on the syrup, often crowding a bottle to its
very mouth, but this did not prevent the birds from
drinking. I am not prepared to say that they never
took an ant as food, but I have stood as closely as is
possible to a bottle while a Hummingbird was drinking from it, and none was taken at such times. When
a new bottle was placed, or the old ones were set out
in the spring and filled, it took from one to two days
for the ants to find the syrup. A small red species
generally, if not always, was the ant to make the discovery, the fruits of which it enjoyed for a very brief
season, a large black ant soon taking possession and
holding the spoils for the rest of the summer.

The bottles, having been removed from the en-
croachments of the ants, were ready for the first test.
One bird being the sole boarder at that time, a level
tea-spoonful of sugar dissolved in water was consumed
by her daily. In time two, three, four and five Hum-

mingbirds having joined her, the quantity of sugar was increased accordingly, a spoonful or two being added to offset any possible waste. In this way more than a pound of sugar was eaten in twenty days, or to be more exact three cupfuls, weighing 9252 grains; which made an average of 462 grains per day. This for the six birds frequently counted as present confirmed the first rough estimate of a tea-spoonful of sugar daily for each bird.

Another method of estimating the amount eaten was devised. On several days the sugar and the water were carefully measured and weighed, then weighed and measured again, after which the syrup resulting from their combination was also measured and weighed, until I felt confident that in a dram of the thinnest syrup served there were 40 grains of sugar, or two-thirds of a gram to every drop. But the syrup usually used was considerably richer than this, easily containing a grain of sugar in every drop; but it seems best in giving the estimates to keep them to the weakest grade of syrup ever served.

In making the test a dram of syrup was measured in a glass graduate, and bottle No. 4 was filled. This was always done in the morning when the bottle had been emptied by ants. A waiting Hummingbird came and took her breakfast, after which the residue of syrup was poured back into the graduate, the bottle being thoroughly drained. Possibly a drop still adhered to the bottle, but the number of minims now in the graduate subtracted from 60 must have given very nearly the amount drank by the Hummingbird. In two summers a number of these tests were made. A bird took for her breakfast from 8 to 20 minims, the average being 15. Using the low estimate of two-thirds of a grain of sugar to each drop, the average breakfast held 10 grains of sugar. A better comprehension of the size of that meal may be gained by remembering

that two large navy beans, or one medium-sized lima
bean also weigh 10 grains. Breakfast and supper were
the Ruby-throats' heaviest meals, but there were many
luncheons between them. By reckoning eight to nine
such meals daily, (and beyond doubt there were that
number), we reach again the first estimate of 70 to 90
grains of sugar as the daily ration. About this amount
of sugar is held by a common tea-spoon when level full;
such a spoon will hold from 110 to 120 minims of
water, whereas one of those heir-looms, a grand-
mother's tea-spoon, is the measure of the standard tea-
spoonful of 60 minims. Referring then to the standard
measure, the bird would be said to eat two tea-spoon-
fuls of sugar daily. An ordinary cube of loaf sugar
contains the equivalent of this amount.

Reflecting upon the bulk consumed by so small a
creature, one naturally desires to know the weight of
a Hummingbird. A little boy brought to us the body
of a male, that had been shut into a machine shed,
where its death may have resulted from starvation.
Its weight was 33 grains. Naturalists in early days
were vexed by the same question as is shown by a
quotation given by Mr. Ridgway in his book on Hummingbirds. It is from "Philosophical Transactions,"
1693, by Nehemiah Grew, who wrote: "I did weigh
one (in those parts) as soon as ever it was kill'd whose
weight was the tenth part of an Ounce *Avoirdupoise.*"
From these weights one makes the deduction that our
Hummingbirds are accustomed to eat of sugar twice
their own weight daily. If human adults ate of sugar
proportional amounts there would be required nearly
300 pounds of this saccharine food daily for the
average person.

No attempt has been made to tame the birds that
came to drink, yet one, perhaps two of them, became
bold enough to drink when a bottle was being filled;

while she thrust her bill into the empty receptacle a spoonful of syrup was frequently held touching the mouth of the bottle, but she did not learn to drink from the spoon. While drinking the tongue was extended about a quarter of an inch beyond the tip of the bill, and two or three drops were sipped before the bill was withdrawn. Once fifteen drops were taken with three insertions of the bill, and at another time the bird drank without the withdrawal of her bill for about the duration of a minute. At such times the bottle was free from ants; probably they were present when the drinking was done with numerous sips. Often a bird preferred to take her breakfast in courses, perching on a nearby dead twig for a minute or two between drinks.

During two of the seasons it was thought that some of the birds roosted on our place, appearing as they did very early, and making a long day for feasting and fighting. In other years the birds were seen to fly eastward at night and their morning arrivals were not so early. One June morning a bird was ready for her breakfast at four o'clock, and took her last drink at night just before the clock struck eight. On some August days there are records of their presence at break of day, in one case it was thirty-eight minutes before sunrise. They usually lingered a short time after sundown, drinking long and deeply before taking their evening departure.

The conviction that the same birds were returning to us summer after summer began to be felt at the beginning of the fourth season. On May 26 of that year the first Hummingbird appeared on the place. The next day the flowerless bottle No. 4 was put out, and in a few hours a bird was drinking from it. For the next three weeks she was seen drinking from this bottle on every day except two, but not in the middle of the day; then for two weeks she was missed, returning again on the first of July.

The history of the fifth season was similar, Hummingbirds having been seen on May 22, bottle No. 4 was staked out and filled for a few days. No bird coming to drink, the bottle-filling had been discontinued, when on June 6 a Hummingbird on suspending wings was seen searching this bottle; not finding syrup in it, she flew to the spot always occupied by the flowerpot holding the artificial flowers, when they were in place. Over this vacant spot she hovered an instant before flying away. On a few other June days a bird of this species was present, and on the 17th one was seen drinking, but her steady summer boarding did not begin until July 9. In the sixth spring the species arrived earlier than usual. No bottles were out on May 7 when a Hummingbird was seen hovering over the customary place for the artificial flowers. As quickly as possible these flowers were put out, but before they could be filled the bird was thrusting her bill into the tiger-lily. She came to drink on most of the days thereafter until June 9, also June 14, 15 and 24, and on July 1 and 2; but it was not until July 16 that she came for constant drinking.

These dry and dull details have been given in full because two theories were based on them. That the birds of former years have returned to be fed seems unquestionable from their searching at once flowerless bottle No. 4, and from the other evidences offered. Because the birds came in May and at intervals in June and July, before becoming steady boarders about the middle of July, seems to indicate that they nested two or three miles away, too far for daily trips after incubation began. The supposition that these nestings were in the woods is founded on the fact that in leaving the birds flew in that direction, also because they were never found about the trees of the four farm-yards that intervene between our place and the woods. That in two summers a mother Ruby-throat returned with her daughter was suggested by seeing on several occasions two birds drinking together from one bottle, a phenomenon that needs explanation when we consider the pugnacious disposition usually exhibited by one drinker toward another.

In further confirmation of the foregoing is the history of the feeding in 1913. Bottles No. 4 and No. 6 were set out on April 30. For two months and a half no Hummingbird visited them. It chanced on July 14 that the stick support of No. 4 was lying on the ground, leaving only No. 6 in position, when my sister saw a Hummingbird thrusting her bill into it. She hastened to fill this bottle, which was the first time it had ever been filled, and it lacked but eight days of two full years since it was first set out. Six days later I was in the orchard a hundred feet or more distant from the bottles, when a Hummingbird flew toward me and buzzed about my head as do no other birds except those that are fed. With greatly accelerated pulse I hurried to the house and filled the bottles. In exactly two minutes the Hummingbird was drinking from one of them; this was the first drinking witnessed in that year. It was one of my most thrilling experiences in bird study. Two marvelously long journeys of from one to two thousand miles each had this small sprite taken since last she had drunk from the bottles, yet she had not forgotten them, nor the one that fed her. She was quite prone to remind either of us when the bottles were empty by flying about our heads, wherever she chanced to find us, whether in the yard or in the street. Once having been long neglected, she nearly flew into my face as I opened the barn door to step out.

The last experiment made was that of flavoring one of the bottles of syrup with vanilla, and later with extract of lemon, to see if the birds showed preference for the plain syrup or for the flavored. Both kinds were served at the same time, and of both the birds drank, showing no choice that could be detected.

It may already have been surmised from the gender of the pronoun used that it is the female only of this species that has the "sweet tooth." Never once in the seven summers has a male Ruby-throat been seen near a bottle. The drinking birds have been examined long and critically, with binocular and without, in order to detect on some of the birds the identification marks of the young males, but without success; moreover, had young males been present they, too, would have been apt to return in later years. This absence of the males led to noting their scarcity in general, and to recording in note-book when and where a male at any time was seen. The entire number seen in the past five years has been six on our place and six elsewhere. It is impossible to do more than estimate the number of females that have been seen; but when it is remembered that on several days in two summers seven have been in sight at one time, it does not appear to be an over-estimate to place their number of twelve or fifteen for each year, or six times more of them than of the males.

The simple experiments herein described are such that they may be tried by anyone having a yard frequented by the Ruby-throat. If any one doubts that the female of this species will choose a saccharine diet, when it is available, let him continue the tests until convinced beyond cavil or a doubt. It is especially desirable that the experiments be made in proximity to the nesting birds in order to see if the mother will feed syrup to her nestlings. Sometimes our Catbirds and Brown Thrashers have come into the porch to the

cat's plate and taken his bread and milk for their nestlings. Upon this hint for needed aid I have put bread
soaked in milk on the fence railing for them, and they
have taken it also. It is reasonable to believe that in
like manner sweet benefactions proffered to a hard-
working Humming-bird mother might be acceptable
to her, and shared by her with her nestlings.

CHAPTER XVII

ARE BIRDS DECREASING IN NUMBERS? *

In replying to a query regarding the decrease of birds in recent years, a careful observer would be quite apt to say that many species are decreasing in numbers, while a few are increasing. Such would be my answer, based on memory impressions, as well as on daily written records. Within the past three years friends have signified their recognition of a keenly felt loss of certain birds, formerly common or abundant, speaking somewhat in this wise: "We seem to have lost our Bobolinks. In this entire summer I have seen a Bobolink only two or three times." While another asks, "Tell us what has become of the Bobolinks, Kingbirds, and Bluebirds? We used to see many of them by the roadside, but now they are seldom met." Such remarks have been made by elderly men, living in the counties of Winneshiek, Allamakee, and Clayton, which occupy the northeastern corner of Iowa. They are men who have known the fields and highways of the region for seventy years or thereabout. One object of this paper is to substantiate these impressions with figures taken from written records, kept daily, based on intensive observations, covering a score of years, and made on the same acres, whose natural conditions have changed very little in that period.

During the twenty years under consideration the changes in natural conditions, which have materially

* Read at the Second Nashville meeting of the Wilson Ornithological Club, December 31, 1927.
From 'The Wilson Bulletin', Vol. 40, No. 1, March, 1928.

affected our bird population, pale before the magnitude
of the changes that preceded them. Of these it may
be permitted to speak briefly. To Farmersburg Township, Clayton County, Iowa, my parents came upward
of eighty-two years ago, in May of 1845. Three, possibly four, homes preceded theirs, but these were built
in the shelter of the woods, whereas they located on
the treeless, trackless prairie wilderness, whose wide
expanse of wild grass was unbroken by any object. The
memories of their older children reach back seventy-
five years, but mine for only seventy years or a trifle
less, when many changes already had occurred. The
Wild Turkey, so abundant on the wooded banks of
rivers, had been exterminated before that day. Prairie
Chickens were still numerous, as were some other
ground-nesting species. The hosts of Passenger Pigeons
still passed in migration, while as late as 1865 the
honking of wild geese, flying northward, caused sleep-
less nights for a young man, recently arrived from the
East. To have kept for sixty years a record of the
coming and rate of increase of bird species would have
been a most desirable achievement. Instead of that I
was sent from home to school in 1869, and for the
next twenty-six years was absent except for brief intervals. For a few years after residence in the family
home was resumed other duties claimed my attention.

The spot where my bird studies have been conducted
became the family home in 1866. It was situated on
the southern edge of a small, frontier village, that the
coming railroads did not approach; consequently it
shared the fate of many another hamlet similarly situated. Our home dooryard contains about an acre of
land. The changes it has undergone in sixty-one years
are characteristic of many prairie localities and have
close connection with the bird species displaced and
those attracted to it. The first change on grass covered

prairie soil, which held no attraction except for ground nesting birds, was the building of house and barn. The barn has provided nest sites for seven species of birds. The next change came with the growth of trees, shrubbery, and berry bushes; the last, important change has been due to lack of pruning and to riotous thickets for the planting of which the birds brought the seeds. The elderberry is the most attractive of these and its bushels of berries find favor in the sight of fall migrants. Drawn by bird-planted bushes, there have come within the past half dozen years to nest the Traill's Flycatcher, Indigo Bunting, Cedar Waxwing and Yellow Warbler. Of the forty species of birds, known to have nested on our premises within twenty-two years, thirty-six of them have nested within the limits of the dooryard. Probably thirteen instead of forty would have numbered the breeding species had the land remained in its original wild state.

The duration of the period whose figures are here discussed is from 1907 to 1927, inclusive, which makes twenty-one years, but I was absent the whole of 1914 to the middle of September, therefore no account is made of that year. There have been other long absences, but these occurred late in the fall months, mainly after migration had ended, or in the winter. There have been short breaks in the summer records, which have not seriously affected the general averages.

A daily record of the birds seen or heard has been kept throughout the year. From about November 12 to nearly the same date in March rarely are other than resident birds to be seen. These are seen from the windows. For the remaining 245 days of the year to window observations is added the list of birds found on a walk over our own acres and along the highway for a distance of a half mile or more, occasionally less. On this walk approximately a hundred acres can be viewed with binoculars for the identification of the larger species and the smaller ones near at hand. The time given to this counting of species would average two hours a day for the greater part of eight months. Shorter hours are offset by the time given on days, when nearly the entire time is devoted to watching the migrating hosts. Since 1905 there have been identified on or from our land 162 species of birds. The largest number in one day was 52. Out of this total of 162 species the annual lists show that from 92 to 109 species are recognized yearly. The records for thirteen years of nearly unbroken observations give an annual average of 103 species, while the average for the past three years is 94 species only.

Even more deplorable than this decrease of species shown by the annual totals are the showings made by the median number of bird species daily present in the three months of June, July, and August, when the lists consist chiefly of breeding birds. The daily average for these three months in the four year periods 1909 to 1912, and 1917 to 1920 was 21 for each, but for the four years 1924 to 1927 inclusive, it was 17. In 1921 for June and July only it was 25 species; for the same months in 1927 the daily average shrank to 16 species. It should be noted here that the decrease of nine species in the breeding months names the same number shown in annual totals, when 94 species instead of 103 is the average. Any bird student, keeping records of this sort, ought to be able to answer, "It is death," to the question, "What has happened to our Kingbirds, Bobolinks, and Bluebirds?" and confidently add that equally with these have the Chipping Sparrows suffered; that beyond our ken have passed a large proportion of the Bob-whites, Prairie Horned Larks, Baltimore Orioles, Vesper Sparrows, Cliff Swallows, Barn Swallows, Warbling Vireos, Maryland Yellow-throats, and Short-billed Marsh Wrens, which until very recent years helped to make longer these daily lists. All are not yet extinct. To restore *some of them* to their former numbers is still possible, if mankind is willing and will act.

The next step will be to outline the status of certain species of the listed birds. In the fall of 1907 I built a rude blind for shelter, while observing rails and other marsh birds in a wet ravine about a hundred yards from our house. For a few years there had been a radical change in the occupant uses to which this bit of marshy land was put, also there had been a succession of wet seasons. Due to these causes the rails flourished in that spot. King Rails were seen on a few days, Virginia Rails were listed on fifty days of 1907 and the following year, and the Sora Rail on ninety-five days. In the spring of 1909 the King and the Virginia Rails were seen only a few times, but the Sora stayed and nested. It is believed that at least two pairs had nests. Our state geologists tell us that the water level in Iowa has fallen 15 feet in the past fifty years. Springs have dried up that formerly had fine flows of water. This happened to the marshy ravine that was the haunts of the rails. In succeeding years a few of them were seen, but in the past six years only the Sora has been listed, and it on only two occasions.

Numerically the Solitary Sandpiper does not seem to have suffered. Far different has been the fate of Wilson's Snipe. Formerly in migration it was seen in flocks, numbering from six to fifteen birds, on a dozen to twenty days of the year. Gradually its numbers fell to one or two individuals, until in the last two years not one was seen. The Upland Plover, formerly an abundant breeding species, is with us no more. A pair here in the summer of 1917 probably was nesting. Owing to crop rotations the Killdeer must change its location yearly, making it difficult to estimate its numbers; however, they do not seem to be greatly reduced in twenty years. In this neighborhood a few Prairie Chickens still survive, but now so far from our home that no longer can their booming be heard in spring. It is three years since the last one was listed.

Fortunately, most fortunately, our county's population is largely rural. Its villages are few and small; its largest one numbering less than 1700 inhabitants. This means that the county is quite free from that urban creature, who calls himself "a sportsman," whose pleasure it is to go forth with a gun and shoot such beautiful, beneficient creatures as the Bob-white. Twenty years ago it was a common bird, heard calling daily in summer, sometimes three or four cocks calling at once. For ten years its numbers held fairly well, then came winters of severe cold and drifting snow, after which Bob-white became very scarce. In the summer of 1918 it was heard only twice. Since then a slight increase in its numbers has been detected.

The so-called sportsman is absent, and I have yet to hear of farmers in this neighborhood shooting Bob-whites, but I have seen some of them show deep concern over injuries done to nesting birds by their plows and mowing machines. It is these implements that have worked destruction; these and the life-sustaining cow. If long ago everyone had become a vegetarian, leaving no one to demand veal, beef, pork, and mutton; if chemists had placed on the market synthetic butter, milk, cheese, and ice cream, the ground nesting birds would not have fared so badly.

The pasturing herds have been inimical to our wild flowers as well as to our birds. Long, long ago there perished a flower of transcendent loveliness; it was gone before we learned so much as its name. But the beauty of other flowers still glowed on all the hilltops.

These in turn vanished. In the tame grass now covering the hillsides may be seen numerous flowering plants,
but the plants are ragweed, thistles, and dock. Last
year the man, employed to cut roadside weeds, slashed
down every evening primrose, jewel-weed, and aster,
and left standing every burdock, thistle, and nettle,
that I passed on my daily walk.

The early settlers of this region planted deciduous
trees about their homes. About forty years ago the
general practice of planting evergreen trees for wind-
breaks began. Their growth has marked a great increase among the Bronzed Grackles. Before that the
Kingbirds were numerous. They seem to hold well
their own against all birds except the grackle. It and
the rare activities of some keeper of bees are the only
known causes for the great decrease of the Kingbirds.

Along with the Kingbirds some years ago the Bobolinks held a constant place on the daily bird lists. Both
species were marked present for seven days in the
week and thirty days in the month until their summer
season was over. Fifteen years ago while visiting a
cousin on his ranch in California he remarked to me,
"I don't know what I'd give to hear again the Bobolinks singing on the old farm in Iowa." Some of his
friends have said that his income is a million dollars
a year. This he declares is exaggeration. Whatever
the figure may be, it has not been lack of the price of
railroad fare that hindered his return in the months
when the Bobolinks sing. Unless he comes quickly all
the millions of the entire globe can not procure for
him in this locality one hour of music of the Bobolink.
Even now the absence of its song makes the world
seem dreary and when a song is heard the occasion is
marked for special recognition. In contrast with
former summers, when a grand chorus of song was
heard each day, in 1927 I heard a Bobolink sing on

four days only. In August the count of individuals in flocks, moving southward, proved that some other localities are more fortunate. To the rice growers on the Atlantic sea-board must be referred those people asking, "What has become of our Bobolinks?"

In 1907 the Red-winged Blackbird was the most abundant breeding species in our neighborhood. Seven of its nests were located on our premises with many more nearby. In the summer just past not seven pairs of these birds were seen on all the acres under my observations. Many dry summers in which farmers could mow the grass on low ground seem to explain the loss among redwings. A similar decline has attended the Meadowlarks. Here both the eastern form and its western cousin are breeding species. Formerly both the Redwinged Blackbird and the Meadowlark could be listed daily, now there is many a break in their records.

For the marked falling off in the numbers of the Baltimore Oriole thanks are due to the Screech Owl. In 1924 a pair nested in one of our maple trees and came daily to the feeding-stick for food. A most enjoyable sight and a brilliant combination of colors were afforded by a Red-headed Woodpecker together with both of the Orioles feeding on the stick at the same time. Later, after the mother Oriole was taken the father strove bravely to feed the three nestlings, but all fell victims to the foe.

Twenty-two of our native sparrow species have visited our home place. While speaking of sparrows let it be said that the English Sparrow has never been listed here, never counted among the birds, it is accounted a pest only, and is with us always. The numbers of our native sparrows *seen* in each migration season depends very much on whether the brook beds are dry or hold water and on what crops the three years crop rotation, practiced by my farmer neighbors, has brought to the brooksides. Enough of these cycles have passed to confirm the opinion that the hosts of visiting sparrows are less than formerly. Among the breeding Fringillidae the status of the Goldfinch alone remains unchanged. The Vesper Sparrow has appreciably decreased. The Dickcissel is always a variable summer resident, sometimes here, sometimes absent. Year after year the spacing of nesting Song Sparrows was the same; six or seven locations were claimed. In 1927 only three of these were occupied. Formerly the Chipping Sparrow was one of the birds to be found constantly on the daily lists. It has not been learned if a foot disease, afflicting the species elsewhere, does so here. But it is known that the increase of its destructive arch-enemies, the Bronzed Grackle and the House Wren, is sufficient to explain its present scarcity.

Any one who has been called upon to write the obituary of a dear, young friend, a friend beautiful and graceful of form, whose coming was like the breath of spring, whose beneficent life blessed mankind and harmed him not, then that person knows full well the emotions felt by any of us when speaking of the swallows—the swallows that were the chief bird joys of our childhood, the Cliff Swallows that built their homes three deep under the eaves of the barns, and the Barn Swallows that built numerous nests within. Hundreds of swallows skimmed the air, where scarcely one can now be found. Last spring, like a token out of the blue, came a flock of Cliff Swallows to the home of a near neighbor. They built twenty-seven nests, almost all of which English Sparrows occupied at once.

In connection with other bird losses it seems fitting to recall the great catastrophe that befell the warblers in May of 1907. Not only warblers, but also vireos, and some of the flycatchers died from lack of food, accompanied by freezing weather. A large portion of our warblers' range was not affected. The area on which warblers suffered death is estimated as upward of one hundred million of acres. In our dooryard of an acre sixteen dead warblers were found. Using this as a basis for computation, it has been said that millions of them perished. In the *Auk* for January, 1908, are two articles descriptive of the calamity, and a short account of it appeared in *Bird-Lore* (September-October, 1915).

It was a bereavement for bird students to have the beautiful family of warblers come so near extinction. If one bewailed the loss, he was sure to be told, "Mourn not! Comfort yourself with the thought of the short time taken by the Bluebirds to replenish their numbers, when nearly annihilated!" Naturally one would deem twenty years sufficient for warbler restoration. In spring migrations before 1907 no attempts were made to count the individuals of the great swarms of warblers that halted in search for food. For sake of later comparisons this was most unfortunate. However, it was estimated that fully one hundred warblers have visited our trees on some days. Over against this reasonable estimate are placed the recorded figures for twenty years, taken on the very same grounds, which were fully as attractive for warblers as they were prior to 1907. It was believed that warblers were not increasing, when a chart of the figures was made it showed that the family was decreasing. Both spring and fall migrations are counted. Only in 1915 did the warbler numbers exceed the beggarly few which came in 1908, directly following the year of the great death. In the entire spring of 1918 the total of eight species, containing twenty-three individuals, was no more than could have been found in one hour of the old days.

Facts so astonishing, so contrary to expectations and

experience, must have an explanation. Beyond doubt
the facts known to be true on one acre are true of the
millions of acres north of it. After the House Wrens
became established here Maryland Yellow-throats were
driven off. Not a warbler's nest had successful outcome until last summer, when the wrens having been
reduced to a minimum and all Cowbird eggs having
been removed from the nest a Yellow Warbler brought
off a brood.

The Bluebird is one of the greatest sufferers from
the evil nature of the House Wren. Not until about
ten years ago were the effects from the intensive breeding of these wrens felt here. Once more the proof-
telling figures show much. My daily records show that
in certain past years I enjoyed the presence of this
beautiful bird for such annual totals as 126 days, 132
days, 136 days, and 149 days. During all of last year
(1926) I saw the Bluebird on four days only, and
this year on eleven days. What does this mean?
Nothing less than that I am being wronged, defrauded,
cheated out of my rights to the pursuit of happiness by
the maintainers of wren boxes to the north of me.

Among the birds here whose numbers have not
changed appreciably of late may be named the Chimney
Swift, Phoebe, Blue Jay, Crow, Cowbird, Brown
Thrasher, Robin and five species of woodpeckers. I
know of no family of birds capable of affording specta-
tors so much entertainment as can the woodpeckers.
The Flicker especially deserves a volume for his history. Although a model of fatherhood, he is mated to
a fickle female, far too often ready to desert him, leaving her nestlings to starve, while she goes off with
another male. His trials are enough without the
addition of a foreign foe.

The latter part of 1913 and until mid-August of the
next year I spent in the Old World, seeing a little of

twenty countries. From the first of June onward my itinerary was planned for seeing birds. The sight of a woodpecker was very rare, marking a red-letter day on the bird lists, and there were but three of them. The first was in January, when a Golden-backed Woodpecker was seen in Delhi, India; the other two were in July in which a Lesser Spotted Woodpecker was seen in the environs of Honefos, Norway, and later a Green Woodpecker was seen in a public park of Stockholm, Sweden. This serious dearth of Old World woodpeckers lacked explanation until a few American ornithologists reported instances of Starlings driving Flickers from their holes and usurping the same. The unchecked spread of the Starling seems to repeat a tragedy, similar to the spreading of the English Sparrow with almost nothing being done to save our valuable native birds. Therefore it is gratifying to hear from one man in North America who is doing some of this protection. Mr. John B. Lewis of Lawrenceville, Virginia, has related his difficulties in protecting one Flicker's home. "In the last two years the Starlings have given me no little trouble. Last spring they would have taken possession of all the nest boxes and holes on the place, had I not made free use of a shot gun. More than twenty were killed in about two weeks, before they gave up and quit the premises. Seven were shot off one flicker house in three days."

In my restricted field of observation five bird species have been increasing. Three of them are among the most destructive and undesirable of our bird citizens. Favoring the increase of Screech Owls has been the advantages offered by many woodpecker holes and untenanted buildings, together with immunity from the shot gun. A close study of their habits brings the conclusion that the farther away are all Screech Owls the better it is for all desirable birds.

The coming in abundance of the Bronzed Grackle has been mentioned and the part it plays in the reduction of Kingbirds and Chipping Sparrows. The farmers like to see the grackle following the plow, picking up the larvae of the May beetle, known as the white grub worm, which destroys their corn. But its good deeds do not seem to counter-balance its harm to other birds.

Among the many melancholy events in a bird history covering a score of years one delightful occurrence stands in bright relief. It was the coming of the Cardinal on its northward advance. Its first appearance in this area was in 1909, and its second visit came six years later. Since 1918 it has been a regular winter boarder, showing in spring a desire to stay for nesting, but is driven off by the Brown Thrashers.

Not so welcome has been the increase of Catbirds. They were plentiful enough before their ranks were augmented. Desirable bushes in which to build nests and an abundant food supply have attracted them. Their gluttony for berries surpasses that of other birds. However great the supply of berries, none is left for us except those under covers, protecting them from Catbirds, Brown Thrashers and Robins.

Here House Wrens have increased immensely in twenty years. Nothing less could be expected, when across the entire continent school children are urged to build and put in place boxes for wrens. A fad or fashion has been started more deadly to many birds than the fashion of wearing bird feathers on women's hats. The disaster following that fashion was not so much the fault of ignorant women as it was the market hunters who killed birds for gain. The disaster following the wren house craze is not the fault of innocent children, but is the criminal fault of those fostering for gain the business of wren house making. They include various classes of teachers and leaders who are selling the birthright lives of many kinds of birds for their own mess of pottage. They have heard the truthful warnings of many who *know* that in summer the House Wren is a constant menace to several species of birds—a menace that is spelling destruction to vanishing birds, greatly needing protection.

Some of us in a few short years have seen great changes in natural surroundings. Having seen the vanishing of some birds from a locality, and other birds take their places; having seen how easily the English Sparrow displaced the beautiful swallows, we can believe that quite as readily the Starling can displace the woodpeckers; moreover, on a small area we have seen the House Wren completely displace warblers and the Bluebird. Those who can lift their eyes to hills once beautiful with wild flowers and now see there naught but ugly weeds realize how easily in nature work the laws of displacement, and how easily good birds are displaced by bad ones.

CHAPTER XVIII

AT THE SIGN OF THE
NORTHERN FLICKER *

The apartment building that displays flicker-signs all the year around is our barn. These signs consist of the holes chiseled through the siding; the marks left by the birds' muddy toes and tails, and the splashes of gastric juice which sometimes adhere to the walls of the barn for a distance of 2 feet above and 7 feet below the hole, and remain many weeks before they are washed off by the rain.

The date of the making of the first hole has not been kept, but as long ago as 1897 a pair of Flickers nested in the space into which this hole opens, a space 4 by 15 by 23 inches formed by a board parallel to the rafters, nailed to the studding which kept the hay back from the wall of the barn. For purposes of observation it was covered with a movable board which had a peep-hole in it. In this accidentally formed cavity three years out of four Flickers raised their young, but in the spring of 1903 there came a frantic female that would not settle in the old nesting place in the east end until the pair had drilled two other holes, one in the west end, and the other in the south side of the barn. Back of each of these new holes a box was placed in the following spring, but these proved too shallow to suit the birds for other than roosting places. Early in 1908 the first boxes were replaced by boxes

* From 'The Wilson Bulletin', Vol. 22, Nos. 3-4, September-December. 1910.

made to hold one hundred cakes of that fair emblem of civilization—soap. These offer a nest room 8 by 12 inches on the bottom and 18 inches deep. In the top of each box a hole was made for observations, and a few inches from the bottom a hole large enough to withdraw the hand while it held a well-grown nestling. This hand-hole was closed by a trap-door, and the bottom of the nest was covered with excelsior, into which sawdust was firmly packed.

One male Flicker has been the subject of study for four summers. The conviction that it is the same bird each season is founded on the facts of his increasing tameness year after year, his unhesitating occupancy of the barn, and the shape of his almost circular malar stripes. On the fifteenth of April, 1908, he had taken possession of the south box, and was calling, drumming and practicing flicker-antics in the presence of a female, believed to be his mate. That he with his spacious, ready-furnished apartment may have proved unusually attractive to the female heart is an incident, which ought not to be too severely condemned by a race of beings among whom male creation is often courted for no superior reasons. Whatever were the underlying motives, it is certain that by the twenty-fourth of the month two females were conducting an ardent competitive courtship which lasted five or six days. It was impossible to detect any new methods in their manner of wooing. There were the same struttings and spreading of feathers, the same dancing, bobbing and bowing that is practiced by the males in a similar situation.

On the evening of April 30, the rivalry having ended, a female was found roosting in the west box, two nights later the male was there. On half of the remaining nights before the first egg was laid the female roosted in the west box while the male occupied the south one. A burning question arose as to which box would be used for breeding purposes. The south one was much better located for human observations, also for bird comfort, it being in the shade of tall maples and a walnut tree. Both holes had been used by the birds during the courting season, and in both boxes the excelsior had been torn up and carried out, therefore the finding of an egg in the south box on the morning of May 15 was a pleasurable occasion.

From what has been related it easily may be seen that the male bird chose the nesting place, and persuaded his mate to lay her eggs there, even when she was inclined to nest elsewhere, and when she had a box quite as good as his.

The preliminaries to nesting this season differed little from those of last. Again the male suffered a dual courtship, but it lasted one day only. Three days thereafter his mate cleaned house although the sawdust was fresh and needed not to be cast out. Again there was a seeming indecision as to choice of box for nesting, and again on May 15 the first egg was laid in the south box. This made the third year when laying had commenced on that date. On other seasons the date had been a little earlier, and once a month later.

Before the eggs were laid in 1908, the male roosted part of the time in the south hole, and the female part of the time in the west hole. While the eggs were being laid, and before incubation began, the male roosted in the box with the eggs. After that, incubation or the brooding of the young at night was performed mainly by the male, but on several nights the female took these tasks, and he went to lodge in the west box, where she generally, but not always, spent her nights. This nocturnal interchange of duties appears to be somewhat unusual. In 1909 the order of things was changed a trifle. The male bird began roosting in the south box on the evening of April 17, and spent every night there until that of June 23, sixty-seven nights in all. With the exception of five nights, the female was a regular occupant of the west box from April 24 to June 3, after which she spent a few nights in the east hole. This desertion of her lodging place may have been caused by unwelcome visits made there by Screech Owls. For it was in this west box on April 5 that a Screech Owl was found sitting on four fresh eggs. This nesting was ruined by a violent wind storm, yet it was believed that the owls occasionally returned to their chosen quarters.

It may be in place to say a few words regarding the popular conception of a Flicker's nest. It is usually described as "a hot, dark hole." The nest in the hollow tree cannot be vastly different from that in the barn. There it is hot when it is hot elsewhere, and it is cold when it is cold elsewhere, even when it is windy outside enough of the breeze enters to stir the feathers on the bird's back. But the worst misapprehension exists regarding the darkness in the nest. It is surprising how much light enters through a hole 2½ inches in diameter. In the case of the south hole in our barn it lights the box sufficiently in the daytime for one to read a newspaper spread on the bottom, when the eye is at the customary distance of about 22 inches.

The number of eggs laid in these barn nests has been from seven to nine, with generally one to three infertile. They were deposited on the hay in the old nest, on the level surface of the sawdust in the new without any effort to hollow out a place for them. Beginning with the laying of the first egg, it is the custom for one of the pair to remain in the hole as a guard for the jewel-like treasures that lie there. A lapse in this guardianship duty must have occurred some time in the day of May 16 last, for an enemy entered and destroyed the two eggs of the nest. Circumstantial evidence pointed to a pair of Red-headed Woodpeckers that in their search for a nesting-place were acting like beings possessed by an evil spirit. The next morning the distressed female Flicker flew about as if seeking a new nest. Her mate sitting in the south hole, called to her, evidently coaxing her to return to the old place, which she did.

A study of the growth of the young by weight has included the weighing and the marking of the eggs in the order in which they were laid. The usual time for depositing the eggs in the nest appears to be the hour between five and six o'clock in the morning. The first exact data was obtained May 20, 1908, when the sixth egg was laid at five o'clock and forty-eight minutes. It was five o'clock and eighteen minutes on May 22 of this year when the sixth egg of the new series was laid, and the seventh was on the following morning at five o'clock and forty-nine minutes. The marking of this seventh egg had been postponed until four o'clock in the afternoon when a little surprise was in store. Beside it lay the eighth egg left there sometime between the hours of eleven and four o'clock. It made the identification of the seventh egg impossible so the two were marked as twins. The weight of one of these eggs was a trifle in excess of that of any of the others, and the weight of the other twin was above the average. Before six o'clock the next morning the ninth egg of the new series—the eleventh one of all—had been deposited. At this juncture a message summoned me to a distant state. My absence extended over the greater part of the time of incubation, which probably did not differ much in history from that of the nests of previous years from which I shall describe the nest activities of this period. I am greatly indebted to a friend, who in my absence visited the barn every evening and ascertained that incubation was performed by the male bird during all of the nights, while the female roosted in the west box every night except three.

By day the duties of incubation seem to be shared about equally between the two birds, who are close sitters, the eggs seldom being found alone. Of the length of the sittings no adequate record has been kept, but those lasting from one hour and a half to two hours have been noted. The bird that is returning to the nest announces its approach by a soft "wick-ah -wick" note, which the sitter answers as a rule, and at once takes its departure, flying past the mate that is hanging to the outside of the hole. It is contrary to Flicker etiquette for both of the pair to occupy the nest at the same time, and never but once have I seen one enter the hole until its mate had left. Then it was the male, who in his headlong haste, blundered in while the mother was feeding the young, and hurried her departure. In the years of close study of this species I have never seen anything that suggested the feeding of one mate by the other and I doubt very much if this is done. The incoming bird enters cautiously, turns, inspects the works of creation without, hangs an instant with one foot grasping the lower edge of the hole and the other the wall below, then with a thud it drops to the bottom of the nest, but never upon the eggs. To cover the eggs the bird goes to one side of them, straddles those nearest to it, then with a hitching motion moves along until all are covered. No matter how wet and muddy it is out of doors the eggs have never been soiled.

After the nesting took place on the sawdust in the south box, a new feature has been added to the routine of the nest. Before the bird covers the eggs or the young, whichever it chances to be, it eats some sawdust. The craving for sawdust seems to be limited to this period of the bird's life since no signs have been found to show that it eats any of the sawdust while it occupies the boxes before and after the nesting time. The amount eaten is considerable. That at one time the male ate three tablespoonfuls is deemed a modest estimate. An attempt to measure the amount both ate by a fresh supply daily showed the consumption of three or more handfuls. The sawdust came from sugar maple, white and red oak wood.

After the bird has arranged itself comfortably upon the eggs it goes to sleep. The female sleeps most frequently with her head turned until her bill rests among the feathers of her back. The male sometimes takes this position but not often. He sleeps with his neck flexed until his bill touches one wing, or with his head straight forward and turned down until it rests on the crown, or, the favorite position of all, with his head lying flat upon the bottom of the nest, thus making as fine a "picture of calm content as mortal ever saw."

From some former nests it had been learned that sometimes the eggs hatched in nine days, but more frequently in ten days after the laying of the last egg. On May 20, 1908, the sixth egg was seen to have been laid at five o'clock and forty-eight minutes. Incubation began that day. On the morning of June 1, the eggs were hatching; four tiny Flickers were squirming in the nest, and as the father raised himself into a standing position, one of the remaining eggs broke slowly open and another Flicker kicked itself into the world. It was a moment thrilling with interest when bird and shell were lifted from the nest, and the shell was found to bear the number six. The hour was nine o'clock and forty minutes. The exact time for incubation had been twelve days, three hours and fifty-two minutes. The seventh egg hatched four hours later, making its period of incubation eleven days and eight hours nearly.

I was anxious to be beside the Flicker's box when their eggs hatched this year. Two periods for incubation had now been furnished, nine days and ten days from the date of the laying of the last egg. Therefore my return was planned for June 2. During the thirty-six hours that the iron horse bore two of us swiftly homeward, crossing and recrossing our longest rivers, and rushing over our most beautiful plains, one question kept recurring with insistent frequency: Was there danger in this case that the period might be shorter than ten days? If so, we should be too late for part of the hatching at least. When at length the Sign of the Northern Flicker had been reached, one peep into the nest revealed the facts that all nine eggs were safe, and dark with the embryos of the living birds.

The next morning being the tenth one from the date when the last egg was laid, and the eleventh from the time incubation began, a very early stand was taken beside the nesting box, but it was not until five o'clock and forty-two minutes that the occupant of egg No. 1 was sprawling in the nest. Three hours later the shells of eggs No. 2 and No. 3 were chipped, but the bird in No. 2, as well as that in No. 4, died in the shell after it had been pierced. The bird from the third egg was hatched at ten o'clock and two minutes, and the one from the fifth egg at ten o'clock and twenty-five minutes. At half-past one in the afternoon a shell that proved to be No. 6 broke open. This was the egg that was laid on May 22 at five o'clock and eighteen minutes, hence its period of incubation had been twelve days, eight hours and twelve minutes, while that of the sixth egg of the previous year had been twelve days, three hours and fifty-two minutes. Although the shell of one of the twin eggs was chipped several hours before dark, both of these eggs were hatched in the night, and the ninth or last egg at ten o'clock and forty-eight minutes on the following day, making its period of incubation eleven days and five hours, while eleven days and eight hours had been the period for the last egg of the clutch of the preceeding year. Roughly speaking, then, the time that our Flickers take for incubation is from eleven to twelve days.

The pellucid color of the newly hatched Flicker resembles that of freshly sun-burned human skin, but so translucent is the nestling's skin that immediately after a feeding one can see the line of ants that stretches down the bird's throat and remains in view two or three minutes before passing onward. This may be witnessed for several days while the skin assumes a coarser red, until it begins to thicken and become a bluish hue, before the appearance of the pin-feathers. These may be detected under the skin on the fifth day at the same time that bristle-like projections about one-sixteenth of an inch long announce the coming of the rectrices and remiges.

Until the young are about eleven days old, they lie in a circle in the nest, their long necks stretched over each other, then for nearly a week they press against the side of the nest. At seventeen or eighteen days of age, their claws having acquired a needle-like sharpness, they begin to cling to the wall of the nest, and when three weeks old they are able to climb to the hole and be fed while the parent hangs outside.

Although the eyes of the nestlings are not open until they are ten days old, yet these organs are by no means dormant. An easy proof of this is made by placing the hand noiselessly over the entrance hole when they are no more than three or four days old, and are lying apparently asleep; up comes every head and they beg for food; getting none they soon sleep, when the experiment may be repeated, gaining from the young the same response that is given when a parent darkens the hole.

That cry of the young which is so often described as a hissing sound, begins very soon after they are hatched. At first exceedingly faint it soon grows stronger and still stronger, and is uttered day and night for two weeks. A parent upon taking its place to brood these wailing nestlings, begins to croon a lullaby and continues this musical murmur until it falls asleep, which often is quite soon. It has no effect in lessening the noise of the youngsters, yet the parent faithfully renders its cradle song until the young cease to make this noise which is about the time they begin to show fear. Of other cries that they make there is the chuckling noise uttered when the little one is in the act of seizing the food-bearing bill, and there is a cry that sounds like a whine. Still another one is a note of alarm given when the young are disturbed by some such thing as the opening of the trap door. This uttered in unison has a very theatrical effect strongly suggesting the chorus of the stage. After they have commenced to move about freely in the nest, they make much of the time a pleasant sound like a chatter or quack, as if talking to each other. And lastly comes the grown-up Flicker "pe-ap," which they begin to call as soon as they climb to the hole. As one sits in the hole it appears the personification of juvenile impudence shouting its mandatory call. A change may be detected in the accent of this note after a feeding, when the fellow, that has received little or nothing having gained the hole, hurls after the retiring parent a yelp that sounds truly derisive.

This arrival at the entrance hole works a decided change in the young Flicker; he utters for the first time a call of his adult years, and he shows pugnacity remarkable because of its contrast with his earlier and later peaceful disposition. The versifier who wrote

"Birds in their nest agree;
And 'tis a shameful sight,
When children of one family
Fall out and chide and fight."

evidently was not familiar with the inside of a Flicker's nest, where they fight like little demons at times. Some broods are much more quarelsome than others. Their battle-ground is in the vicinity of the hole. The one in possession of the hole maintains his supremacy there by occasional withdrawals of his head from the hole in order to deliver vigorous blows on the heads of all within his reach, causing them to shrink downward. This is the case with the stronger ones, the weaker ones frequently are driven from the vantage place. When the hole is large enough for two to thrust out their heads together, they draw within after the serving of a meal and fight furiously, while a waiting third may slip up and gain the coveted hole. But all their fighting days seem to be confined to a few in the fourth week of their lives.

They have other occupations besides fighting during the last ten or twelve days spent in the nest. Preening themselves comes first, immediately followed by the amusement of running out their long tongues. This organ is extended the length of an inch and a half from the tip of the bill which seems extreme for such small birds. It is run over the wall of the nest, through each others feathers, or over a hand introduced into the box. The tongue is extended straight out from the bill, and the withdrawal is straight backward at times, but at other times it is whipped around almost at right angles to the bill, then disappears like a flash. They peck good-naturedly at each other and at their own toes; they hammer with the point of the bill, and of course they sleep much of the time either on the bottom of the nest or clinging to its walls. In sleep the head rests in various positions; when it is turned backward one can see exactly where the bill is placed; on these half fledged little creatures there is a naked strip between the feathers of the dorsal tract and those growing on the wing, upon this naked surface the bill rests, hence not under the wing but back of it—*parapternum,* beside the wing, describes it.

In 1909 the eggs, when fresh, weighed from 106 to 111 grains, and the same eggs just before they were hatched weighed from 91 to 96 grains. The young birds freed from the shells weighed from 83 to 85 grains. The hour for hatching was reckoned from the time an egg burst open; the rest of the act of exclusion from the shell took place either in my hand or in the weighing bag, hence there was no chance for the nestling to receive food before the first weighing. The first little Flicker was not fed until it was two hours and twenty-two minutes old, then the mother inserting her bill very, very gently fed it until its weight had increased 3 grains.

In very early life a meal is served to baby Flicker with many insertions of the parent's bill, as many as thirty-four have been counted, but from eight to twenty are the orinary number, decreasing to three or four before the young leave the nest. A record made during a continuous watch of six hours and thirty-two minutes shows that each parent fed five times; that the father delivered his supply with eighty-two insertions of the bill, while the mother used but forty-one. Probably the father brought more food since on every count he proved himself the more devoted parent. In grasping the bill the point of the youngster's bill is at right

angles with that of the parent's, thus the opening between the food-bearing mandibles is covered after the
young have attained a few days of age, and any over-
dropping of food is prevented. This accident frequently
happens in the early days of the nest, then the mussed-
up ants that fall are carefully picked up by the frugal
parent when the feeding is over.

Those persons, who have watched and weighed birds
from the hour of their hatching, realize what an advantage is held by the first-born. The few meals it
receives in advance of the others give it a start that
makes it stronger, its neck longer, and its mouth wider,
so that it easily holds the lead in the race for food.
This great advantage may be seen by comparing the
daily gain of the oldest Flicker with that made by the
others in the record for 1908, which is of nest life
normal in all respects.

This record shows that the increase in the average
weights is upward of 100 grains per day for the first
eleven or twelve days, after that from 25 to 40 grains
daily. All my records show that there is a period of
four or five days somewhere between the thirteenth
and twenty-second day when there is little increase, or
sometimes a decrease in weights for a few days. Several other species, whose growth by weight has been
studied, have furnished similar examples, and as this
period of very slight increase, or possibly decrease in
weight occurs not far from the time the nestlings begin
to show fear, and their wing-feathers burst from
enclosing sheaths, it is probable that three points of
interest center about this period of their lives.

Although Flickers remain in the nest much longer
than many of our common birds, and their rate of
growth is very fast at first, yet the scales show that
this growth is not proportionately very much greater
than that of some other birds. Taking the following

species on the ninth day of their lives, we may find that
the Flicker weighs twelve times as much as it did when
hatched. Phoebe and Red-winged Blackbird have each
increased their weight ten times, the Song Sparrow and
Catbird eight times, while the Mourning Dove weighs
but seven and a half times its first weight.

Numerous attempts have been made to ascertain
the amount of food brought to the nest for one meal.
The young were all removed from the nest except one
hungry fellow that was weighed just before and after
the visit of the parent. The increase in weight must
have been that of the dinner just delivered. Experiments show that to a nestling weighing 743 grains was
given a breakfast that weighed 76 grains, to one weighing 1430 grains a dinner of 118 grains, and to another
that tipped the scales at 1530 grains a supper of 103
grains. Probably the weight of the average load is not
far from 100 grains.

The number of daily visits increases with the age
of the nestling from about ten on the first day to four
or five times that number later. Six or seven meals
may be served within an early hour, as many as four
arriving within seventeen minutes, while at other times
nearly an hour may intervene between two visits.
When the young were eighteen days old, during a
watch of four and one-half hours, twenty-five meals
were given to five nestlings that wore distinguishing
marks. Three of these are positively known to have
received five meals apiece, and two received four apiece,
if the two undetermined feedings went to the latter
pair, then each one was fed at the rate of one meal
every fifty-four minutes. On the following day a count
was made of meals given during four hours, which
numbered twenty-two. At this age the young Flickers
every hour partake of food to the amount of one-
sixteenth of their own weight, or in one day consume

their full weight of food, yet the table of growth shows that it does not add to their weight to any noticeable extent.

In delivering the food the parents give Scripture measure, yet the young are never too full for utterance. With the food literally hanging over the edges of their bills they clamor for more until the parent leaves the hole. From this exposed food there comes a strong odor that fills the box and penetrates to the nostrils of the observer for three or four minutes after the feeding is over. The odor is not a disagreeable one, but strongly reminds us of that of a slightly over-ripe orange. It remains for the entomologist to tell us if this is the aroma of emmet jam. The filled-up fledgling slowly slips down to the bottom of the nest, there to sleep for a half hour or more; but before tranquility is restored to the nest there is a violent shaking of wings.

The subject of the cleaning of the nest would not be discussed here at length if it had not long been somewhat of a mystery to many, and if Flickers had not often been called very untidy house-keepers. The fact is they are very solicitous to keep a cleanly nest. Like many other altrical birds, the Flicker eats the excrements for several days, generally for nine or ten days, then it begins to carry them out after feeding, often going out three times with the dejecta before settling down to brood. If none of these are lying in the nest when the parent enters, it begins after the feeding to solicit them. This is done by biting the heel joints sometimes, but more often the fleshy protuberance that bears that budding promise of the tail. That this nagging is no gentle measure may be judged from the way the nestling cries and tries to wriggle out of reach, for the parent is not content with three or four bites, but frequently inflicts as many as a dozen on one bird before it turns its attention to another. The victim of one parent's cleanly habit may receive the attention of the other parent in a very few minutes, and be worried until it yields a second excrement, then soon fall under the blows of the first parent again. Such triple importunities do occur, but not often. By such means the parents keep the nest scrupulously clean for three weeks.

The fecal matter is enclosed in a tough white sac that will withstand much rough handling without breaking. When the young are from fifteen to eighteen days of age the weight of these dejecta is the greatest. One of these weighed 146 grains, from a nestling of 1666 grains, another of 156 grains from a bird of 1908 grains, and another of 207 grains from a bird of 1828 grains. Statistics of this period of their lives show that each nestling is fed about once an hour, and the nest is cleaned for it once in two hours. When fledglings begin to move about the enclosing sac is no longer formed. With the Flicker it disappears gradually; from the time they commence to climb the excrements decrease in size to about 30 grains, and one or two are dropped by each fledgling in an hour. The parents struggle heroically with the new conditions, but nature is against them. By the time the young take possession of the entrance hole they cease entering the nest at any time. But the tidiness of the parents does not extend to the ridding of the nest of the egg-shells which are rarely carried out on the day of hatching; they may lie a week before they are taken out, or are broken into tiny fragments.

Until 1909 the only menace to young Flicker life was a plague of lice. An infested English Sparrows' nest had been routed from their nesting place shortly before a pair of Flickers settled there. They had reared a lusty brood to about their eleventh day, when the second generation of the plague, introduced by the sparrows, broke out. There were some chicken lice, but of chicken mites (*Dermanyssus gallinae*) there were myriads. Drastic measures were necessary: the nest was scalded with boiling water, then treated with a soap and kerosene emulsion. Daily the little Flickers were hand-picked for vermin, and dusted with sulphur until the plague was abated.

This year trouble began because of three very cool days when temperature did not rise above 55 degrees, and because there was a nestling twenty-nine hours younger than the eldest one. Flickers, like other birds feed more the young that receive the food most readily. The youngster that has the widest mouth, or can suck the hardest gets the lion's share. Jostled to one side, the baby of the brood soon became so weakened by the cold and the lack of food that it would fall over in its attempt to seize the parent's bill: before it could rise again perhaps the meal had been served. When it did secure the bill it was so weak it could not suck with a strong pull and was dropped by the parent in order to feed those that took the food with greater ease. From cold and starvation the baby died, aged four days.

The next morning one of the twins was passing through a similar experience. It was found very cold and straightened out in the rigor of death, but gasped a little when taken in the hand. It was carried into the house to the fire and warmed thoroughly; when returned to the nest it was too weak to hold the bill after grasping it, and fell back unnourished. Then it was that a human will rose up against what has been termed Providence, which in plainer English is often merely parental stupidity and indifference among mankind as well as among birds. Earthworms were dug, beheaded, and washed for the little starveling, for which it eagerly opened its mouth, but it could not swallow until the worm was started down its throat by means of the bent end of a wire hairpin. This was true of the strongest of the Flickers: they made no effort to swallow until the hairpin, to the length of an inch or more, had been thrust down their throats; upon this they would suck vigorously with a loud smacking noise; but even then it was an onerous task to feed them, for earthworms, even when decapitated, are very sensitive about the order of their going, and positively refuse to back down a young Flicker's throat.

This year the young of the brood were named from the color of the cotton string each wore upon its left foot as a distinguishing mark. Very briefly the history of raising little Redfoot from death's door is this: After a long hard struggle in the feeding of the first worms it was sufficiently nourished to be returned to the nest, still it stood slight chance in the contest against the stronger ones. In this disadvantage Grayfoot, the other twin, shared; therefore the other nestlings were frequently taken from the nest and fed earthworms giving the twins opportunities to gain the whole meal. Later a better scheme was devised; by introducing a hand into the nest Redfoot was held in readiness for the return of Father Flicker, and by offering Redfoot's mouth to him first, the little one received all it could take. From extra attention through six days Redfoot made such rapid growth that it was able thereafter to hold its own, and the figures of the record show that as far as weight is a requisite it went forth into the world as well prepared as any.

On the warm, pleasant day following that of the successful resuscitation of Redfoot, both twins had received extra feedings from the father, and could hold on to the bill like little leeches; after the daily weighing they were occupying the nest by themselves for a few minutes, when the mother came in. If alienists were called in to pass judgment upon what followed I am sure they would pronounce it a case of "brainstorm." Certainly it bordered on the extraordinary; probably there was a shock to the mother's nervous system caused by the absence of the rest of the brood, however it may have been she very roughly shook the twins about as they held tightly to her bill; then she stopped feeding, solicited an excrement, obtained and ate it, after which she began feeding again—an unheard of thing to do—then with Grayfoot hanging to her bill she dashed out of the nest. Possibly she was alarmed by some noise, but I heard none. On the preceding day mistaking her arrival for that of the father, I began to open the trap door whereupon she flew out like a flash. For the hapless little creature the ground in ever widening circles was searched fruitlessly during several hours, scarcely a leaf remaining unturned; if it was not killed by its fall to earth, it perished most miserably.

The study of former Flicker nests revealed the fact that it is the male bird that shows the fearlessness and devotion that we are wont to find more prominent in the mother in most species. Until the cases of starvation in the nest of 1909 occurred, great pains had been taken not to disturb the natural activities of the nest; only in taking out and returning the young at weighing time did any one so much as show a hand. At such times the father, eager to return to brooding, frequently came down and touched the hand. This year it was decided to let the hand touch him. To patting and stroking he fearlessly submitted although evidently not relishing it. He suffered the hand to poke under him in taking and returning the nestlings and finally he did not shrink from it when it held up one of the twins for him to feed. This so-called tameness, which more truly is the engulfment of fear by the overwhelming instinct to brood and care for the young, gradually disappeared, and by the time the young ceased to need brooding he was as timorous as before. His timidity, however, was far less than that of any other Flicker that has been a tenant of the barn.

Generally the sounds that aroused fear in this species were made by some one back of their nest, yet the bird always sought the hole and looked for the cause of alarm outside. After two seasons of experience with the five-fingered terror that entered the hand-hole so often, and removed their young, they failed to learn to look for any disturbance from that direction. Another illustration similar to this is the careful inspection of the hole before entering it at night; a Screech Owl or other enemy might be lurking there, and experiences through millions of generations, have created an instinct of caution akin to that racial instinct that leads human beings to search for the hidden enemy, the man under the bed.

It has already been mentioned that this year the male Flicker covered the eggs every night; he also stayed with the young every night until they were three weeks old, brooding all of them until nearly two weeks of age, when they began pressing their breasts against the side of the nest, and he could cover the tails of two or three only, after which for two or three nights he sat upon the bottom of the nest apart from the young; then for four nights he hung upon the wall of the nest near the hole; thereafter he stayed with them no more. The date of this desertion is coincident with the fledglings' attainment of the entrance hole, which is the time the parents begin to fail to keep the nest perfectly clean. The parents fed so late in the evening that it was often impossible to identify the brooding bird without the aid of a flash-light lantern; this did not disturb him and he sometimes slumbered on regardless of it.

Pronounced individual characteristics could be recognized in the fledglings; Blackfoot and Whitefoot were over-bearing little gluttons; Pink was the pert one of the brood; Blue was a spunky little creature, the hardest biter of all; Redfoot was timid and demure, perhaps the early ordeal of cold and hunger had a sobering effect on it. As models for drawing or painting the little Flickers are the best posers of any species I have tried. They have posed for their pictures from one to two hours on occasions when there has been scarcely a movement other than the winking of their eyes.

As the eggs hatched in the order in which they were laid, so the fledglings went forth in the order in which they were hatched; Blackfoot early in the morning of their twenty-sixth day, Whitefoot and Pink late that afternoon. The next day the father brought at least one meal to Blue and Redfoot, but most of the time they fasted. Late in the afternoon Blue flew from the nest, leaving Redfoot to spend the night alone.

The next morning Redfoot still clung to the hole, although good strong branches swung invitingly only 4 feet away. For two months and a half the Flickers' nest had claimed more than its share of attention. Of the twenty-five species that have been found nesting on our grounds, more than half of that number had nests there this year. Many of these were advantageous subjects for study, and were demanding attention on that morning of June 30 while the little Flicker timidly lingered. Somewhere in the tree-tops was Blue and the two answered call for call. The hand might still caress the form of the little bird as it hesitated to make the frightful plunge. Finally, at nine o'clock and eight minutes, standard time, there was a flash of feathers, light streamed through the erstwhile darkened hole, for the wilderness of green had enfolded little Redfoot.

Both Whitefoot and Blue were seen and identified on the mornings following their departure from the nest. For six days Redfoot remained in the tops of the maples; sometimes it could be heard crying for food, and sometimes a parent could be seen trying to coax it away. On the morning of July 5 both parents were seen to leave its neighborhood, and it soon flew to an old apple tree, then along a fence: this was its first excursion. Several times thereafter it was identified by means of its crimson badge. For a few weeks all was very quiet in Flicker-land. On July 22 weaning time must have been near at hand, when the parents appeared followed by three youngsters, and one begging for food was pecked a decided refusal by the mother.

On the nights of the eighth, ninth, tenth and thirteenth of August, a young Flicker roosted in the old nest box. On two nights in July and two in September the father occupied the west hole. Possibly it was the unusual dryness of the summer that caused him to desert his old lodging-place. I believe him to be the timid Flicker that began roosting in the west hole in August, 1906, but soon changed to the east hole: that he came again the next summer, and before the middle of July had cleared out a boxful of trash carried in by English Sparrows, but did not begin to roost there until August 3, then, excepting a few nights, was a regular lodger until September 29. By the end of that season he had become quite fearless.

Of all our birds the Flickers are the earliest to retire at night, sometimes going to their lodgings an hour before sundown, the customary time being about a half hour before sunset. Generally they go out soon after sunrise, but on cool autumn mornings they have been known to linger much longer. During a rainstorm in the middle of the day they have been seen to seek their apartments, also in fine weather they have been found there enjoying the seclusion thus afforded. It sounds like a simple matter to say that barring about two dozen nights, a certain Flicker roosted in the barn every night from April 19 to October 2, yet this ascertainment involved an examination of the holes from the outside once every evening for six months, sometimes three or four times if the visit be made too early; if too late then a loud clapping of the hands may be insufficient to wake the heavy sleeper, and a sharp blow on the barn wall or a continuous bombardment with any convenient missiles may be necessary to force the lodger to show himself. To examine the boxes from the inside too greatly disturbs the birds. Many unsuccessful attempts were made to see just where and how the Flicker roosted in the box; at last the fearless male furnished the much-sought opportunity. Not far from the hole he clung to the upper edge of the siding, and slept with his head turned backward, his bill resting in his interscapulars.

In the summer of 1908 three Flickers roosted in the barn; the one in the east hole was timid, making it difficult to learn of his movements; however, it is certain that he went to roost there at least half of the nights from July 12 to September 25. The next spring a bird of corresponding behavior returned to this hole on April 12 and continued his roost there for almost a month. The bird in the south hole was a regular lodger from the seventh of August to the first of October, excepting two nights when he was frightened away. The occupant of the west hole was the father of the brood raised in the south box, where he took lodgings on April 15 and stayed there the greater part of the time until the young ceased to need his care. This box was cleaned thoroughly as soon as the young had gone out, but apparently it was regarded as the nursery, and not as a sleeping apartment by this Flicker, who returned to his old quarters in the west end on the sixth of July, preferring it to the cooler place in the east end. On some hot evenings he must have found there a temperature of 100 degrees, the thermometer having shown a mark nine degrees higher two hours earlier. Before July 20 he had failed to come in on four nights, after that he came every night until that of October 2. He was there as usual on the evening of the first of October, whether he began his southward journey at some time in the night or at an earlier hour than he was accustomed to go out, no one can tell. He wore no tag, therefore gave no one a pretext for killing him; he returned in safety the following spring, and this, it is hoped, he may continue to do for many years to come.

Flickers in 1910

Some points of interest in the summer life of the Flicker, omitted from the preceding paper, together with a resume of the history of this species for 1910, are given in the following pages.

In this portion of northern Iowa the young Flickers meet with few destructive enemies and a goodly number go southward every autumn, yet there appears slight, if any increase, in their numbers when they return in the spring. To each of the old nest sites there returns a pair; these nests in my immediate neighborhood are about a quarter of a mile apart: outside of the villages every farm-yard, that has suitable trees, usually furnishes a home for a pair, but as there are only two or three farms upon a section of land the houses average about a half-mile apart. In placing themselves for the summer how large a space does a pair demand?

To provide more roosting places, also to see if more than one pair of Flickers could be induced to nest on our grounds the nest-boxes in the barn have been inceased from three to seven. Three springs ago a suitable box was nailed upon a willow tree that stands about 25 rods from the barn, and the following spring another was placed in my bird-blind, which is situated near the willow tree. When the Flickers returned in 1910 the last mentioned boxes were occupied by a nesting Screech Owl and her mate, thus once more reducing accommodations to the boxes in the barn, where, as hitherto, but one pair nested.

One determining factor, perhaps the principal one, in the spacing of their homes may be the area necessary for their food collection. The places they usually frequent for food are pasture lands and newly mown fields. With binoculars I have followed the flight of a parent Flicker to the barn from a pasture nearly a half-mile distant, while far too many ant-hills existed near at hand. This choice of open and closely cropped fields for feeding may be the chief influence that leads them to seek prairie homes, although thousands of wooded acres stretch along the Mississippi River, their western border being but two miles to the east of us. Besides our barn, the only known buildings in the neighborhood inhabited by this species are an ice house, used for nesting, upon a farm three miles distant, and the amphitheater on the county fair grounds, used for roosting, a quarter of a mile away.

The advent of the first Flicker in 1908 was on March 26: for the following spring it was on April 4, while this year it occurred on March 23, and eight days later three of them went to roost in the barn. Among them the tame old male could not be found; his last journey may have been the long one from which none return. It is hoped that he died full of years, as he certainly

did full of honor. The greatness of the debt of grati-
tude due him was not fully realized until the timidity
of his successor made it apparent. The wildness of this
bird precluded the former freedom of nest study: and
his offspring, either from heredity or example were
wilder than any brood of previous years.

The courting in 1910 was conducted by the males,
and was a very inconspicuous affair. The mother of the
nest is believed to be the same as that of last year. She
bore no distinguishing marks, but her familiarity with
the place and the readiness with which she took up her
roosting quarters in the old west box pointed to this
conclusion. The four new boxes had been placed in the
southwest corner of the barn, occupying a space that
might have been enclosed in a tree 2½ feet in diameter.
The entrances to two of the boxes were on the south
side and the others on the west. In the lower box upon
the south side roosted the male before the eggs were
laid. As has been related, the tame old male of recent
years was a masterful fellow and rather insisted that
the laying should be done in his box. This year the
eggs were deposited in the box of neither parent, but
in the lower one of the new boxes opening toward the
west—a box in which there had been made no demonstrations of choice before the laying began. Here the
male at once took up his abode and later performed the
usual duties of incubation and brooding.

The first egg was deposited on May 5, a date ten
days earlier than that of any year except 1906. On
the morning of May 9 the hour of deposition of the
fifth egg was six o'clock and ten minutes, that of the
sixth egg was five o'clock and fifty-four minutes on
May 10, and of the seventh was five o'clock and forty
minutes on the following morning. The morning the
eighth egg was laid the mother went to sleep several
times upon her nest, then sat outside the nest upon a

perch; thinking that the clutch had been completed, the watch was discontinued a few minutes after six o'clock. The next morning the nest was not visited until a late hour, hence it was not due to any known disquietude that the female neglected her own nest and laid her ninth egg in the box above, having its entrance 14 inches to the right and above her nest: there the egg was allowed to remain for nearly a month, when it was probably eaten by one of the pair.

Five of the eggs hatched upon May 22, making a period of nine days from the laying of the last egg, a shorter period than that of any previous nest except that of 1905. Since incubation of a somewhat inconstant nature begins upon the day the sixth egg is laid, it was a bit of good fortune that it was the female, instead of the timorous, complaining male, that was at home when the sixth egg broke open at two o'clock and eight minutes in the afternoon of May 22, making its period of incubation twelve days, eight hours and fourteen minutes, which was exactly two minutes longer than the incubation period for the sixth egg in 1909. The order of the hatching was irregular, the second egg being the fourth to hatch and the first one last.

The number of young reared in these barn nests has invariably been five or six. None died in the nest until 1909, infertile eggs reducing their number to the above figures. This year the last two Flickers hatched, lively little fellows that struggled hard for food, but apparently received none, died from starvation at the end of their second day. That the father was a poor forager is attested by the daily average of weights of the brood, which, during the latter portion of their nest-life, was lower than any previous records; nevertheless the young began to leave the nest when twenty-five days old, which is earlier than some broods leave. The smallest nestling lingered two days longer; its stay

might have been of still greater length if unintention-
ally it had not been frightened out of the nest about
noon of June 18.

Some seasons the parents take their young away
from the neighborhood as soon as possible, but in
others, as was the case this year, they remain constantly
about the place for several weeks until the family ties
are loosened. These ties do not appear to be entirely
broken during the rest of the summer, there being
times when apparently the whole family has a joyful
gathering on the roof of the barn, or in the top of a
dead willow tree. Again just before their hour for
going to roost, four or five of them, having found a
luxurious bed of dust, disport themselves therein with
evidently as keen enjoyment as a duck finds in water.
Flickers, like other members of the Woodpecker family, have little use for water. During many hours, all
of which taken together would amount to weeks, I
have watched from a blind a pool of water much
frequented by the birds for drinking and bathing purposes. Near it stands the dead willow visited daily
by Red-headed Woodpeckers and Flickers; there the
former have never been seen to drink, and the latter
on two occasions only. The first time it was the tame
old male that backed down a fence post to the surface
of the water and drank while clinging to the post.

Aside from occasional rather curious exhibitions of
courtship, the late summer interests in the Flicker
center about his food habits, his moult, and his roosting. All seven boxes in the barn have been used for
roosting purposes this year, only five, however, at one
time. For the first time a female has had a chance to
occupy a box after the nesting season was over: formerly she was driven out by the males. In its summer
roosts the Flicker is one of the most immaculate of
lodgers. When he leaves for the south after several

months of occupancy of a box, no droppings of any kind can be found there except some of his moulted feathers, remaining as little tokens of the excellent bird that spends just half of the year as a sharer of our home. But in the nesting boxes some signs of the Flicker's inhabitancy are permanent: these are the places hewed by their chiseling bills. In the last box used this was very slight; in the south box where they nested for two seasons a hole as large as a half dollar was made through the half-inch boards, which would have formed an opening into the barn if it had not been for the batten back of it. It is in the old east hole occupied for so many years that this hacking is most prominent. Below the entrance hole the siding of the barn in places has been hollowed out to half its original thickness, and the board parallel to the rafters, that helped form the cavity, has been cut half way through in that portion of it that is opposite the hole. Evidently this was done to enlarge the space; the other cuttings probably are the result of the bird's natural tendency to enlarge its nesting chamber while sitting, or it may originate from the bird's habit of hammering with its bill at such times. This hammering, which is often heard before the eggs are laid, seems to be a call, and when done while the bird is incubating, it may be for the same purpose, since it appears to be indulged in toward the close of a long sitting, when the bird shows signs of restlessness by frequently going to the hole to look out.

A BIBLIOGRAPHY OF THE
PUBLISHED WRITINGS OF
ALTHEA R. SHERMAN *

1905. Some Observations at Weedseed Inn. Wilson Bull., 17 (1) : 1-4.

1906. My Neighbors' Homes in Clayton County, Iowa. Wilson Bull., 18 (3) : 81-83.
Decrease of Icteridae in North-eastern Iowa. Wilson Bull., 18 (4) : 134.

1907. Another Provident Melanerpes erythrocephalus. Wilson Bull., 19 (2) : 72.

1908. The "Farthest North" Record of the Cardinal in Iowa. Wilson Bull., 20 (2) : 102.
August Notes from a Watering Place. Wilson Bull., 20 (3) : 146-150.

1909. The English Sparrow and Bird-boxes. Bird-Lore, 11 (5) : 217.
Migration Halts. Wilson Bull., 21 (1) : 38-40.
Bohemian Waxwing in Northeastern Iowa. Wilson Bull., 21 (1) : 49.

Five Notes from the Upper Mississippi Valley. Wilson Bull., 21 (3) : 155-158.

---

* Compiled by Fred J. Pierce and reprinted from *Iowa Bird Life*, Vol. 13, No. 2, June, 1943.

This number of *Iowa Bird Life* was a memorial issue to Miss Sherman. A biography entitled, "Iowa's Woman Ornithologist: Althea Rosina Sherman — 1853-1943," by Mrs. H. J. Taylor, occupied the entire issue (pp. 18-33, with nine photographs).

1910. An Acre of Birds. Bird-Lore, 12 (6) : 230-232.
        Effects of Weather in North-eastern Iowa,
        Spring, 1910. Wilson Bull., 22 (2) : 117-118.
        At the Sign of the Northern Flicker. Wilson
        Bull., 22 (3-4) : 135-171.

1911. Nest Life of the Screech Owl. Auk, 28 (2) :
        155-168.
        The Keeping of Notes. Bird-Lore, 13 (4) :
        203-204.
        A Vireo Tragedy. Bird-Lore, 13 (4) : 205.
        The Village English Sparrow in the Grain-rais-
        ing Region. Wilson Bull., 23 (2) : 129.

1912. Diurnal Activities of the Great Horned Owl
        (*Bubo virginianus virginianus*). Auk, 29 (2) :
        240-241.
        Relative Number of Birds in 1912. Bird-Lore,
        14 (6) : 347-348.
        Position of Mourning Dove Nestlings. Con-
        dor, 14 (4) : 153.
        Moments with the Leconte's Sparrows. Wilson
        Bull., 24 (1) : 18-21.
        Bob-white (*Colinus virginianus virginianus*).
        Wilson Bull., 24 (1) : 49-50.
        Robin (*Planesticus migratorius migratorius*).
        Wilson Bull., 24 (1) : 50-51.
        The Brown Thrasher, (*Toxostoma Rufum*)
        East and West. Wilson Bull., 24 (4) : 187-191.

1913. Carolinian Avifauna in Northeastern Iowa.
        Auk, 30 (1) : 77-81.
        The Nest Life of the Sparrow Hawk. Auk, 30
        (3) : 406-418.
        The Extermination of the Wild Turkey in

Clayton County, Iowa. Wilson Bull., 25 (2): 87-90.

The Increase of the Cardinal in the Upper Mississippi Valley. Wilson Bull., 25 (3): 150-151.

Experiments in Feeding Hummingbirds During Seven Summers. Wilson Bull., 25 (4): 153-166. (Reprinted in the Report of the Smithsonian Institution for 1913, and in Avicultural Magazine, issues of Sept. and Oct., 1915.)

The Cardinal Arrives at Lansing, Iowa. Wilson Bull., 25 (4): 205.

1915. The Rock Wren at National, Iowa. Auk, 32 (2): 234.

The 'Whisper' Songs of Birds. Bird-Lore, 17 (2): 129.

The Great Destruction of Warblers: An Urgent Appeal. Bird-Lore, 17 (5): 375-377.

Birds by the Wayside, in Europe, Asia, and Africa. Wilson Bull., 27 (1): 243-271.

Birds of 1915: Too Few and Too Many. Wilson Bull., 27 (2): 350-352.

Birds by the Wayside, in Egypt and Nubia. Wilson Bull., 27 (3): 369-393.

1916. The Nest Life of the Western House Wren. Wilson Bull., 28 (2): 91.

A Peculiar Habit of the House Wren. Wilson Bull., 28 (2): 94-95.

Birds by the Wayside: In Palestine. Wilson Bull., 28 (3): 106-122.

Birds by the Wayside: In Greece. Wilson Bull., 28 (4): 157-171.

"Incubation Period of Killdeer." Wilson Bull., 28 (4): 195-196.

1917. Summer Records for 1917. Wilson Bull., 29 (3): 163-164.

1919. Historical Sketch of Park Region about Mc-Gregor, Iowa, and Prairie du Chien, Wisconsin. Iowa Conservation, 3 (1): 11-14; (2): 35-41.

1920. "The Grizzly, Our Greatest Wild Animal" (book review). Iowa Conservation, 4 (1): 19-20.

Bird Conservation. Iowa Conservation, 4 (3): 72-74.

1921. The Bohemian Waxwing in Iowa in Vast Numbers. Auk, 38 (2): 278-279.

1922. An Open Letter. Iowa Conservation, 6 (1): 13-14.

A National Bird Day. Iowa Conservation, 6 (2): 26-28. (Reprinted in the Condor, 25, 1923 (1): 15-20.

1924. "Animal Aggregations": A Reply. Condor, 26 (3): 85-88.

1925. The Problem of the House Wren. Bird-Lore, 27 (2): 97-100.

A Society to Protect Wild Life from the Protectionists. Condor, 27 (3): 124-125.

Down with the House Wren Boxes. Wilson Bull., 37 (1): 5-13.

Additional Evidence Against the House Wren. Wilson Bull., 37 (3): 129-132.

1926. A Skunk Entrapped by Nature; Periodicity in the Calling of a Chipmunk; Fox Squirrels' Nest in a Barn. Jour. Mammalogy, 7: 331-332

1928. Are Birds Decreasing in Numbers? Wilson Bull., 40 (1) : 29-38.

1929. (No title) A note on woodpecker holes. Bull. Iowa Ornith. Union, (2) : 12.
(No title) A note on Red-bellied Woodpecker and Ruffed Grouse. Bull. Iowa Ornith. Union, (4) : 24.
Summer Outings of Bats During Fourteen Seasons. Jour. Mammalogy, 10 (4) : 319-326.

1930. A Choice of Birds. National Plant, Flower and Fruit Guild Mag., March issue. (Reprinted in Iowa Bird Life, 1, 1931 (2) : 17-19).
The Old Ornithology and the New. Wilson Bull., 42 (1) : 3-10.

1931. Migrating Blue Jays. Auk, 48 (2) : 272-273.
A Sustained Interest in Iowa Birds. Iowa Bird Life, 1 (1) : 5.
Studying Iowa Screech Owls. Iowa Bird Life, 1 (1) : 9.
The Gambel's Sparrow at National, Iowa. Wilson Bull., 43 (3) : 154.

1932. Red-winged Blackbirds Nesting in Treetops near Top of Hill. Auk, 49 (3) : 358.
Downy's Mate or Daughter? Bird-Lore, 34 (3) : 202-203.